'An incredibly important and beautifully written account of perseverance and passion by one of the pioneers of research on gender in academia. In this book, Pat O'Connor continues to inspire new generations of feminist scholars and academic leaders with her honest and intimate story of her own gendered career path.'
— Marieke van den Brink, Professor Gender & Diversity Studies, Radboud University, Nijmegen, the Netherlands

'A 'Proper' Woman? is a beautiful, beautifully grounded, and often moving and inspiring, text – combining (auto)biography, life writing, life story, story-telling, an accounting of a career, and a case study of a woman, and women, in and around the university world, and beyond. The book contributes to and across several areas, including Studies of Higher Education, Gender Studies, and Critical Studies on Men and Masculinities; it has been a personal privilege to read it.'
— Jeff Hearn, Hanken School of Economics, Finland; author of: Age at Work; Knowledge, Power and Young Sexualities; and Men of the World

A 'proper' woman?
One woman's story of
success and failure
in academia

Reimagining Ireland

Volume 126

Edited by Dr Eamon Maher,
Technological University Dublin – Tallaght Campus

PETER LANG
Oxford - Berlin - Bruxelles - Chennai - Lausanne - New York

A 'proper' woman?
One woman's story of
success and failure
in academia

Pat O'Connor

PETER LANG
Oxford - Berlin - Bruxelles - Chennai - Lausanne - New York

Bibliographic information published by the Deutsche Nationalbibliothek. The German National Library lists this publication in the German National Bibliography; detailed bibliographic data is available on the Internet at http://dnb.d-nb.de.

A catalogue record for this book is available from the British Library.

Library of Congress Cataloging-in-Publication Data

Names: O'Connor, Pat, 1950- author.
Title: A 'proper' woman?: one woman's story of success and failure in academia / Pat O'Connor.
Description: New York: Peter Lang, 2024. | Series: Reimagining ireland, 1662-9094; vol. 126 | Includes bibliographical references and index.
Identifiers: LCCN 2023032572 (print) | LCCN 2023032573 (ebook) | ISBN 9781803743059 (paperback) | ISBN 9781803743035 (ebook) | ISBN 9781803743042 (epub)
Subjects: LCSH: Women in higher education--Social conditions. | Women college teachers--Social conditions. | Discrimination in higher education. | Marginality, Social.
Classification: LCC LC1567. O26 2024 (print) | LCC LC1567 (ebook) | DDC 378.0082--dc23/eng/20230815
LC record available at https://lccn.loc.gov/2023032572
LC ebook record available at https://lccn.loc.gov/2023032573

Cover image: Butler Claffey Design, 1998.
Cover design by Peter Lang Group AG

ISSN 1662-9094
ISBN 978-1-80374-305-9 (print)
ISBN 978-1-80374-303-5 (ePDF)
ISBN 978-1-80374-304-2 (ePub)
DOI 10.3726/b21197

© 2024 Peter Lang Group AG, Lausanne
Published by Peter Lang Ltd, Oxford, United Kingdom
info@peterlang.com – www.peterlang.com

Pat O'Connor has asserted her right under the Copyright, Designs and Patents Act, 1988, to be identified as Author of this Work.

This publication has been peer reviewed.

Dedicated with love and hope

To the next generation:
Emma, Suzanne, Mags, Claire and Lizzie

And to the generation after that:
*Eoin, Conor, Harry, Ciara, Isabel, Leo, Jeff, Bobby, Alannah, Maia,
Clara, Robyn, Art, Fia, Blaise and Oscar*

Contents

Acknowledgements

I am indebted to my sister, Stella Reeves, who has been a steadfast support to me since we were children, particularly since the death of our parents forty years ago. I am grateful for her many kindnesses, including tolerating me publishing this memoir. My nieces, Emma, Suzanne, Mags, Claire and Lizzie in their very different ways have enriched my life, as have their children: Eoin, Conor, Harry, Ciara, Isabel, Leo, Jeff, Bobby, Alannah, Maia, Clara, Robyn, Art, Fia, Blaise and Oscar. Friends, colleagues, acquaintances, and strangers have shown me many kindnesses throughout my life and these have enabled me to maintain that kind of naive optimism which has been so important in sustaining me.

The original impetus to write this memoir came indirectly from my brother-in-law, Tommy Reeves who forwarded the link to Silver Threads, an online memoir writing group sent to him by his daughter/my niece Claire. I am grateful to them for this and to Tommy for his work on my mother's family history (which I draw on in Chapter 1). Cathy Fowley, the co-ordinator of Silver Threads and the other members of that group provided early encouragement and ideas. Miranda (Mo) Doyle, the leader of the Faber memoir writing course, and the other participants on that course provided helpful insights and suggestions. Finally, I benefitted from City University and Curtis Brown memoir writing courses as well as from the Writing and Meditation sessions run by Emer Philbin Bowman.

Stella Reeves, Julia Brannen, Deirdre O'Toole, Sarah Moore Fitzgerald, Eugene O'Brien, Ellen Hazelkorn and Tom Lodge read earlier drafts of the manuscript and I am grateful to them for their encouraging comments and suggestions. Brian Langan and Eamon Maher provided editorial assistance and I appreciated this. Tony Mason, the Commissioning editor for Peter Lang responded to the manuscript with heart-warming speed and alacrity and I thank him for that.

There is some limited overlap in content between this memoir and the chapter on 'A Standard Career?' in *Generation and Gender in Academia,*

edited by B. Bagilhole and K. White, published by Palgrave Macmillan
and I am happy to refer to that publication. The sub-section on *Gender
Equality in the Health Services* in Chapter 4 draws on some of the material
in the 1996 *Economic and Social Review* article and I am grateful for permission to draw on it. The academic article: 'An Autoethnographic Account
of a Pragmatic Inclusionary Strategy and Tactics as a Form of Feminist
Activism', *Equality, Diversity, and Inclusion* (2019), 38 (8): 825–40 deals
with a part of my work life, but is obviously very different to this memoir.

The evocative image on the cover was created by Niall Toolan for
Butler Claffey Design who used it for my book, *Emerging Voices: Women
in Contemporary Irish Society,* published by the Institute of Public
Administration, Dublin in 1998. Catherine Griffin helpfully suggested
that I re-use it. That was facilitated by Gerry Butler, Signal Design, and I
very much appreciated that.

This then is my story. There are particularities of time and location.
The critical moments in my life will be different from many others. Other
women may be less naive than I or more adept at learning the lessons of
life. But the similarities are there.

But this is my story.

Prologue: The fork in the road

Seán and I walked slowly, holding hands, listening to the sound of the sea as it sucked the stones on the shore. In the gathering dusk of that balmy September evening, we headed for a celebratory drink in Mulligans, an old-fashioned pub in Greystones. The country was in a fever of excitement around the Pope's visit to Ireland in 1979, with a Mass in the Phoenix Park the previous day. It was a moment for re-affirming Catholic values, especially the importance of women's lives of service and self-sacrifice. Although I was a member of the institutional Roman Catholic Church, I had no interest in the Pope or his visit. I had read enough to know that, despite his genial personality, the message he was promulgating as regards the position of women was not one that I could support. The only thing on my mind was my Master's thesis. Relieved and excited, I had flown back from London to submit it to University College Dublin. The duplicate copy, with my name emblazoned in gold on its hard blue cover, was in Seán's car – a ridiculously long, 526-page tome, dedicated to him because he 'had loved the pilgrim soul'[1] in me.

Sporting my Vidal Sassoon haircut and silver owlish glasses, I wore my blue dungarees. I felt confident and at ease now that I had at last finished the thesis. Seán wore his rust and white striped cotton top and cords: his brown eyes, black curly beard and quizzical 'please be kind to me' eyebrows were as attractive as ever. I was 28; he was 32.

He had invited both sets of parents to what was meant to be a celebration of my Masters'. I was surprised since our parents had little in common, and rarely met but I was too preoccupied to query it. We heard children's laughter in the distance. Suddenly he turned to me and said: 'Let's elope. We can tell them now.' I could imagine my life: four or five children, living miles from a one-horse town in Kerry, in the little cottage in the middle

---

1   Yeats, W.B. (1892) 'When you are old', https://www.poetryfoundation.org/poems/43283/when-you-are-old. accessed 29 May 2023.

of nowhere that he had bought as an alternative to a suburban 'bird cage', and that we had decorated together before I went to work in London. I could imagine years of cooking and cleaning, too like my mother's life for comfort. Seán's life would change little: he would still be playing Gaelic football; training the ladies soccer team; playing the violin in local trad sessions; still singing in the chamber group near his engineering workplace. What was my alternative? Doing a PhD in London, maybe eventually having a stimulating research and teaching career. He had gone to work in Cameroon while I was still at university. When he came back, he got a job in Kerry while I was working first in Dublin and later in London. I loved the intensity of our long-distance relationship, with its weekends and holidays together and long satisfying phone calls. I was lonely at times, still on short-term contracts and had published nothing. But there was the hope that I might make it. Marriage and children seemed inevitable – but my feeling was that they were best deferred for as long as possible.

'It's not the right time,' I said. 'I want to do the PhD.'

We were at the door of the pub.

'Let us enjoy the Masters', I said.

I knew that he would be disappointed, but there was no point dwelling on that. I pushed open the door, still holding his hand, as the sound of the sea sucking the stones faded in the distance.

I had gambled for the third and last time. Was I a 'proper' woman?

Like Dolmens round my childhood[2] ... sometimes

Context

I grew up in Ireland in the 1950s and early 1960s. This was yet another period of recession and emigration, as the country struggled to recover from the effects of 'The Emergency', an Irish euphemism for its neutrality during the Second World War. Unusually for the time, both my parents went to university, graduating from University College Cork in the 1930s. Both were from farming families with declining family fortunes, and as such were very unlikely candidates for university education. Both were also from Cork, a county in the south of Ireland which is popularly seen as 'the rebel county' because of its ability to produce dissenters: people who in Irish terms are 'great craic', with a nice line in parochial arrogance reflected in the belief that Cork is the centre of the universe. We lived in Cork until I was eight years old. In truth, my parents never really left there and were perpetual migrants in their own country.

---

2   Montague, J. (1972) 'Like Dolmens round my Childhood: The Old People', *The Rough Field*. Oldcastle, Co Meath: Gallery Press.

Memories and moments

There is a photograph in my living room of the four of us at my sister's communion in east Cork. My sister, Stella, looks calm and happy with her long, blond ringlets and pretty communion dress. Her right hand is in our mother's right hand. Although the photo is in black and white, I recognise my mother's cream, linen button-through dress. She is seated on a padded stool, with her left arm resting behind Stella's back. My father stands behind them in a tweed suit, with a boat in full sail on his tie. I am maybe three years old and am sitting high up on a dark polished display unit. My ankles are crossed, but in the opposite direction to my mother's. My straight brown hair is fixed in place with a fancy clip. My feet are miles off the ground. There is nothing to hold on to, and no-one holds on to me. My right fist, the one nearest to my father, is almost clenched; my left holds on to the hem of my pretty dress. I am not smiling.

There are other photos. I am five but I am big for my age. I look the same size as my sister Stella who is three and a half years older. We are sitting on the front ditch waiting for the visitors. Big bows in our hair. My sister is barely smiling in her green party dress with the white collar. She does not like parties. My bow is smaller and took ages to fix on my short straight brown hair. My grin is bigger. I like parties. I am wearing my favourite pleated red skirt, my red and white stripey jumper and my white blouse.

The visitors are the Cooks. They are friends of my Mammy and Daddy. Their Daddy got a big job in a bank in Michelstown. We have not seen them for a long time. My Mammy has baked a sponge for tea and we are going to have it and chocolate biscuits. My Mammy has been busy cleaning the house all week. She says that we must put our best foot forward. I am not sure what that means.

They have two children: Amanda who is Stella's age and Tony who is the same age as me. I am all excited. We take turns on the swing in the monkey puzzle tree in our big garden and then we play chasing and catch me if you can. That is fun. Amanda and Stella go off to explore. Tony and I sit down on the path in front of the house and I get my box of marbles from my bedroom. The stripey orange one is my favourite. I have had it since I was very small. I love to hold it in my hand before I go to sleep. He has brought his box and we start to play. My pink marble hits his grey one. I win it. Then it is Tony's turn. His blue marble hits my stripey orange one. He puts it in his pocket. I offer him my green one. Then his own grey one. He will not swap. The stripey orange one is much nicer, he says. I start to cry. Then I start to roar. I hit him with my fists. He will not give it to me. He starts to cry. My Daddy comes out of the house. I love my Daddy. He puts his hands on my shoulders and shakes me hard:

'You must learn to play the game. You lost. That is the end of it. Stop crying.'

I sob but more quietly now. He has never been this cross with me. I want my orange stripey marble. But I want my Daddy more.

The sponge cake is nice and I have two chocolate biscuits. We play hop scotch and try to climb the monkey puzzle tree. They leave and it is time for bed. I look for my orange stripey marble. It is not in my box of marbles. Then I remember what happened. And how cross my Daddy was. It takes a long time for me to go to sleep. I think maybe my sister was right. Visitors are not that great.

I never remember my father shaking me after that. I never saw the Cooks again. There were good times. On weekdays, particularly during the summer, my sister and I and any other children around, would pile into the car in east Cork in layers, with the big ones underneath and the small ones on top. My mother driving, we would head for the sea – usually Garryvoe with its sand dunes or Redbarn, with its miles of sandy beach. She was a nervous driver. She was not good at reversing and had the odd altercation with ditches and gates.

'Was anyone killed' my father would ask.

The answer invariably being no he would then say:

'You had no accident.'

Togs and towels, a big brown plaid rug, banana sandwiches and red lemonade were all in the car boot as well as a teapot, loose tea, a drop of milk in a bottle with a paper screw as a stopper and cups. Neither a flask nor a gas stove ever found its way into the boot. But my mother did like a cup of tea. I loved the sea, the wild freedom of it. None of us could swim. Regardless of the weather, the children were all expected to go in. Shouting and screaming with excitement we would splash around until we got so cold that it was time to come out. Shivering we passed the towels around. The fine sand seeped through our toes like silk.

At my mother's instigation, one of us would knock at the nearby summer cabins and ask for some hot water to make the tea. In retrospect I am amazed that no money was ever offered or expected and this request was never refused. Tea made, we crowded round the rug for the picnic. It was at this point that, as I remember it, large rain drops frequently started to fall. A muddle of socks, sand and banana sandwiches were gathered up in the rug as we ran pell-mell for the car across the sand, clutching our sandals and wet togs. We piled into the car to a chorus of:

'He won't move over'; 'she is hurting me'; 'move your legs'; 'he pinched me'.

As my mother slowly and carefully turned the car we all knew that, despite the rain, it had been another great day at the seaside.

My father was rarely with us on these expeditions because of his work in the creamery (cows did not keep office hours). But on Sundays, he drove us to the seaside. He too loved the sea. Unlike my mother, he went in. He could not swim but with his hands on the sea bed, it looked as though he was swimming. I thought that was ingenious.

Like most other cars in the 1950s ours was a black Ford. It is the only car registration I have ever remembered: ZB7239. It was part of the family. My father used to put a blanket and newspapers on its engine every night. When I was ten or eleven, the steering went. Someone told me that it was squashed down to the size of a briefcase. That haunted me. Most things I don't get attached to. But some things, like ZB7239 and the stripey orange marble, creep into my soul. Their familiarity or beauty or the memories embedded in them mean that they become part of me.

Dislocation

My mother, my sister Stella and I sit high up in the Silver Bullet, squeezed in beside the driver of the long, articulated truck with its consignment of shoe polish, its name emblazoned in large print on the side. It is a hot July day in 1959. I am 8 years old and Stella is 12. We are in our Sunday best dresses. Mine is red and white with a big bow at the back. We are leaving our home with its huge monkey puzzle tree and wooden swing. I liked my own comfy bedroom; the breakfast room where my mother boiled Lucozade when I was sick; the big sunny kitchen. Opposite our house was the station with its signal box and the station master, Mr Saunderson, who let us move the levers and open the railway gates when the trains had passed. We are leaving behind Mrs Saunderson whose cigarette ash was always about to drop on to her ironing and who put the weak baby piglets into her Aga oven to keep them warm. Marie Saunderson was the same age as Stella, and had seen Santa and his sleigh travelling over our chimney.

That day in July, our house was in a fever of activity. While our belongings were being loaded up into the Silver Bullet my refuge was another neighbour's kitchen, Mrs Enright's, where I laboriously copied down the words of Kelly the Boy from Killane ... 'Seven feet was his height with some inches to spare ...'. My tongue stuck out as I concentrated on my task. In retrospect I can see that I was seeking refuge from the emotional vortex of the move in the controllable world of learning. I have no recollection of being called home by my mother or of what must have been tearful farewells.

I did not understand it then, but our house was the creamery manager's house, and when my father lost his job as the creamery manager, the house went too. Maybe the Enrights had been involved in the heave which had cost my father his job, and us our home. In any event I never saw Mrs Enright again. There was no other work for my father in the little village of Mogeely in East Cork, with its one shop where we bought pennyworths of sweets wrapped in a poke made of newspapers, the huge Catholic church where we went every Sunday and the three pubs.

My father got a job as an office clerk in Dublin, a position he was over-qualified for, but there was no demand for creamery managers there. My mother told us to say that he was an office manager. He had gone on ahead to look for somewhere for us to live, staying with his thin, red-haired, generous and slightly querulous brother (Uncle Pat). Since there were already five children in their small house, there was no room for us. The plan was that we would all stay, temporarily, my mother stressed, with her brother, Bill and his wife in Mount Merrion, a posh middle-class suburb. Meantime, we had to get to Dublin. Money was short, so we got a lift there in the Silver Bullet.

There were no motorways then and, apart from farm machinery and lorries, there was little traffic on the two-lane road that wound its way from Mogeely up through Fermoy, with its six-foot-high pencil on the pavement, past the fairy tale Rock of Cashel, through Horse and Jockey (which was just a village), past the cottage decorated with shells, to Portlaoise and then Naas. It took hours. My mother, although upset, made conversation with the driver: about the weather, the roads, the crops and the price of eggs. Daunted by the enormity of the change, we sat staring out of the windscreen before we dozed off in the blinding sun.

Eventually we were on the outskirts of Dublin. To my mother, born and reared in Cork, Dublin was a foreign country. She became so overwrought that she could not remember her brother's address (like most houses in Ireland at that time they did not have a house phone). All she could tearfully say over and over was that it was on a hill. Scared, we sat in silence as the increasingly irate driver drove up and down endless roads and looked for hills. After a long time, she remembered: it was Mount Merrion and it was on a hill. It was not a good beginning.

We stayed with Brother Bill very briefly. My father had found a house for us to rent in the newly built suburb of Walkinstown. He described the house enthusiastically to my mother:

> 'Sheila, it is new and has a sound roof. It is not far from Pat's [his brother's] house. You can see cows out the back window. It even has a name: Mount Carmel.'

To him it was perfect. He took us to it. It was a terraced house in a working-class area, with a small garden at the front and a bigger one at the back, both overlooked on all sides. The kitchen was tiny. There was a dining room, a sitting room and three bedrooms, including a small box room. It was a big come down from the spacious, detached creamery manager's house on its own grounds that we had left. My mother's disappointment was palpable. She said nothing. It was accessible via a large complicated five-road intersection that terrified her. She never drove a car again.

It was the end of an era.

A normal unhappy childhood?

I have always had the feeling that something went wrong in my child-hood. Or rather a series of things. But then what childhood did not go wrong in Ireland of the 1950s and 1960s? I have no doubt that I was not an easy child to rear. There is a family story about my wanting a big pram, a 'high nellie', similar to one that a neighbouring toddler had – not a doll's pram but one for myself to sit in - and kicking up such a fuss that even-tually I got one. That story reflected my fearsome reputation as strong-willed, and the implacability of my demands even as a very small child. Obedience was an important virtue for children then and docility was valued. Neither of these were my strong suit. My reputation also included relentless independence (illustrated by my mother's frequent reference to me as exemplifying the attitude of the little red hen in the children's story, who said 'I'll do it myself'). This belied the dependency that I craved.

There were early traumas which another child might have more easily transcended. I had trouble with my tonsils when I was three or four years old. At that time, it was normal to have them taken out. I remember being on my own in the hospital, a strange place, hearing sounds coming from the dark corridor. I was terrified. I remember having a tube down my throat. After that I drank nothing but cold water until I went to university when I was 16. My sister remembers me being brought home from hospital looking ashen. In a household where Santa often brought household items, that year he brought me a spectacular tiny grand piano with keys that could be played.

When I was six or seven years old, my sister got tuberculosis (TB). My mother, with considerable courage since TB was both highly contagious and hugely stigmatising, cared for her at home. When she recovered, everything in the room had to be burned to prevent the spread of the disease. Meanwhile, the station master's wife, Mrs Saunderson, allowed her daughter, Marie, to go in and out of my sister's room to play. I was left to my own devices. I hung out with the neighbourhood boys. The dares were scary. Running, climbing, eating bugs, doing horrible things – I was afraid of doing them, and of not doing them. The forfeits were worse. Being in a kind of shed. No walls – just potato sacks hung from a corrugated iron roof, flapping in the wind and held together by a nail pushed through a chestnut conker. Focusing on that. Bad things happening. Being afraid to tell. Was there abuse by one of the boys? I cannot remember. I do remember being unable to explain to my mother why I could not receive holy communion and pretending that it was because I had accidentally broken my fast by eating crumbs.

I was always in trouble at home for giving cheek and being disobedient. My mother found me hard going. I remember her beating me after we moved to Dublin. She said that it was 'for my own good'. I hated it. Not only the physical pain but the indignity of it and the attempt to break my will. I cannot remember being beaten in Mogeely. But I do remember praying, unsuccessfully, that the long bamboo cane that she used would get lost when we moved from there to Dublin. I cannot remember when it moved out of the house in Walkinstown and was used to stake the St Joseph's lilies beside the front door. But I do know that it was not soon enough. I hated being a child. I could not wait to grow up so that no one would ever do that to me again.

Yet I was reared to challenge authority outside the home and to resist peer pressure. 'This above all: to thine own self be true'[3]: was one of my mother's favourite phrases. When I was 11 or 12 years old, I read Anne Frank's diary,[4] and my mother encouraged the conclusion that if the

---

3   From William Shakespeare's play *Hamlet*, Act 1, Scene 3: line 78, https://www.fol ger.edu/explore/shakespeares-works/hamlet/read/1/3/, accessed 29 May 2023.
4   Frank, A. (1952). *The Diary of a Young Girl*. Elstree, UK: Valentine Mitchell.

Germans had been more questioning of authority, the Holocaust might have been avoided. When I did not want to play hockey at secondary school, she did not insist. When I did not want to stay in secondary school for study at the end of the school day, there was no question of making me do it.

Whenever possible, I hung out in Uncle Pat's house. Aunty Kitty (his wife) was a larger-than-life figure. Tall, thin and wiry she ruled the house by the sheer force of her personality. Diagnosed with cancer after the birth of their fifth child, she took up French and amateur dramatics, determined to live in the face of death. There was sometimes no food left there at the end of the week after she gave her housekeeping money to a visiting African priest, to Uncle Pat's frustration and the children's dismay. She valued principles even more than her children. I was fascinated. She was sick for six or seven years and was in the hospice before she died. Hers was the first funeral I went to and my first really close contact with death. I was 14 and it rattled me.

After we moved to Dublin, my mother's fervent prayer, frequently repeated, was that she would be spared until my sister and I were 18 years old. I had nightmares from nine or ten years old about dying; about my mother dying; about death. Terrified, I would wake and make my way to my parents' room sobbing and she would let me sleep at her side of the bed. It happened to Aunty Kitty. It could happen to anyone, maybe to me? I grew agitated and anxious. Life was difficult but death was terrifying. It was my first brush with mental ill-health. My mother stepped in. I remember nothing of that time, except the feeling of not being able to cope with homework – of feeling that it was all too much. When I hit another wall in London in the early 1980s and was prescribed medication, I recognised the tablets. They were the same ones I had been prescribed in Dublin in the 1960s.

Meanwhile I hated the tension in the small narrow blue kitchen in our house in Walkinstown. One of my mother's many mottoes was: 'idle hands are the devil's workshop'. During term time, on weekdays, all we had to do was to study hard and do well at school. Every Saturday we poured Rentokil into the holes left by woodworm in the furniture we had brought from the creamery house in Mogeely. We skated on the floors polishing the lino and on Sundays after we gone to Mass, we wrote to our grandmother and helped our mother with the baking. In our teens, if we wanted new clothes, it was taken-for-granted that we would make them. Simplicity patterns were in vogue. Ever ambitious, one of my first attempts was a green, 1920s style dress with a dropped waist and pleated skirt. The pattern was complicated and I struggled. Eventually I finished it. The iron was too hot and it left a large brown mark on the left-hand side of the bust. It was unwearable.

During the holidays there were plenty of jobs for us to do including tidying under the stairs, a long dark tunnel with little air that contained the gas meter and was always in a total muddle. In our early and mid-teens, we did the house maintenance work with our mother: painting walls and doors and pasting and hanging wall paper. My father was useless at DIY. His attempts at hanging pictures were legendary: the hole got bigger and bigger as the rawl plugs disappeared into it; he swore as he hit his fingers with the hammer and still the job remained unfinished. None of us liked going up ladders. I can remember my mother standing at the foot of the double ladder on the outside of our two-storey house encouraging me as I struggled to paint the windows and the gutters. No one seemed to worry that I might fall. It had to be done. Someone had to do it.

Every day, winter and summer, a small innocuous man drove the Downes bread van up and down the road selling bread. It seemed a meta-phor for our ground hog life. The joys and traumas of east Cork had been replaced by a grey narrow sameness in Walkinstown, where fear and anxiety lurked in every corner. It looked like a normal childhood.

'School days are the happiest days of your life'

'School days' according to my mother 'were the happiest days of your life'. I started school at 4 years old and I was happy in the two-teacher school in Castelemartyr, a mile from our home in Mogeely. I blossomed under the influence of roundy, kind Miss Brown in her brown jacket and skirt who never hit us; and tall thin Miss Fitzsimons with her red chiffon scarf, who was a bit more severe in demeanour, but never hit us either. Each of their rooms had several classes in them. I liked to listen to the older classes' lessons and pick up what they were learning.

With the new school year looming after our move to Dublin, my mother decided that we would go to the Loreto, on Crumlin Road. On the first day my mother walked me down St Patrick's Road, St James' Road and St Peter's Road. Then across the intersection, with its bewildering mesh of roads. Over to the green double-decker bus stop. She saw me on to the bus and told the bus conductor to let me off at the Loreto on Crumlin Road. Then she was gone.

The Loreto National School was a huge, grey, forbidding building behind very large black iron gates. I was terrified, but followed the crowd. I was initially put in second class, where there was a constant undercurrent of violence. The teacher there threw dusters, boxes of chalk – anything to hand – from the back of the room, venting her frustration at anyone and everyone. The class was huge, fifty children, and if any were missing, two of us were sent out to bring them in since the state's financial support for national schools was based on attendance. A long bamboo cane was used frequently, leaving red weals on our palms which we cooled on the copper ink wells embedded in the desks.

Playing in the huge cement yard was a nightmare. A favourite game in that bleak, grey playground involved guessing the names of film stars from their initials. I had never even heard of film stars in Mogeely. I still remember that PB (Pat Boone) was one of my failures. The other children called me Corky the Cat, because of my Cork accent. A doctor's daughter in my class was particularly nasty about my Cork accent and my total ignorance of pop stars. I told my mother. She gave me an umbrella and told me to hit the doctor's daughter with it, and hard:

'Attack is the best means of defence,' she said.

The next day I waited at the bus stop. There was always a lot of pushing and shoving there so it was easy to give her several good digs with the umbrella 'by accident'. It was the survival of the fittest.

The lessons were no problem. I had benefitted from my experiences in the little two-teacher school in East Cork where firm educational foundations had been effortlessly laid. I loved to learn and was a good all-rounder, but particularly good at mental arithmetic. In Dublin, I was moved up to third class, where I was the youngest and out of my depth socially. But again, the lessons were no problem. The teacher, Miss Nolan, was calm and kind and reminded me of roundy Miss Brown from the school in Castlemartyr. At the end of the year, she resigned her post to go to teach in Africa. And we were back to the reign of terror. In fifth class, I was made prefect, which exacerbated my pariah status with the other pupils, as well as provoking more caning from the teacher because I could not control the class in her absence.

Before our confirmation, entirely incongruously, we were taught the cuckoo waltz by one of the Loreto nuns in the yard behind the huge grey building. I loved to dance so learning that too was easy. Our photos were taken there in our confirmation outfits. I loved my pink frilly nylon dress, my lilac coat and pink broad-brimmed hat, white gloves and shoes. It was a flash of colour in a grey and troubled world. With the state Primary Certificate done (in my case at 11 years old), our time was over. I had made no friends there.

I went to the secondary school next door, run by the Loreto nuns. It was 1962 and free secondary level education did not yet exist. My sister Stella, says that I got a County Council Scholarship there but I have no recollection of that. I can still remember the brown envelope, with the window in the front, that arrived every August and the tension in my mother's face as she opened it. As well as the fees, there was the cost of the pale green gymslip, the plaid green blouse, the dark green tie, beret and gabardine coat that had to be bought in Greene's, an old-fashioned expensive shop in Dolphin's Barn. But my mother was determined that we would go to the Loreto. Somehow, year after year the money was found.

I had grown accustomed to the dog-eat-dog environment of the national school and had learned to fight my corner. I did not realise that different rules now applied. One of the other students picked on me.

'It is starting again,' I thought.

I lifted my right hand and slapped her across the face. I can remember the stunned silence in the room. Loreto Schools were famous for producing

girls who were young ladies. I must have been punished but I have no recollection of it. There was no caning there. That was a mercy.

The religious ethos permeated the day. There were the prayers we all
said shuffling to our feet at the beginning of each 45-minute class; the
AMDG (All for the honour and glory of God) that we wrote on our class
exercises and homework; the daily trips to the chapel for prayers at 11 a.m.
There were the May Processions through the streets. In fifth year we all
became Children of Mary, and wore our blue cloaks to the annual processions, second in line only to the first communion children with their
white dresses and veils.

In sixth year I agonised over whether to spend time at the May processions or on studying for the Leaving Certificate. God inevitably won
out. I was then still fully committed to the institutional Roman Catholic
Church and loved the drama of these occasions: the tar melting on the road;
the banners swaying in the light breeze; the rise and fall of voices raised in
unison in the rosary responses and the singing of 'Queen of the May' as
the procession moved through the streets of Crumlin and Dolphin's Barn.

We had an annual retreat in secondary school: three days of silence.
Although I was a talker, I liked these days. The silence, where there was
structure and meaning, made it possible for me to relax. I loved the feeling
that life made sense, that our work and our efforts were directed to some
higher end. But there were harbingers of future doubts. These went back
to when I was at primary school where I read about the perfidious Jews
in my missal at Easter. (I had to ask my mother what that word meant). I
was horrified by the existence of Limbo, the place where unbaptised babies
went and where they could never leave to go into the presence of God. I
thought it was strange that unmarried motherhood was so stigmatised since
after all, Mary Mother of God was an unmarried mother. I was terrified
by some of the Passionate Fathers, with their short black capes with the
flaming hearts embroidered on them, who led the retreats and threatened
us with eternal damnation. My mother was unusual at that time in freely
criticising individual priests and the institutional church while being a daily
Mass goer. Thus, I saw no contradiction between my enjoyment of quiet
retreat times and my questioning of the church.

Even as a young teenager, I noticed that the nuns who taught us were called Mother, whereas those who worked in the kitchens were called Sister and were looked down on. I was not impressed. Much later I learned that the Sisters were the ones who came in without a dowry: money talked it appeared, even in the relationship with God. The lay teachers were single women, because at that time (the 1960s), the Marriage Bar still existed (that is to say, a ban on married women being employed in second-level teaching or in the public sector). No-one thought this was in any way odd. They wore black gowns, like those now worn at graduation ceremonies. Miss Walsh, who taught Geography, had travelled to India on a motor bike. Miss Murchan, the History teacher, was a tiny slip of a woman whose sarcasm could shatter glass. The teacher of Irish, Miss O'Brien, was a country woman with a strong Kerry accent. Mother Marie Estelle was our Maths teacher up to the Intermediate Certificate (the first state examination at second level, now called the Junior Certificate). My love of Maths diminished under Miss Newman who taught us for the Leaving Certificate. I struggled with geometry cuts, solving them to my own satisfaction, but not in a way that was acceptable to Miss Newman. The only science subject we were taught was the (quaintly named) Physiology and Hygiene.

I made a few friends there but rarely met them outside school. The only thing I really enjoyed was debating and extempore speaking. I loved the still, breath-holding silence that descended when the audience were really listening. I loved the challenge of having to think on my feet. Most of all I loved being listened to, being able to persuade others and to win the argument. I was leader of the debating team at junior and senior level. This meant not only making the opening address, but also highlighting the weaknesses and inconsistencies in the other teams' argument in the summing up at the end. Although I was always nervous before a debate, once it started, I felt alive. As seniors, the teacher made us learn off what we were going to say. I hated that. It reduced the spontaneity and the fun. We were beaten in the senior final by the much posher St Stephen's Green Loreto school. The spontaneity remained in the extempore speaking competitions where a topic was given ten minutes beforehand, to speak on for five minutes. That was exciting. I won senior and junior medals for extempore speaking, with a warning from the judge against the excessive use of rhetoric in speaking at senior level on the 1916 rising.

We got books as prizes in secondary school. I was surprised years later to find that I got first in the class each year from second to sixth year. I did not remember it that way: another girl, Mona, always seemed to be at my heels. Although I was a reader, I instinctively distrusted the attempt to mould me and I did not read most of these books. The only one I can remember looking at was *101 Great Lives*[5] which I won when I was 14 and doing the Intermediate Certificate. I noticed then that the overwhelming majority were men. I remembered only two of them being women: Queen Elizabeth 1 and Marie Curie. As a nationalist it was unthinkable that I would identify with the former, so that left Marie Curie. Education was the way out, but she was a scientist. Looking at the book, fifty years later, there were five other women referred to: Florence Nightingale, Joan of Arc, Gertrude Bell, Elizabeth Fry and Queen Victoria. Even at that age, feminine service or martyrdom was as unattractive as royalty or serving the British Empire.

I was frequently first in the class in religious doctrine. I took to heart the Parable of the Talents in St Luke's Gospel, and resolved not to follow the example of the man with the one talent who buried it, rather than using it. I loved learning but I hated the subordination that increasingly seemed to be a necessary pre-condition for it. My acceptance of that was on a strictly time-limited basis. By sixth year my patience was wearing thin and I expressed my barely concealed resentment by being always almost late for classes, not late enough to be sanctioned but late enough to be disruptive.

If 'school days were the happiest days of your life', even as a child I wondered what the rest of my life was going to be like.

Being Irish, the Gaeltacht and the céilís

I was very conscious of being Irish, and proud of it. In most schools at that time, the History curriculum stopped at 1916 and was nationalist. My

---

5　Pringle, P. (1963). *101 Great Lives*. London: Ward, Lock and Company.

mother had changed her name by deed poll in her teens from the English version Julia to the Irish version, Sheila. Both the War of Independence and the Civil War were particularly vicious in Cork, my parents home county. They remained fascinated by Irish politics and public affairs.

On the fiftieth Anniversary of the 1916 rebellion, I was asked to read the 1916 Proclamation[6] at the school. I loved that and fully embraced the vision of Ireland that it expressed. I was conscious that there was unfinished business in relation to the North of Ireland. A frequent visitor to my Uncle Pat's house, Mr Drummond, had been interned in the Curragh in Kildare by the state after the failed Seán South attempt to take the North. In retrospect I can see the possibility that I might get involved in the IRA was one of my mother's unspoken fears. It was later concretised with the emergence of Bernadette Devlin as a leader of the Civil Rights movement in the North. Articulate, headstrong and strongly nationalist, my mother knew that if I decided to take that road no one or nothing could stop me. Preoccupied with deciding on a career, that thought did not occur to me.

Like many Irish children in the 1950s and 1960s I was sent to Irish dancing classes as a child, and later to the Gaeltacht. I went to An Graigh in the Kerry Gaeltacht for a month every year for seven years from when I was 11 years old, initially with my sister and later with two of my first cousins (Uncle Pat's children). When I saw the beauty of Clogher strand and the Minaun for the very first time I had an immediate feeling that I could be happy there. I loved the freedom and the dancing, with nothing to do except speak Irish (and not get pregnant: although that was never spelt out). I don't know how my parents found the money to send me there. But I do know that I loved it, and I suspect that it was a break for them too. We had no classes to attend. A month of freedom. We had an identity: 'The girls from Maire Breathnach's house.' I learned to do all the usual céilí dances as well as set dancing in the Bru, the hostel just up the road where the boys from Cork schools stayed. Our accommodation was

---

6   The 1916 Irish Proclamation, https://www.museum.ie/en-IE/Collections-Resea rch/Collection/Resilience/Artefact/Test-3/fb71e3dc-2e95-4406-bc46-87d8d 6b0ae5d, accessed 29 May 2023.

basic. We slept four or five to a room. There were no wardrobes so we hung our clothes from the string that held up the curtains. It was fun.

We visited the homes of men like Seanin de Hora, who were Sean-Nós singers. It was entirely innocent. We walked from An Graigh to Krugers, the local pub, several times a week to dance. It never occurred to us to drink alcohol. The attraction was the music and the dancing. The men, farmers and fishermen, would come in from the fields and the sea and would start to dance. These men rarely lifted their feet but their whole body swayed with the music. They danced Kerry Sets with five or six parts, lasting over forty minutes. In and out between there was old time waltzing: the endless circles creating a kind of trance. Being a good dancer was a mark of distinction, and I was good.

In Dublin, one of those first cousins (Mary), my sister and I went to céilís at the Mansion House or the Clarence Hotel during the holidays and especially on St Stephen's night. We got ready in our house, and the craic was mighty as we decided what we would wear. There was no alcohol at the céilís. For enthusiastic dancers like myself, the main risk was overheating. I got redder and redder and sweatier and sweatier as the night wore on. We were under strict instructions that we were to dance with any man who asked us (unless he was very drunk), because to refuse was impolite. I discovered to my amazement that most young men in Dublin could not dance: it was like their bodies had been torn up from the soil and had become stiff and wooden. I noticed for the first time that I seemed to attract more than my fair share of older men which I did not appreciate, but at least they were good dancers, so that was something.

I was confident, cocky, able to look after myself and I loved dancing. My sister was much quieter and quite shy. It still amazes me that when I was 15 or 16 (and my sister 18 or 19), we were sent by my mother to adult dances at the Garda Club, the Television Club and other venues in Dublin.

I minded myself and no ill befell me. And I did enjoy the dancing.

The people who made me

Both my parents were unusual in leaving behind the dreams and night-mares of their different farm inheritances and family traditions and going to university, despite, rather than because of their family backgrounds. My mother met my father on the road near her home in Cahermone, after they had both graduated from University College Cork. She was, he said, 'the saddest girl he ever saw'. Since he had been engaged before, they signed a statement before two witnesses (one of them my mother's sister, Betty) in which he promised to marry her within a year. He did, in 1940 when she was 27, despite the opposition of her parents. They started married life in a rented flat in Middleton in east Cork, just over four kilo-metres from her home place. At a time when Irish couples overwhelm-ingly referred to each other as Mother and Father in the presence of their children, they always used their first names: Denis and Sheila.

My mother

My mother was a woman who did not thrive in the limited, restrictive, procrustean bed of Irish femininity. I was 34 when she died. A lifetime after her death, I am beginning to see that although she was not the kind of mother I wanted, she was the kind of mother I might have been.

She was a child when the Black and Tans set fire to Cork city and tore up the floorboards in her home in Cahermone looking for guns. She was a child too when her disabled sister, Eily, was taken by pony and trap to hospital in Cork and subsequently died. She worked as an unqualified school teacher in her late teens. Then, she entered a convent and was sent to a novitiate in Waterford, where she was asked to leave because she walked in her sleep. Still searching for a different kind of life, she went to University College Cork to do a BA in her early 20s, as a mature student, on six old pence a week, despite opposition from her mother ('All this studying will ruin your eyesight,' her mother said, and it did ...). She loved boarding at La Retraite and doing 'pana' (promenading) in Cork city. Those were her halcyon days. She got first-class honours in English and History in her first two years. Then, unable to decide which subject to specialise in, she continued with both and ended up with a Third-Class Honours BA degree. Her professor said that if he knew it was so important to her, he could have given her a higher mark. She was haunted by that for the rest of her life.

After their marriage, there were five or six miscarriages, many of them alone while my father cycled to work in creameries in east Cork. She was told she would never bear a living child. But then she had my sister, and four years after, in her late 30s, she had me. A lover of ideas, literature and political argument, domesticity did not agree with her. She read nine library books a week to escape into her own world after we moved to Dublin. She walked. She did the housework, the cooking, the cleaning, all the usual chores and looked after us because it was her duty. She loved a good fire, and built one with skill by scrunching up newspapers and rolling others to make paper twigs to get the fire going: the words she loved burning as the newspapers curled up in the heat. I can remember her animation as she tucked her feet under her and settled in the arm chair with a lighted cigarette to discuss religion and politics with my father and my father's brother on Friday and Saturday nights. The rest of the time, with a grim stoicism she carried on in her narrow, monotonous, unfulfilling, lonely life in Dublin.

Her dream was of a pill that you could take in the morning that would substitute for all meals during the day. She mastered a small number of dinners. Sunday was bacon and then as money got a bit more plentiful, roast chicken. Monday was cold meat. Tuesday was shepherds' pie. Wednesday was pot roast. Thursday was fried liver. Friday was fish fingers. Saturday could vary. The rest was fixed. It reduced the time and effort involved. Got it over with. At that time, it was normal for working fathers and school going children (even those who like us were a bus ride away) to come home for dinner during the week. To go to a café for lunch was unthinkable. Dinner at home was at 1 sharp. If you were late, it did not wait. There was dessert, usually stewed apples and custard or stewed rhubarb and custard, lovely runny custard and occasionally a crumble as a treat. Then one biscuit. Over time she became a good baker, except when visitors were expected. Then the sponge cake invariably failed to rise.

So strong were her friendships in east Cork that I can still recall hearing their names: from Middleton, where they first lived after they married, there was Mrs Daly, who had a daughter, Noelle, a day older than I and Doc Leary, whose wife gave me her engagement ring to play with; and from Mogeely, Mr and Mrs Saunderson. Those friendships did not survive the move. Only her relationship with her best friend from her university days, Rita (whom we called Aunty) who ran the post office with Uncle Jim, survived it. He had a heart condition and when we later stayed with them for holidays, we would hear her shouting in her sleep: 'You are dead Jim, you are dead.' Slightly scatty, she once put an electric fire into our bed to warm it and accidentally set fire to the bed clothes. Yet there was always fun and hugs there. My mother only ever made two women friends in Dublin, neither close: Mrs Roche a west Cork down-to-earth nurse was a good neighbour, and Mrs Flanaghan, who was quite 'hoity toity' and whose attraction as a friend, as children, we never really understood.

I cannot recall my mother ever initiating a hug when we were children. Yet I can see in retrospect that she was a woman that young people liked and found easy to talk to. Aunty Rita's children visited as young adults when they came to work in Dublin. Aunty Betty's daughters (her sister's children) stayed over during several summers when they were teenagers. Other young people, children of acquaintances in east Cork, also visited.

She tried primary teaching for a while in the national school in the Loreto in the 1960s when I was in my very early teens. She found it hard: the classes were huge and the children difficult to control. As a married woman, she could not get a job as a secondary school teacher because of the Marriage Bar. To my shame, I told her that I did not want her to work. After a time, she gave up.

I wanted a warm, physically nurturant mother who was homely and a good cook. My mother's interests were outside the home. I have spent my life working for a world that values such mothers. The irony that I could not accept my own mother, who exemplified that, is not lost on me.

My father

In my father's time, you just got on with it:

> 'Those whiz-kids and their job satisfaction,' he used to say contemptuously. 'In my time you were lucky to get a job. And to keep a job. Any job.'

My father loved working. Or maybe he just needed work. He always did 'nixers' (part-time jobs), mostly the accounts for various businesses, in addition to his full-time job. He added up columns of figures on green and red lined paper on the shabby oak table in the living room, with the ready reckoner to hand, as the talk ebbed and flowed around him. And he held forth, took off his glasses and laid them carefully open and upside down on the table and mopped his forehead and his eyes with a large grey white handkerchief. 'Those whiz kids' he would say, warming to the topic.

He went to University College Cork in the 1930s to study Agricultural Science in order to become a creamery manager. This was partly funded by a scholarship, and partly by the dowry of his unmarried aunt Minnie (his father's sister) who lived with them. He was the only one of his five brothers to get that opportunity. He never talked about his college days. While he was there the family fortunes declined, and the educational level of each brother was lower than the one before. A jovial man, he seemed to pull away from the financial chaos created by his own father. His marriage to my mother deprived his parents and brothers of his income in the 1930s at a time when they needed it badly: something that could have fractured the relationships between the brothers. It did not do so.

He was stocky with an open face. Black hair until the day he died. An intelligent man: reputedly sixteenth in the Leaving Certificate in his year; thirty-fourth in the Civil Service Exam. One of his mantras was: 'It is not what you know, but who you know', contrasting with my mother's strong belief in the importance of what you know. And yet, he was not sufficiently ruthless to be successful. Inevitably loyal. And impossibly un-lucky in those who were the recipients of his loyalty. When he lost his job as creamery manager there was politics involved and he backed the wrong man: a what-you-call-it bluffer. The other men he worked for? one was a charming fly-by-night; and the other, a weak ineffectual man. Time judged them, not I. But Dad was loyal to them.

> 'If you had served your God with half the zeal that you had served them, He would not in your need have deserted you',[7]

was my mother's frequently repeated verdict as the years wore on.

Hopelessly impractical, when we had no car for several years for our annual holidays in Cork, he borrowed the large red van from his workplace. It only had two seats in the front. What could be simpler than to put a couple of armchairs in the large windowless area for my sister and me? We loaded up two armchairs from our dining room. At every turn and twist in the road the armchairs slid on the steel floor of the van. It was hilariously crazy, our dad's practical impractical solution.

His 'hail-fellow-well-met' attitude of 'treating the prince and the pauper just the same' involved a disregard of hierarchy and a love of company. There is a photo of him in his suit and tie (with a woolly cardigan underneath the jacket), sitting with four other men from the creamery in east Cork when he was in his 40s. They all are holding glasses, maybe whiskey? He sits facing the camera, his face totally open, with a beaming smile on his face. Because of my mother's aversion to alcohol (and worry about alcoholism in his background) they never went to a pub in Dublin. He did join a Fianna Fáil Cumann in the 1970s but grew disillusioned with the party. His social life became narrow: only including his bosses, his brother (Uncle Pat), and for a time Tom O'C, a local excitable man who was also interested in politics. This loss of male camaraderie must have pained him, but he never mentioned it. He ended up drinking at home after my mother went to bed: very rarely getting drunk, just drinking steadily.

A workaholic, my father believed in the value of a job well done, regardless of its level or salary: 'Trifles make perfection, girl. And perfection is no trifle.' I was reared on such sayings. This one reflected, I later concluded,

---

7   Loosely adapted by my mother from William Shakespeare's play *Henry VIII*, Act 3, Scene 2: 'Had I But Served My God, With Half The Zeal I Served My King', https://genius.com/William-shakespeare-henry-viii-act-3-scene-2-annotated, accessed 1 June 2023.

a need to value the more menial work that he had ended up doing. But I took it to heart. When I was learning to write in the grey green copy books with copper plate writing that were part of home and school in the 1950s, I struggled so hard to make the letters, to do it right, absolutely right, that I rubbed a hole in the page in the pursuit of that perfection.

He was a determined optimist who felt that life was against him:

'If it were raining soup,' he would say, 'we would have a fork.'

Yet he was a proper Mr Micawber[8]: 'Something will turn up. We never starved a winter yet.' And we did not. Troubles he used to say grow larger with nursing. So, he did not nurse them. He lived in hope of better days. He did Spot-the-Ball and the Fashions competitions in the *Sunday Independent*, religiously, every week. He had a few small wins before I was born, but nothing after that. Yet defying the Gods and working on the laws of probability, he persisted. A larger-than-life figure, when he answered the phone, he would never say his name but would boom: 'You know the voice.' That kind of arrogant parochialism, that confidence, I loved it. In Dublin, after he put the key in the door, the booming voice would ask: 'Anything strange or wonderful?' It was an invitation to hold forth. Many years later I realised that, unlike most women of my generation, I assumed that men would find what I had to say interesting and would appreciate me holding forth.

He was one of the main people who taught me how to drive. He let me practice by driving him to work through all the traffic to his office in Harcourt Street when I was 16 and an undergraduate in Earlsfort Terrace in University College Dublin, with never a cross or impatient word. Yet we argued vigorously at the kitchen table, much to my mother's chagrin. But he thought I was wonderful. He bored me sometimes, exasperated me often and was pitiable and awful on the very rare occasions when he was drunk. But I loved him.

8   A fictional character in Charles Dickens novel, *David Copperfield*.

My seed and breed

My seed and breed on both sides were Irish and rural and yet they were individualists, in what was a highly collectivist, conforming society. From them, I inherited a disregard for social convention.

My grandmother, on my mother's side, Margaret Kelleher (nee Donovan), was the only one of my grandparents I met as a child. She was a tiny severe woman, always dressed in black. I never heard her laugh. She did not allow my father to smoke cigarettes in her home in Cahermone, in East Cork: an act of assertiveness that struck me as unusual, even as a child, in a society where men's wills prevailed.

The only room in that house that was really used was the kitchen, a stone floored, dark room with one small window, a big black cast-iron bastable pot hanging over an open-hearth fire and a large rectangular table with green benches on both sides. It was a lean-to structure, attached to a fine Georgian house with large windows in the elegant sitting and dining rooms which were down the corridor from the kitchen. By the time she died in 1962, the timber floors in those rooms had been eaten away by woodworm and were unsafe. There was no bathroom and no running water in the house in her lifetime. An attempt had been made to sink a well in the yard, but as it was limestone, it had failed. Water had to be drawn by a horse and barrel (a puncheon) every day. There were extensive out buildings in lovely old stone around a huge cobbled yard. In retrospect I can see that it reeked of better days.

My grandfather's people (the Kellehers) were far more 'respectable' than my grandmother's. His father (my great-grandfather) was a self-made man, born in 1830, before the famine. His will was seven pages long and was signed with an X (he was illiterate). He had a magnificent family grave constructed, with foot high railings and a plinth crowned by a large statue of Christ the Shepherd costing £70 (an indication of the family's social aspirations). He got land from the Land Commission in the then home place of Castleview. In his will in 1904, he left Castleview to my grandfather, Patrick, on condition that he married a woman with a dowry of £500 in her own right (equivalent to roughly £60,000 today). If he did not marry such a woman, it was to pass to his next son and so on, under the same conditions. The executor of the will was another son Timothy, a clerical student (later a parish priest). He picked a 'suitable' girl for my grandfather but he refused to marry her.

My maternal grandmother (nee Margaret Donovan) came from a small neighbouring farm in Whiterock, less than a mile away. She did not have the required dowry but saw my grandfather in Midleton and said: 'That's the man I am going to marry.' She was reputed to have had a waist of 18 inches. Three years after his own father's death, my grandfather married her. There is a photograph of their wedding in July 1907: she, standing, a slip of a girl of 23 in a high Victorian blouse buttoned at the neck, with bouffant sleeves over a heavy woollen floor-length skirt, hair piled high on either side of a narrow severe face, and my grandfather, Patrick Kelleher, 38 years old, moustached, seated, in a three-piece suit and watch chain with incongruously unpolished boots. Her arm rests proprietorially on his shoulder. In accordance with his father's will, although he had worked the farm in Castleview for over twenty years, he was disinherited. An uncle bought a smaller farm for him in Cahermone, but it had no water. The rift between him and his brothers was never mended. His descendants were not buried in the fine Kelleher family plot, exemplifying a kind of homelessness in death, which is a very Irish kind of tragedy.

After her husband's death in 1943, my maternal grandmother ran the farm on her own with two of her unmarried sons (my uncles). They spent their lives hoping to inherit the farm and arguing with each other until first my grandmother and then Dinny, the oldest brother, and finally Pad, the youngest, died. Betty, my mother's only living sister, did not finish nursing training. She loved shopping, travel and a good time, and was always referred to by my mother as a 'right glig' (not a steady responsible person). My mother's remaining brother, Bill, who got a job in the civil service in Dublin, was always referred to by her as Brother Bill.

My father's people were from North Cork and according to one of my father's brothers (Uncle Jack) they would drink the local river, the Aabeg, dry. But there was an element of social ambition way back. My great-grandmother, Bridget Lillis, came as a young servant girl to the house and married my great-grandfather, Denis, in 1878 although he was much older and in poor health. The land was good, but the farm was small. Her occupation was described as a farmer on their marriage certificate. With extraordinary vision, she sent her oldest son, Dan, to Glasnevin Agricultural College in the 1880s on a two-year course to qualify as a creamery manager. Perhaps because the stories of her influence were so powerful and her sons so weak, for her grandsons (my uncles) she became a terrifying ghost.

Her son John, my paternal grandfather, inherited the farm, and married Mary Ann Regan in 1914, who brought in a dowry of £300. His only sister, Minnie, got that dowry, but remained unmarried, living with her brother and effectively rearing her nephews. Because of my paternal grandfather's rakishness, they were threatened with eviction in the 1930s and lived an impoverished existence, trapping and selling rabbits.

My paternal grandfather John, died before I was born, and his wife, Mary Ann, two years after it. They too became homeless in death, losing the family grave in Buttevant Abbey, reputedly through my grandfather's drinking and gambling. From then on, the family was buried in Annakisha. Even that gravestone – a six-foot high Celtic cross – harked back to better days, supplanted by plain headstones on either side.

We did not go to my father's home place in north Cork until August 1964 when I was 13. The excuse was that his three brothers' bachelor life style there was rough and ready. The house was a traditional poor Irish cottage, with a cement floor, small windows, two bedrooms and a kitchen. It had running water but no toilet and there was a large heap of manure too close to the door for comfort. There was a strong feeling that the brothers liked and protected each other and knocked some fun out of life. My father and his brother (Uncle Pat) and their families came down from Dublin that August and we all met up there. The 'Dublin crowd' never visited 'en masse' again. In the autumn of that year, the youngest brother Ned (who had epilepsy and was physically handicapped) died, and some years later Dave died too. When the last brother Jack was still living, I visited him there. He was an intelligent, innovative, if somewhat contrary man who 'adopted' a cousin and signed over the farm to him. I noticed that old car seats were used as armchairs, with the TV hung from the roof at a judicious angle. It typified the O'Connors' prioritisation of comfort, achieved unconventionally.

My inheritance from both sides was declining family fortunes, combined with a disregard for social convention and an awareness of the cost of romantic love from my mother's side and rakishness from my father's.

Making and not making choices

Context

In the late 1960s there were shreds of hope, culturally and economically. Ireland was moving from a predominantly rural agricultural society to a more urban one. However, the institutional Roman Catholic Church still dominated all aspects of public and private life in what was culturally a very static grey society, where men controlled the public areas, and where to be 'really' Irish was to be male, catholic and a supporter of the (largely male) Gaelic Athletic Association. In the 1970s differential pay scales for men and women ended when Ireland joined the European Economic Community (later the European Union (EU)). During this period too, the conflict in Northern Ireland became more overt, with bombs going off in Dublin in 1974. Thus, neither national economic well-being nor political stability was a given.

Women's power base was in the home. Indeed, it was the only arena where most women could dream of having power. Public power was not a respectable aspiration for a woman. Mary, the mother of Jesus (Our Lady) was venerated: submissive, invisible, putting her own needs aside, accepting stigma and loss with grace – this was womanhood at its best. I was not so sure. I liked the idea of a mother figure looking out for me but the ideal of womanhood she embodied sat uneasily with my values.

What to become?

I was set to be 16 years old doing my Leaving Certificate (the final state examination) because I had gone to school at four years old, and had skipped a class after we moved to Dublin. All the jobs that might be considered by a girl from a small family with a lower middle-class background were unavailable to me at that age (e.g. primary teaching, which my sister had done, the civil service or the bank). I refused to repeat the Leaving Certificate. I was just about old enough to be admitted to university. I had, for a girl at that time, a surprising sense of my own importance. I also had a precocious appreciation of professional expertise. I persuaded my parents to spend some of their hard-earned money sending me to University College Dublin for a day when I was 15 years old to be assessed, with a view to identifying my future career options. In neither of their cases had their degrees led to a sustainable career. They did not feel able to provide career guidance – nor indeed would I have accepted it if they had done so.

After a day doing all kinds of assessments, it became clear that my abilities were mainly numerical followed by verbal. My spatial abilities were particularly bad – scoring 25 out of a possible 100. I had a strong sense of social justice. At 15 years old I wanted to change the world and saw no reason why I could not do it. A list of possible careers was identified – including a BA (in history, politics, or English), law, primary teaching, hotel management or social science. Possibly reflecting the fact that my mother did a BA, I cannot recall even considering that. Law was dismissed because we had no contacts; hotel management seemed unrealistic given my lack of practical domestic skills. Social Science had only begun to be offered in University College Dublin in the early 1960s. It had an aura of the prestige associated with science, but was reframed by the word social. I had no idea really what it was – but I decided that was what I was going to do. In retrospect it was an inspired choice for someone whose outsider-ness made the taken-for-granted world appear exotic.

The report from University College Dublin indicated that at age 15, I was in the superior range in the general population but average in a university population at a time when only five per cent of school leavers went to university. Ironically, since my highest score was in the numerical area (97th percentile) it was not possible for me to do honours maths in the Leaving Certificate. Like most girls in single-sex schools at that time, this was assumed to be beyond us and our female teachers. I took six subjects at honours level and got honours in all of them. My best subjects were history (93 per cent) and geography (89 per cent) – and although I remained interested in both I never considered doing them at university. My next best subjects were English (85 per cent) and Irish (82 per cent). These were followed by French and Physiology and Hygiene (75 per cent). I got 89 per cent in pass maths. At that time, it was possible to get into university with two honours – although there was a further hurdle in social science since it admitted only 100 students. I had no worries about making that 100 – but the fees would have to be paid. I assumed that I would live at home. It never occurred to me to get a part-time job – nor was that expected of me. There was a County Council Scholarship of £160 per annum and I decided that I would try to get it.

I grew increasingly anxious and irritable. I cannot remember the specific trigger, nor the aftermath. All I can remember is lifting my right fist and smashing the mirror hanging on the wall by the back door in our small kitchen. Since breaking a mirror brought seven years bad luck, this added to the pressure. Recognising my anxiety and my ambition, my father promised that regardless of whether I got the County Council Scholarship or not, he would give me an (Irish) pound a week. This was a substantial sum of money, to him and to me. I got the scholarship and was able to 'lend' him back the money. Relieved of total financial responsibility for me, he bought a second-hand family car – a Volkswagen. It was a clear lesson in how educational success brings many different kinds of rewards.

I got a blue hard-covered little booklet as a student card when I started my degree in Social Science at University College Dublin. Because that degree was so new and could not mount a full programme of subjects, I had to choose Arts subjects in first year. I chose English; Irish, Philosophy and Economics. My greatest intellectual stimulation came from English. The most exciting lecturer was Denis Donoghue who lectured on Shakespearean tragedy and comedy on Saturday mornings to 500 students in a vast lecture hall in Earlsfort Terrace-then the main campus. He argued that the greatness of man was reflected in his ability to survive in the Shakespearean comedies and that his vulnerability was reflected in the heroes' fatal flaws in the tragedies (these were the 1960s so 'his' went without saying ...). My disposition was to the heroic. But this idea fascinated me, and still does.

My first cousin, Mary (Uncle Pat and Aunty Kitty's eldest daughter) was doing Arts, and also studying English and we animatedly discussed these ideas coming home on the bus and continuing at the lane which linked our two estates after his lectures on Saturdays. But I struggled in the English tutorials (and confided in my mother about this). I was amazed then to come first in the Arts faculty in English in University College Dublin that year. If I had continued with English, I have no doubt that I would have been an enthusiastic, happy and fulfilled second-level teacher. A possible desire to choose a different route to my mother's, or a reluctance to abandon my dreams of changing the world meant that I continued with Social Science. That decision dramatically changed the course of my life.

The head of the department of social sciences was then an adjunct bishop in the Roman Catholic Church, and the heads of the departments of psychology and ethics were priests. That seemed in no way odd to anyone at the time. Neither did the fact that 90 of the 100 students doing Social Science were women, most of whom were middle class and many of whom saw university as simply an enjoyable interlude and/or a way of meeting a 'suitable' husband. I made friends with two women – but joined a study group of men. The men, like me, were very focused on study. They seemed somehow less complicated than the women and my parents' address in a working-class area (where I lived while at college) seemed less important to them. The fact that I was a woman was ignored by me and presumably by them. I was an asset in a study group since I never missed a lecture or a tutorial.

I was in second year when the so-called Gentle Revolution occurred in Earlsfort Terrace, where University College Dublin was at that time, with mass meetings in the Great Hall there in February 1969. These were dominated by confident, entitled, middle-class male students who could not manage the political process – amendments to amendments to proposals and counter-proposals meant that we ended up voting ourselves into knots.

Much of their attention focused on poor facilities, especially in the library in Earlsfort Terrace. I was then living in Walkinstown, a working-class area where most young people did not even finish second-level schooling. We frequently went on holidays to my maternal aunt's house in Cork, where (like many rural families at that time) they did not have a toilet. Arguing about facilities was a luxury I could not afford.

I had identified a career in social work as one of my future options and had already done a short placement in a centre for troubled adolescent girls. A longer work placement had to be done in the summer of second year in 1969. A three-month one as a pre-release social worker was available in Baltimore Psychiatric Hospital in the United States. Possibly because it was an opportunity and/or because of my own unacknowledged mental health issues I applied for it. I had never been in a plane; never been outside Ireland; never been in paid work. No-one I knew was interested in going there. I was a very young 18 year old. I neither asked my boyfriend Seán nor my parents what they thought of the plan, nor considered whether they might approve/have reservations about it. I arrived at John F. Kennedy Airport on my own in a heat wave, wearing an off-white Aran cardigan knitted by my mother and with 40 lb of luggage. The Student's Union had arranged accommodation and orientation for a couple of days in New York. I did not like the city. It was too hot; the buildings were too big; the cars were too long. It was too much. I did the tourist sites – but was happy to leave and get the bus to Baltimore.

Baltimore Psychiatric Hospital was a very large public hospital with 3,000 patients and roughly 1,000 staff on a green campus site outside the city. There were frequent violent thunderstorms in the afternoon and the endless sound of crickets in the evening. My responsibilities were two-fold: firstly, to prepare elderly men who had become institutionalised for release back into the community; and secondly, to help adolescent boys deal with various psycho-sexual issues. Neither of these was related in any way to what I was doing in college nor indeed to my own interests. Both were very challenging for me, although I had a kind and helpful super-visor – the first Black woman I had ever met.

In my free time I loved to walk barefoot in the grass. Staff lived on campus and any such bohemianism was discouraged since it made it difficult to differentiate between staff and patients – illustrating the fragile and arbitrary line between the 'sick' and the 'well'. To save money I had made much of my own wardrobe for my trip – including a very light pink cotton dress with flower buds on it. I was asked not to wear it since it became see-through when I was standing in the sunlight waiting for admission to the adolescent ward and was leading to disruption there. I was mortified. It clarified my ideas about my future career.

While I was there, I learned that I had come first in second year Social Science and that my prize was £50. Without discussing it with my parents or anyone else I decided to use it to see America. I had made an initial foray to Washington with a female mature student from University College Dublin who was also on placement in Baltimore. It was eventful since we were followed by a man unknown to either of us. That was unnerving. My fellow student was not interested in taking a month-long trip around America. My choice was to go alone or not to go. Using almost all of my prize money, I bought a monthly round America Greyhound bus ticket for 99 dollars. My only contact was a friend of Sean's brother who was living in San Francisco. With the help of a guidebook – *Let's Go* – I planned my route, booked accommodation along the way and set off on my own. I was on a very tight budget. I was terrified – but it was an opportunity.

My plan was to cross America without getting off the Greyhound bus. This I reckoned was how the initial pioneers did it – well sort of anyway. It was amazing rolling across the endless plains, seeing the sun go down, sleeping on the bus, and seeing the sun rise again and still be rolling along. Seeing the colossal arch at St Louis was extraordinary: 'Go west young man' was what they had said and here I was: going west. At one point a young man got on the bus, and sat beside me. We fell into conversation. He had what was clearly a lovingly made and very large lunch. I had little money to spend on food and stared at the silver foil around it. He mentioned that it included roast chicken. I love roast chicken. He seemed reluctant to eat it. Before he got off a few hours later he thrust it at me and said: 'You need this more than I do.' He then left the bus. It was delicious. I ate it all. It was the first of those extraordinary acts of kindness by strangers that were to dominate the trip.

I saw the canyons in the Midwest: Grand Canyon – at that time so underdeveloped that it was hard to get a sense of its vastness and depth; Bryce Canyon, an orange wonderland with rock sculptures created by the wind that you could wander through and Zion Canyon, pink and white mountains that blew my mind. I stayed in a timber hut in Zion Canyon. This was a challenge as I was afraid of the dark and was on my own there. I slept badly. I was due to get a bus from the reception area, but overslept. The man at reception was not only sympathetic – but drove me at break-neck speed so that I caught up with the bus.

I met a Vietnam veteran in Los Angeles who took it upon himself to protect me. When I eventually managed to persuade him that I wanted to sightsee on my own, he gave me a small knife to protect myself. A kind but worrying gesture. I had booked a cheap hotel for my last night there and shortly after checking in I was disquieted to hear a lot of shouting and slamming of doors, raised voices and arguments about money, and by a much larger number of people than would usually occupy a hotel room. I began to wonder if it was a venue for prostitutes and their clients. Nobody had bothered me so far – but I was now too uneasy to sleep. I checked out around 11 p.m. saying that I had a late-night bus to catch. I had no money for another hotel. There was nothing to be done but to spend the night in the bus station. I did not realise that this was forbidden as my bus was not going until the following morning. I spent much of that strange uneasy night hiding out in the toilets, trying to look as if I was going somewhere.

A bit unnerved, I headed for San Francisco a couple of days early. I found my way to my contacts' house, bringing a gift and looking forward to relaxing and being looked after. It was not to be. When I arrived, the couple's child had meningitis and they were understandably extremely worried about her and in no mood for visitors. After a short stay I moved on and explored San Francisco on my own. I liked it as a city with its hills and trams and my feelings of personal safely returned.

I made my way back across America in the Greyhound bus-taking a more northerly route this time – again astonished at the sheer vastness of the country and the easy generosity of the people who 'adopted' me – saying that they had sons and daughters of their own and hoped that strangers would look after them as they looked after me. It was my first ever trip abroad -and it was incredibly brave, even foolish. It reflected my need to grasp opportunities, despite my fear. The mental and physical toll it exacted only became clear when I realised that my periods had stopped during the trip. They started again when I got back to Dublin.

I found social science interesting but not riveting. The questions asked were very important but the answers were less satisfactory. The passion I had felt in English lectures never re-appeared. Social policy and social administration were easy but I struggled with sociological theory – particularly those theories that implied that the existing social structure was functional and so inevitable. Simmel's ideas on interpersonal relationships were more interesting[9] (reflecting an interest in the micro and the meso that has persisted). Professor Damian Hannan lectured us on sociology of the family, and although he was not a great lecturer, he provoked me to think about power and love in the family.

I graduated with a first-class honours Degree in Social Science at 19 in 1970. I was delighted but also unnerved since I knew just how little I knew. For my graduation, I bought a midi-length purple dress with a key-hole neckline. But at the last minute, I changed my mind and wore a white high-necked Victorian blouse with bouffant sleeves under black wool dungarees with gold buckles at the front and a red rose pinned at the high-lace trimmed neckline. Mary, my first cousin, who graduated at the same time with a BA, wore a fashionable brown midi-length suit with leather trim. I was totally happy with my rather eccentric, dramatic, romantic outfit. Recently it has occurred to me that my blouse was not dissimilar to that worn by my maternal grandmother in her wedding photo; with my mother sporting a carnation rather than a rose in her graduation photo.

It was unthinkable that I would not get a job straight after I graduated – and a good job. After my experiences in Baltimore Psychiatric Hospital, social work (which was the choice of many of the female social science graduates) was out. I felt that I did not know enough to teach. It had to be research – an unusual choice for a woman. Fortuitously, Professor Damian Hannan was starting a new project on work, power and emotional support in families. Ideal.

9   Simmel, G. (1964). *Conflict and the Web of Group Affiliations*. New York: Free Press.

'Trivial' interests? a research career in a man's world

I applied for and got a three-year contract job working on Professor Damian Hannan's project at the Economic and Social Research Institute in Dublin. Formerly the Economic Research Institute, it was struggling at that time to accept sociology as a 'real' discipline. I bought myself a stunning bright red Dr Zhivago style coat with black fur around the neck, the sleeves and the hem. I was on my way.

It was 1970. Married women were still obliged to retire from the civil service and second-level teaching on marriage. There were higher pay rates for men (seen as 'natural' since they would have a wife and family to support). There were few women researchers in the Economic and Social Research Institute at that time. Most of the women were located in the large room on the ground floor that was the typing pool. Their status was linked to the men whose work they did: with the (male) professors being the most prestigious. As a woman, I did not fit into the predominantly male research hierarchy – but neither did I fit into the female typing pool.

For most of that first year, I was out of the office interviewing farmers and their wives on Professor Damian Hannan's project. Since both the husband and wife had to be interviewed, and separately, we worked in teams of two. I wore a duffle coat and boots to increase my rural acceptability and to reduce any possible embarrassment arising from the suggestion that the husband and myself adjourn to the office car to do the interview if a second room was not available in the house. My Cork accent grew stronger. I felt very comfortable interviewing these farmers, although they were often puzzled about our focus on what to them were the take-for-granted 'natural' arrangements in their farm families. But then, things changed. A new Director of the Economic and Social Research Institute was appointed: a male Irish economist, Professor Kieran Kennedy. At much the same time my supportive line manager, Professor Damian Hannan, left to take up a professorship at University College Cork. The previous Director, Professor Michael P. Fogarty, a genial Englishman, had co-written a chapter on *Dual*

Career Families[10] (an unthinkable concept in Ireland at that time). Before he left, he had agreed that I could use the remaining two years of my contract to work on my own project on how middle-class women felt about housework and child care.

The new Director's secretary summoned me to his office. I felt anxious. I walked down the corridor – past the office doors of the male professors and their (predominantly male) research assistants, past the large beech doors of the Director's office on the left and on into the light-filled spacious women's bathroom at the end. I needed to think. This new Director might threaten my plans. I combed my short brown hair, checked my double-breasted long orange jacket and just above the knee skirt. I straightened my back, took a deep breath and put my chin up (my father's exhortation in all difficult situations). I was ready for him.

I knocked firmly on the Director's door. A tall, physically large man greeted me, and ushered me into a chair opposite his impressively large desk. He cut to the chase: 'With the departure of Professor Hannan, the question arises as to what your workload will be for the next two years.' I explained that his predecessor had promised that I could do my own project and said that he was morally obliged to honour that commitment. The shadow of a frown passed across his broad face.

'What is this project of yours', he asked.

I explained it as best I could, slightly unnerved by his obvious impatience. He was hostile to my topic ('trivial' he said). If I had to study marriage and the family:

'Why not something important like the sexual relationship between husband and wife?'

I said I did not agree with him. Thinking to impress him, I mentioned that I hoped to write it up and submit it as a Master's thesis. To me, a

---

10   Forgarty, M. P., Rapoport, R. and Rapoport, R. N. (1971). 'The Reconciliation of Work and Family Life: The Dual Career Family'. *Sex, Career and the Family*, Chapter 9. Oxfordshire: Routledge.

Master's was like Everest: impressive but daunting. 'Why would you want to do that?' He asked. 'You will marry.' I was dumbfounded. How did he know I would marry? And even if I did, why could I not do a Master's thesis? I told him that his attitude was completely wrong.

No one had ever dismissed my ambitions before. I was furious but also unnerved. Then he delivered his coup de grace: 'You will be reporting to me. My secretary will set up frequent and regular meetings to report on progress.' I tried to protest: he knew nothing about sociology; my topic was not his area of expertise; I would prefer to work on my own without time-wasting interruptions. He now looked irate. He got up. The meeting was over. I went back to the bathroom and looked at myself in the mirror. My face was white. I was shaking. This man had no interest in my work or my future. He thought marriage was the height of a woman's ambitions. It was not going to end well.

Although still appearing publicly confident and bolshie, I became a nervous wreck: retching and crying in the bathroom before each meeting. I had never accepted authority and had no skill in dissembling. He was unable or unwilling to deal with someone who had never grasped the essence of line management. I told him that he was wasting my time: not a strategy likely to gain his support. There was no meeting of minds. I carried on grimly with my research, designed my questionnaire and embarked on collecting data from 100 interviewees. My boyfriend, Seán, was working for a German company and I fantasised about doing a PhD in Germany. Somehow, I persuaded my (to me) impossible boss to pay for me to attend nine hours German a week (he wanted me to do French since I had honours Leaving Certificate French. But I was not for turning).

I began to notice 'odd' things. Most of the time the researchers ate lunch (mine was banana sandwiches) seated together in a very basic canteen-like room at the Economic and Social Research Institute on Burlington Road. The conversation was general and frequently turned to rehashing topics discussed on the then popular *Late Late Show* – such as equal pay for women, the position of the catholic church, the Northern Ireland troubles etc. Politics and religion were the meat and drink of conversation at home. I was used to arguing about them. I invariably launched in with my contribution or drew down topics that I was interested in. I was frozen out. Eventually I recognised that it was taken for granted that the male professors would lead and dominate the conversation, and that their opinions would be treated with the respect they apparently deserved. The junior male researchers appeared to accept this situation (many years later I recognised this as a kind of pragmatism, reflected in an unwillingness to challenge male power directly in such situations, not least because of the expectation that such power would eventually be theirs). I was not comfortable with this situation but felt unable to challenge it. I began to eat my sandwiches alone on Patrick Kavanagh's seat on the canal bank: a strategy that improved my digestion but not my career prospects.

When my three-year contract ended at the Economic and Social Research Institute, not unsurprisingly, unlike the other (male) research assistants, it was not renewed. There was no leaving 'do'. It was 1973. I was 22 years old. The position of women in Irish society was changing. I had finished the data collection for my Master's thesis and was asked to do a piece in *The Irish Times* on it for its end-of-year review. I was invited to join a women's activist group.

But I could not focus on anything beyond the need to get a job. My Master's thesis was unfinished: the analysis had not moved beyond basic description and the theoretical chapters and interpretation still had to be done. The thought of going full-time and finishing it never occurred to me. I was facing unemployment. There were very few jobs for sociologists in 1970s Ireland, especially ones for women with questionable attitudes to line management.

If my research career was to continue, I had to look elsewhere.

Going to London: A new challenge

Like so many Irish people before me, I got a job in London. That job was a three-year contract as a researcher in the Social Research Unit at Bedford and Royal Holloway (now Royal Holloway) University of London, working under Professor George Brown, whose research focused on the relationship between life events and the onset of depression and who had got funding for a project on measuring the factors that increased/reduced women's vulnerability to depression.[11] I flew out and did the interview. I was offered the job. I had no other job offer. In my heart I knew I was going to accept it, but I went through the motions of discussing it with Seán before accepting it and getting ready to move to London. He came over on the boat with me. I watched the figures of my parents getting smaller and smaller on Dun Laoghaire pier. I wore maroon bell-bottom trousers and a voluminous cream shirt – some of the old panache had disappeared. But there was hope: a new phase was beginning.

Through the Irish grapevine, I 'inherited' a small damp bedsit on the top floor of a three-story house in Brook Drive, an old working-class area in Lambeth. There was a gas jet on a green tiled fireplace; a shelf as a kitchen area (no fridge); a chair and small table to work at; a single bed and a lovely big window that looked out over the roofs of London. On the second floor, there was a tiny dark toilet with a sink on the corridor. These were shared with the elderly Irish man next door to me on the third floor who never appeared and coughed incessantly, and with an attractive young Polish man and his laid-back English girlfriend on the second floor. They were friendly and hospitable and frequently invited me in for coffee or a glass of wine.

I was excited to have my own place at last. The damp problem was easily solved: two electric blankets – one above and one below- so that I was like a toasted sandwich in winter. There were public baths in Lambeth so that solved that problem. In my naive enthusiasm, I bought dark green crockery from John Lewis and orange Le Creuset cast-iron pots (because I liked the colour). To celebrate life, I bought brownish ochre goblets – almost like chalices. The limitations of my bedsit for entertaining became obvious the first time I had two colleagues round for a meal. One of them got claustrophobia and had to rush out of the room. I was mortified. During the heat wave in 1976, the absence of a fridge became a problem. On the way home from work, I bought liver to fry on the little gas ring in my bedsit. I left it for 30 minutes on the window sill – my improvised cooler. By the time I

11   Brown, G. W. and Harris, T. (1978). *Social Origins of Depression*. London: Tavistock Publications.

opened it, the stench was unbearable. To solve this problem, I became a sort of vegetarian at home but since food was low on my list of priorities, I could never organise the soaking of lentils which was necessary at that time and so lived on huge litres of yogurt.

My landlady was a tiny kindly woman and an excellent professional cleaner, who lived in the basement of the large three-storey house. She liked to keep an eye on things and hence insisted that she clean the bedsit every week. That was no problem. I loved coming in to the room on the day she cleaned: everything was spick and span and to a standard that I could never even approximate. I got plenty of letters: Seán's neatly typed; my father's handwritten, on huge foolscap pages and my mother's and sister's hand-written on normal stationery. My landlady had met Seán when he came over with me at the start and having a romantic streak, she allowed me to receive calls from him on her phone in the basement flat at the weekends if she was not there. Perfect.

The focus of the project I was employed to work on was mainly meth-odological. On a day-to-day basis, my work involved doing long face-to-face interviews with married women in Acton about themselves and their lives and developing a framework which could identify and measure possible factors protecting them from depression. I enjoyed interviewing and worked amicably on the project with an American woman, Mary-Lou. We were part of a larger group of researchers from all around the world. Although I had not finished my Master's thesis, I was able to register for a PhD, without paying any fees because I was employed by the university. My boss agreed that I could use some of the data from the new project for the PhD. I decided that I would focus on women's very close relationships, mainly very close ties with friends, mothers and sisters. I was interested in the mental health impact of having an intimate confiding relationship with both a husband and a friend or a relative who was defined as very close and who was seen at least every two to three weeks. It seemed to me that women got a lot of support from these relationships but the ideological climate at the time suggested that male partners were the key supports in their lives. In Irish terms this topic was as ahead of its time as my Master's thesis, reflecting as it did, a prioritising of women's experiences and their lives.

I was still very anxious, although this was not obvious. I found the project time scale of three to six years worryingly long. I occasionally did some teaching on the medical sociology course at Middlesex Hospital and loved the immediacy of that experience. I also took students on placement from Middlesex University and found that very rewarding (one of them, a mature student, Jane Nelson, became a lifelong friend).

It was the 1970s – a potentially difficult time to have an Irish accent in London with the IRA engaged in a bombing campaign. I experienced no anti-Irish racism myself but was very aware of this possibility when knocking on doors to interview women in west London. But picking up an English accent was unthinkable. I had what purported to be an office car – a very old van – to get to/from interviews. Never a good driver (although I had passed my Irish driving test at 17 years) and still spatially handicapped, I drove round London. When Seán came to visit, he hated me doing the driving, although he was one of people who had taught me how to do three-point turns before my driving test. Hyde Park corner was a particular challenge to me: visibility was limited in the van so I just accelerated confidently and hoped no one would hit me. When my sister and her family came to visit, it became clear that the only routes I knew to anywhere started from the office, which was then in Harley Street. Wherever I was going, I had to start from there. It was a completely mad strategy – but effective.

I made friends at work and outside it, but had little time for socialising. I was still determined to finish the Master's thesis. A (male) former colleague at the Economic and Social Research Institute was doing the analysis of the data for me for free. At regular intervals I got wodges of green printouts with the latest batch of analysis which I proceeded to spend the evenings wading through and writing up. After six months it emerged that there were technical problems with the analysis. I had wasted six months interpreting data that were incorrect. I walked the streets of London. Then, grimly I came back to my small damp bedsit, dumped the work I had done and started again. I could not type and hired a lovely Indian lady to type the thesis up chapter by chapter. I saw my Master's supervisor, Professor Damian Hannan, on my visits home during the holidays. The M.Soc.Sc. grew to PhD length. The whole thing took years.

I was (unconsciously) afraid to challenge patriarchal power and was barely aware of feminism. Ann Oakley was doing a PhD looking at women's attitudes to housework, supervised by my boss and PhD supervisor. She adopted a feminist perspective on the assignment of these activities to women and published several books on the topic.[12] I took years to finish my (first class honours) M.Soc.Sc. and I failed to publish anything out of it. Having been ahead of the wave, I managed to miss it.

While I was living in Lambeth, I had the same dream several times. I was standing outside a crashed aircraft which was starting to go on fire, with the possibility of an explosion. I had managed to escape but there were other people trapped inside. I always had an internal struggle as I decided whether or not to risk my life by going back in to try and rescue them. I always decided to go back in. There was the effort of physically hauling them out; and having done that, always finding that they were dead. I never tried to understand that dream then or to wonder why it was repeated. I just hoped that it would stop which it did eventually. Looking back now I wonder if it reflected my difficulty in choosing to, as I saw it, sacrifice my own life in a futile attempt to justify my mothers' sacrifices?

At the weekends I explored London. I took the bus that passed by Big Ben and the Houses of Parliament, which seemed the ultimate experience to me. I explored the Kings Road, Chelsea and all the places I had heard about and never imagined seeing. For the first year it was very exciting. I came home for Christmas and Easter. I told everyone how great my life was; that London was exciting. It was. But I was lonely. I had proved that I could survive; that, with my A to Z, I could explore London. But I wanted to come home. It took years before I could admit that to myself. Like so many emigrants before me, one of the unspoken conditions of emigration is that you have to at least look successful before you can return. In a contract job, in a grotty bedsit, with an incomplete Masters and vague hopes of a PhD, I was not in that category. There were still no jobs for unemployed sociologists in Ireland. In 1976 I got offered a further three-year contract in the Social Research Unit, funded by a Medical Research Council grant. With no other options, I accepted it.

12   Oakley, A. (1972). *Sex, Gender and Society*. London: Temple Smith Ltd; Oakley, A. (1974). *The Sociology of Housework*. London: Martin Robertson Ltd; Oakley, A. (1976). *Housewife*. Middlesex: Penguin.

I began to notice that in the Social Research Unit where I worked there were lots of other young women in similar research positions, doing part-time PhDs, all supervised by our boss. There were very few men. None of the young women seemed to be making much headway with their PhDs. Furthermore, the much older and most senior female researcher who worked very closely with our boss, had not yet finished her PhD. We were generators of ideas, but credentials seemed to elude us, destined apparently to all sit at the feet of our master indefinitely. I began to wonder.

After six years at the Social Research Unit, it was time to move on. But that was not easy. My boss, who was also my PhD supervisor, did not want 'his women' to move up or to leave. One of his research assistants, Dr (later Professor) Julia Brannen – who became a lifelong friend – applied for a new job and he contacted her potential new employer and tried to stop them hiring her. Fortunately, despite this she got the job. Anticipating similar problems, I went part-time for an initial six months in 1979 when I got a three-year contract at the National Institute of Social Work. Again, there was no leaving 'do'.

Survival rather than success had become my priority.

A different kind of experience

My three-year contract at the National Institute for Social Work in Tavistock Square London, was as a research officer on a project concerned with the community needs of frail elderly people living in their homes or in a variety of supported environments in North London. The project was led by Professor Ian Sinclair, an idealistic Oxford don who had worked on the frontline in probation and residential care services prior to becoming Director of the National Institute for Social Work. This time I negotiated for a research assistant who would share the data collection. I enjoyed interviewing but was determined to spend time on the analysis and writing up before the end of the project. This was particularly important since although I had finished my Master's thesis, I was still doing the PhD and was working on an article with my now former boss/PhD supervisor.

I had moved from the damp bedsit in Lambeth after four years, initially to a house-share in East Finchley with a male colleague whose standard of housekeeping was way above mine, which was incredibly convenient. Later I shared a house with three others (which became four when Steve, Maggie's partner joined us) in Palmer's Green. There my bedroom had a long, very trendy but depressing black wall and a window that looked out at a high cement wall. I became lifelong friends with Maggie Coster and Steve Scarlett, an artist couple who many years later became special needs assistants to survive economically. I was able to cycle – slowly – to work from there: with children ironically calling out, to my considerable amusement: 'Miss, miss your back wheel is turning' – since I was so slow. I found cycling really helpful in taking out the aggression that seemed to be endemic in me.

The Director who was also the lead researcher on the project had a relaxed, self-deprecating style and was genially patronising – kind and helpful but emitting a feeling of superiority. There, Irishness was a quaint and colourful addition. We all worked in adjacent offices. It was friendly and sociable, with a whip around for office drinks on a Friday for everyone from the Director to the janitor (who was also Irish). The Irish were stereo-typed and were assumed to be, and soon became, the life and soul of the Friday drinks sessions. I found being patronised and protected infinitely preferable to my other gendered experiences. In my work experiences so far, these seemed to be the only options available to women.

However, I was and remained puzzled by one thing. The research team included a female senior colleague and a female research assistant as well as a male research officer at the same level as I was, who was the project leader's clear favourite. I could not understand what was the basis for this preference: he was solid, rarely innovatory, not a particularly hard worker or remarkable in any way. Twenty years later, still trying to understand the dynamics in research teams, I took the train from London to York to ask my then boss why he had favoured him all those years before. There was no clear answer to my question. The fact that he was a man seemed to have something to do with it. It also seemed that it was partly because he was emotionally undemanding and reliable (whereas I was seen as more volatile but interesting ...). I seemed to be a problem even to those who liked and valued me. Many years later I wondered if his preference simply reflected homosociability.

When there I was invited to attend an informal circle of what to me were elderly iconic men. John Bowlby's early work on maternal care and mental health[13] had been widely interpreted as prohibiting maternal employment. I had read his books on *Attachment*,[14] *Separation*[15] and *Loss*[16] which I thought had much more to offer. I was also familiar with and admired the work of Murray Parkes on bereavement.[17] My boss, Professor Ian Sinclair, invited me to join them and other distinguished men for an informal evening in one of their houses. Although I was then in my late 20s, I was unaccustomed to meeting powerful iconic men. My early confidence had by now entirely deserted me. I was daunted. I knew that I was going to be the only woman there – and that I was more than thirty years younger than most of them. I did not know enough. Coming up to the evening I felt more and more anxious and became physically sick. I still went. But I have no recollection whatsoever of the meeting. Suffice to say I was never invited again.

I did drafts of chapters for the forthcoming book from the project while I was still working there.[18] After I left, I published a number of articles from the data, looking at these frail elderly people's friendships,[19] their relationships with their children[20] and the sources of meaning and identity in their lives.[21] On just one occasion, I prioritised the personal over work

13 Bowlby, J. (1965). *Child Care and the Growth of Love*. 2nd edn. Middlesex: Pelican.

14 Bowlby, J. (1971). *Attachment*. Middlesex: Pelican.

15 Bowlby, J. (1975). *Separation, Anxiety and Anger*. Middlesex: Pelican.

16 Bowlby, J. (1980). *Loss, Sadness and Depression*. London: Hogarth Press.

17 Parkes, C. M. (1972). *Bereavement: Studies of Grief in Adult Life*. Middlesex: Pelican.

18 Sinclair, I., Crosbie, D., O'Connor, P., Stanforth, L. and Vicery, A. (1988). *Bridging Two Worlds: Social Work and the Elderly Living Alone*. Hampshire: Avebury.

19 O'Connor, P. (1993). 'Same-Gender and Cross-Gender friendships amongst the Elderly', *The Gerontologist*, 33 (1), 24–31.

20 O'Connor, P. (1994a). 'Very Close Parent/Child Relationships: The Perspective of the Elderly Person', *Journal of Cross Cultural Gerontology*, 9, 53–76.

21 O'Connor, P. (1994b). 'Salient Themes in the Life Review of a Sample of Frail Elderly Respondents in London', *The Gerontologist*, 34 (2), 224–30.

there by going to Ireland, ostensibly for Listowel Writer's week, but in fact because I needed to see Seán, my now ex-boyfriend. I had planned the trip prior to the confirmation of the chief scientific officer's visit to the Institute (a visit that was related to its funding). The director accepted this and it had no repercussions.

Despite the romantic chaos in my life during this period (discussed in the next section) and the ongoing pressure arising from trying to work on the PhD in the evenings, I found the National Institute for Social Work more supportive than any of my previous work environments. It was also the first time I had a 'send-off'. My confidence began to return. However, I was still unable to utilise the contacts I had acquired either at the time or subsequently.

I was still focusing on survival rather than success.

Being a 'proper' woman ...

In the Ireland I grew up in it was very clear that domesticity, self-abnegation and self-sacrifice were key motifs in defining a 'proper' woman. My mother did not fit this image – or at least not happily so. I had been raised to think that I should 'make something' of my life. Although emotionally fragile and often fearful, I was driven, rarely invisible and never submissive. In an attempt to conform to the required domestic stereotype after I graduated and started work at 19, I did an evening Cordon Bleu cooking course. If I was going to conform, I was going to be exceptional. The highlight of my culinary achievement was cooking beef wellington for friends on my 21st birthday. Things went more or less downhill after that.

I was even more deficient in the area of self-abnegation and self-sacrifice. I had reservations about the idealisation of marriage – reinforced by reading *The Future of Marriage* in the early 1970s.[22] It seemed to me that marriage was very good for men, but a lot more problematic for women like me who did not want the 'whole package' of domestic responsibilities

22   Bernard, J. (1972). *The Future of Marriage*. New York: Vail-Ballou Press.

and the underlying expectations about self-abnegation and self-sacrifice. I had seen at close quarters the cost and the consequences of that choice in my mother's life. I was in my early 20s when Seán first proposed marriage in the Partry Mountains in Mayo. At the time most of his friends were getting married and buying houses in suburban Dublin. Was this to be my future? I was horrified. My life was just starting: I had absolutely no desire for a cage – however gilded. I went to London rather than settle for that dream or for the little house that he had bought, as an alternative option, in a remote part of Kerry. But I did not want to lose him.

A long-distance relationship offered space for both of us to pursue our careers and interests. By now, with my encouragement, he had left Kerry and gone to work in Paris. I thought I would like to live there at some stage. I really liked him – loved him – but he was not the be-all and end-all of my life. I was not possessive and I was busy with my job in London and my part-time PhD. I knew that he was less career oriented than I. I could imagine an eventual future when he might take most of the responsibility for running a house and caring for the children – but I was not sure that I was strong enough to forge that kind of a marriage contract. I was in no hurry to settle down and made that clear the second time he proposed.

Meanwhile he had a lovely little apartment in St Germain Du Pre in Paris. It was July 1980. I flew over from London. We went for a bite to eat in a chic local restaurant. I ordered coq au vin and a glass of red wine. Conversation flowed easily as it always did. I talked about my move to the National Institute for Social Work and the PhD. Suddenly he said that he had moved on. He was involved with someone else. It was over.

'I will give it all up' I said. 'The job and the PhD. I will come to Paris.'

'Too late' he said.

I excused myself and stepped out into the warm Parisian night. In the dark street outside I vomited violently. I was devastated. But there was also a tiny flicker of relief. I had made the gesture. I had offered to give it all up. I didn't really want to do that. What was wrong with me? Years later I tried to explain to a male colleague how conflicted I felt about prioritising my own career. He fell around laughing. He thought it was hilarious that I would even consider giving up my job, PhD aspirations and life in London for a man. That seemed entirely daft to him. But did it mean that I was incapable of loving? That I was somehow deficient as a woman? I was not so sure. But when the chips were down, I had offered.

That night I cried so much that when I woke the following morning my face was bloated and distorted. Many years later, I learned that this was Bell's palsy brought on by emotional distress. My return flight was not until the day after. I went to see Chartres Cathedral. I barely registered its gothic spires and beautiful stained-glass windows. I was shell-shocked.

My face returned to normal within a few days but my devastation continued. On my trip to Paris, I had worn my favourite outfit: a soft, olive green tweed knickerbocker suit. It had a high mandarin collar, a long, belted jacket and knickerbockers that ended just below the knee. I wore it with long black boots. I loved it. It was comfortable, stylish and green. Green is of course the colour of the heart in the chakra system. To my considerable surprise mine was broken. Even more disquietingly I was no longer sure who I was or where I was going. I felt abandoned and bereft. How could this be? I was a strong, independent, ambitious young woman who had always called the shots in our relationship. Beneath it all I was a weak snivelling romantic. My strength was an illusion.

I felt I could not exist without talking to him. I continued to phone him occasionally while I was in London. I had got him to promise way back that if we broke up, he would not marry for a year afterwards. He kept his word. Then the next blow came. He rang to tell me the date of his wedding. I bought a bottle of whiskey – something I had never done before. I went back to my room in the rented house-share in Palmer's Green, and proceeded to drink it. I was devastated. The future that I had seen as inevitable had disappeared – and with it my confidence, ambition and sense of self. Who was I? What did I want? I no longer knew. I rang the Samaritans. I quickly realised that I did not want to die. But living was a problem. I went on a four-day week at the National Institute of Social Work and tried to keep my crying to my day off. I was appalled at the disappearance of the independent woman that I thought I was.

He got married – and not to me. When I came back to work in Ireland in 1982, I continued to wear the green knickerbocker suit, now with a black shawl, like the old women of the west of Ireland in the 1940s. Eventually the elbows of the jacket became threadbare. I still wore the knickerbocker trousers with another wool jacket until they too fell apart. A series of black shawls knitted by my sister became part of my wardrobe, signalling my grief and loss, protected by my sister's love and care. I had no phone for ten years. It was the only way I could stop myself from phoning him.

I continued to feel a profound and inexplicable self-disgust. I was it appeared, incapable of self-sacrifice. If this was the price of love, why could I not pay it? What was wrong with me? I was not a 'proper' woman.

Finding yet again that people are good and kind

On the brink of returning to Ireland permanently, at Easter 1982, now in my 30s, I needed to go somewhere that would provide structure and make no emotional or practical demands. A small booklet called The Directory of Monastic Hospitality provided the solution. I chose the Cistercian monastery on the Island of Caldy. There, guests were fed and welcome to attend the services, or not. I spent most of my time sitting on grassy hillocks staring at the sea. I loved Compline, the prayer at the end of the day, when the monks in their long white robes and hoods bent their backs and chanted:

> 'You will not fear the terror of night, nor the arrow that flies by day, nor the pestilence that stalks in the darkness, nor the plague that destroys at midday.'[23]

I loved the idea of being minded and protected from real and imaginary dangers. Although I no longer accepted many of the rules of the institutional Roman Catholic Church, I loved its calming rituals and the order and meaning that religion created. But it required submission – reflected in those bent backs. I wished I could bend the back. I had very briefly considered entering a religious order that served the poor in my teens – but

---

23   Psalm 91: 5–9, https://biblehub.com/niv/psalms/91.htm, accessed 1 June 2023.

concluded that there was an insurmountable problem – obedience. That was still a problem. I was not willing to give up my autonomy, my freedom to shape my own life. But I wished I could be free of the terrors of the night and the arrows that flew in the day. Just keeping going was as much as I could manage.

I met a couple who were also staying there. Eric Harber was a part-time academic, a left-leaning, white South African in his late 40s and his partner who was a much younger, rather conventional middle-class woman – a lawyer. She did not sail. Eric was part of a syndicate that owned a fifty-year-old converted yacht moored off the west coast of Scotland. He initially drew it in the sand and asked me if I would be interested in buying a share. Later he showed me a photo of the boat – Joanna – elegantly beautiful-long and low. Difficulties in transferring my pension meant that I had a nest egg. During the summer holidays, with Seán no longer around, I had been taking sailing lessons in Glenans in the west of Ireland. With nothing more than that photo to go on, I agreed to put a substantial portion of my nest egg into the syndicate. The boat was moored in Oban in Scotland and it was agreed that we would meet up there the following July. There was the minor detail that I was afraid to swim out of my depth. Even in the swimming pool, I liked to swim by the wall. But I ignored that. This was an opportunity.

The boat needed three people to sail her. I sailed at different times with Eric or Chris White as skippers and with an assortment of other men as crew. Eric was an excellent cook and a general all-rounder in survival skills. We remained friends for several years. Chris was an English Quaker, a single parent and social worker in his late 30s, who asked on our first trip what my needs were. This was the 1980s and in Ireland asking a woman what her needs were was uncommon. My need, when I eventually figured it out, was for silence and solitude for an hour every day: preferably on land. I was not confident or competent enough to kayak to land on my own. So, without any slagging or further commentary, I was kayaked by the skipper to the nearest shore every day. This arrangement reflected the prioritisation of my needs – a prioritisation that Irish society so disapproved of. I was delighted with the arrangement – and it did not strike me as in any way odd.

The boat was old, small and damp: a former timber racing yacht with no engine which had been converted to a cruiser after the Second World War. There was no toilet: so, you either went over the edge of the boat or waited until the boat came to shore in the evening. My berth was over the kitchen and underneath the hatch. There, if it was fine and the hatch was open, I could see the stars. Even with the hatch closed I could hear the clinking of the halliards – a reassuring sound. I loved the gentle rocking of the sea. Minor inconveniences like bathrooms and damp could be worked around in such convivial and beautiful settings.

My limitations as a crew member were obvious to both skippers. I was too weak to lift the anchor; too stroppy (and incompetent) to cook. My dreadful sense of direction and poor spatial ability meant that I was not to be trusted with the charts. As a crew I was willing and cheerful – a social lubricant in every situation. That was a role I was very comfortable with. For the first time in my life, I was in a situation that required total and instant obedience. Debating what we should do when the boom was swinging overhead was out of the question. Somewhat to my surprise I adjusted to the situation. Our lives depended on it. I completely trusted both of the skippers. It was a holiday. No principles were involved. On one occasion the boat hit a rock which was not on the chart and got holed. On another occasion, the mast broke when we were out of sight of land. But in each case the skippers behaved calmly and confidently and brought us safely to land. Obeying competent men on holidays in a life-or-death situation it emerged was not a problem for me.

We sailed up the west coast of Scotland for two weeks every summer over a six-year period, beginning at Oban. We sailed to Eigg, Canna, Skye and to the outer Hebrides – to Barra, South Uist, Lewis and Harris. The scenery was stunning. Over the years there were a couple of days when it was so stormy that we could not leave the harbour. We talked and read then. By this time, I was living in a house on my own. But if truth be told it was a busy but lonely life. I loved the easy amity of life on board. I loved coming into harbour as the sun was setting and having a glass of wine with our meal on deck (a meal I had not prepared) and enjoying good conversation. In the company of these men, who had started off as total strangers, I never felt in any way fearful. My naive assumption that everyone was good and kind yet again proved to be true.

One of the last gifts I got from Seán was a colourful dark blue, yellow and red woollen romantic 1920s cloche hat with a rosette over the ear. Like the orange stripey marble in my childhood, it wiggled its way into my heart. I lost it in a little village in Lewis where we were moored overnight. I left a description of it and my name and address in the local shop before we sailed on. Many weeks after I returned to Ireland a package arrived containing the hat. A lorry driver had found it – it appeared to have blown into the back of his lorry. It was magical when it reappeared against all the odds.

Yes. People are good and kind ... at least on holidays ....

Coming home

Context

In the 1980s the statues of Our Lady were apparently moving in grottos around the country. There were extremely high levels of unemployment and huge numbers of young people leaving the country for work. In 1983 an amendment to the Irish Constitution was passed which gave equal rights to life to the foetus and to the mother. Referenda related to the availability of abortion and divorce were both lost. There were a series of personal tragedies involving women who became iconic, representing as they did the treatment of women by Irish society. Eileen Flynn was sacked from her job as a secondary school teacher in Wexford because she was living with a man who was separated from his wife (there was no divorce at that time). A young schoolgirl, Ann Lovett, died giving birth in a grotto: the question of whether incest was the source of the pregnancy was unspoken. The Kerry Babies case involving Joanne Hayes was a chilling reminder of men's power in the Gardaí, in the Roman Catholic Church, in the judiciary and in politics. She was wrongly accused of murdering her newborn child – and an entirely male tribunal compounded the original wrong by changing the focus from an investigation of police practices to an inquisition into her sexual life.

In 1982 I got a job in Ireland and I came home ...

Starting teaching .... A new career?

Full-time research did not suit my anxious, extrovert disposition, but there were very few academic jobs in higher education in Ireland. It never occurred to me to revisit my old lecturers in University College Dublin to explore options, or to talk to the kindly supervisor of my Masters. I turned to family. My sister, Stella, kept an eye on the advertisements for me. Eventually a lecturing position was advertised as course director in child care in Waterford Regional Technical College (later to become Waterford Institute of Technology, and in 2022, the South East Technological University (SETU)).

Most of the workload involved teaching adults, who were then part-time students on block placement, on the National Diploma in Child Care. They were working in centres for children who were, in the terms used at the time, emotionally disturbed, socially disadvantaged, delinquent or mentally handicapped. The idea of lecturing them on Principles and Practice of Child Care was daunting. I knew nothing at all about children. The only time I ever minded my nieces the electric cooker went on fire and I reached instinctively for water to put it out. (My sister fortunately pre-empted my action). I had a good understanding of social disadvantage and some insight into emotional disturbance (based partly on my research in the 1970s on the factors protecting women from the onset of depression; and partly on a sample of one – myself). But to an institution that wanted to improve its status, my CV looked impressive. I was offered the job on condition that I passed the oral Irish exam.

I dithered for three months about accepting the offer. I knew the extent of my ignorance. Could I do this job? My discipline was sociology and that was a very small part of the teaching load. I had done no research even vaguely related to this area. But I needed to come home. The immediate problem was passing the oral Irish exam. Although I had gone to the Gaeltacht in my teens and had studied Irish in first year in University College Dublin in the late 1960s, nine years in London had taken their toll. I contacted anyone I knew who spoke Irish and practised frantically.

I rented a car and invited my parents to come away with me for a short break during which time I would do the Irish oral exam. My father was frail and fearful, having been diagnosed with terminal cancer six months before, but was willing to come: and noted with black humour that the name of one of the places where we stayed was Dunromin. I had stopped driving in London a few years earlier when I changed jobs and lost the office van. I assumed that like riding a bicycle, this was a skill that would come back to me. I was wrong. My parents never knew that every time I went to overtake another car I came out in a cold sweat. We all survived. I passed the oral Irish exam. I accepted the job offer in May 1982 and prepared to move back permanently to Ireland.

I identified Dunmore East as a possible place to live. It seemed to be small enough to have a sense of community but not so small as to be claustrophobic. It also had a reputation for eccentrics. I thought I just might fit in. After I went back to London, I put an ad in the Munster Express, the local Waterford paper, looking for an apartment with a sea view in Dunmore East. It was more than thirty years before apartments appeared there. But an enterprising woman – Mrs Quinlan – wrote back to say that she had a little house overlooking the sea for rent. Sight unseen – not even a photo – I sent on the deposit and the first month's rent. My worldly friends in London were convinced that either no house would exist or that it would be a shack on the beach. They were wrong. When I arrived, it was a real house with a sea view: the key was in the door and a bottle of milk in the fridge.

I started my new job in September 1982. All of my classes with the part-time students on the National Diploma in Child Care were in the old Military Barracks, a run-down cluster of buildings a mile away from the main campus with no canteen or any kind of facilities. The students, who were eminently practical people, soon organised themselves: bringing kettles, cups, milk etc. My first lecture to them was in Sociology, outlining core concepts such as society, structure, roles, norms etc. It was a dismal failure. I saw their eyes glaze over. They were competent responsible people who thought from the concrete to the abstract -whereas my mind went in the opposite direction. They thought about the children they knew and the kinds of experiences they had at home and at school; whereas I thought about societal structures and cultures which created inequality and marginalisation. I was also teaching them Principles and Practice of Child Care, which they certainly knew more about than I did. I realised that the traditional lecture format was not going to work. In desperation I decided to use a different approach: one which many years later I recognised as student-led learning. For each class I identified a 'reading': I marked up a text with start and stop signs – picking out clear key sentences. There were difficulties identifying pieces that were small and clear enough to be manageable. It was tedious – but that was no problem. They took turns 'volunteering' to present the ideas in each piece. I made clear that I expected them to show up with it done. I joked with black humour, that if they were dying, their first thought should be to pass on the reading to someone else in the class. They never failed me.

Predominantly from working-class backgrounds, they did not know what was meant by critiquing texts and were afraid of speaking out of turn or being critical. I asked them to identify first what they liked/disliked about each piece, and then to push that feeling up from their stomach to their head, and then to identify what they saw as its strengths and weaknesses and what questions it raised for them. To strengthen their confidence, I wrote their thoughts on the board as they spoke. It worked. They loved it. And so began the process of developing their capacity for critical thinking and their confidence to do it.

I had never held a full-time teaching job and had very little experience of lecturing apart from giving a very occasional lecture in medical sociology in London. This was one of the jobs I was least qualified to do in my entire forty-six-year career. It was also one of the most successful. Running into these students many years later, they invariably said how much they enjoyed these particular classes and how much they learned from them. I realised that sometimes not being the expert is the secret of success.

My appointment as course director on the National Diploma in Child Care, which had seemed totally incongruous, had a kind of logic. I always had reservations about 'the family' as a site for the upbringing of children and as a source of women's satisfaction, unconsciously reflecting my own experiences. Women were still overwhelmingly expected to be the main carers of children. It seemed to me that not all women were suited to the

24 × 7 care of small children – and that if women were unhappy, children were likely to be too. The sexual abuse of children was beginning to be recognised, but a substantial amount of it occurred in families and this was still not being faced. I was very comfortable thinking about how families might be supported and alternatives valued. In a context which stigmatised such arrangements, this was a useful perspective.

The job began to restore my early confidence. At 36 years old, with the Masters and the PhD eventually submitted, and with a permanent job, I took myself in hand. I told myself that if I had not published a substantial amount before I was 40, I would have to give up the dream of being a published academic. That terrified me. I had no other dreams. I started to publish. During this time, I also read and thought a lot about children and their care. I began to recognise that, under certain conditions, caring for children could be satisfying and stimulating. I briefly considered having a child. But at this stage I was not in a relationship. The only context available appeared to be single motherhood. I could see how totally constraining that was and I could not see myself managing it.

I found teaching deeply satisfying and enjoyed the immediacy and strange intimacy of the classroom. I mixed easily at break times with anyone and everyone. The older teachers were going nowhere so there was no backbiting or cutting down to size. Outside work, I hung around with a younger crowd of academic staff and thoroughly enjoyed that. I never hung out socially with the students. Yet my boss at the time noted that:

> 'In a very real sense she lives in and for her students, always demanding more and more both of herself and them ... [she is] utterly tireless in the pursuit of the highest standards.'

The fact that child care was seen as a low status, trivial area by many of my (male) colleagues entirely eluded me for many years. I had, quite unconsciously, developed the ability to shut out the negative evaluation of the area and by association, the negative perception of me and of my own competence and ability.

I was very surprised when an attempt was made to get rid of me as course director on the National Diploma in Child Care and to replace me with a newly arrived male colleague. The process was subtle and relentless.

A colleague lent me a book by La Rouche called *Strategies for Women at Work*.[24] I followed the advice on 'how to deal with a no – holes – barred barracuda'. It worked. On a course developmental weekend, I calmly challenged my newly arrived male colleague. He folded. I felt strong. I knew that I had won that round but worried about whether I could keep it up. Not long after that he left the job. I was waking up to the reality of power and beginning to see my own 'fatal flaw'.

Diary: 28 Jan 1989

> I know that my fatal flaw is that I only 'pander' to people I genuinely admire-and even then, I don't see why I should not be validated in return. In other words, I have never learned the art of managing the male ego. Yet I like nurturing egos – and freely give support to anyone I feel like giving it to. But just because one is a man to expect this of women – ugh. Yet they do.

At that time Dr Venie Martin was head of adult and continuing education (many years later she was awarded an MBE for her work in the University of the Third Age). A Northern Irish, incredibly efficient, energetic woman, she built on casual corridor conversations and proposed a Saturday morning class in women's studies. Four of us were to be involved: Venie herself, who was a manager with a background in hard science; Jane Steward, a gentle and courageous Anglo-Irish woman with legal expertise; Ann Jordan, an English woman interested in philosophy and myself, an Irish sociologist. We were all white and middle class, although from very different cultural and disciplinary traditions. None of us had ever studied women's studies – but in 1989 there was a momentum for change, reflected in a desire to examine the position of women in Irish society.

The turn out for the Saturday morning classes was impressive. For my session, I used Ann Oakley's work on the myths surrounding motherhood,[25] helpfully summarised with hints on teaching it by Leonard and Speakman in the Open University *Changing Experience of Women Series*.[26] These myths

---

24 La Rouche, J. (1985). *Strategies for Women at Work*. London: Unwin.
25 Oakley, A. (1976). *Housewife*, pp. 186–211. Middlesex: Pelican.
26 Leonard, D. and Speakman, M. A. (1983). *The Changing Experience of Women: Unit 9. The Family: Daughters, Wives and Mothers*. Milton Keynes: Open University Press.

included the myth that all women need to be mothers; that all mothers need their children (because of 'maternal instinct'); and that all children need their mothers. Most of the women there could relate to the idea that the situation in which women were expected to bring up their children was frequently not ideal: typically involving isolation, total responsibility, often compounded by money worries and lack of status, with the assumption that mothers would 'naturally' know what their children needed and be totally fulfilled by meeting their needs. This led to a discussion on poverty and an invitation to Kathleen O'Neill, an articulate Dublin working-class feminist to speak to us on that topic. That session was a moment of tension and illumination. Kathleen saw us not as women, but as middle-class women. We survived and continued the classes for a number of years. But the reminder that although many women share important experiences, they are not all similarly positioned – and that privilege is often taken for granted – was made very clear in that Saturday morning class.

In my late 30s, I saw an opportunity for the development of a new degree in social work. It would enhance the institution and add to the greater good by educating professionals in an important area. Full of enthusiasm I gathered a team around me and we produced a credible document for academic approval. The timing was excellent and there was a strategic opportunity to get professional validation for the course. It was all very exciting. My PhD and publication track record gave it and me credibility. However, there was a problem. Neither my immediate line manager, nor the director/president of Waterford Regional Technical College would back me. I was very puzzled. Instead, they backed a degree put forward by a male colleague, who had no PhD or publications but who had footballing expertise. My assumptions were called into question.

I had assumed that if I had an idea that would improve the system, and if I argued persuasively enough, it would be adopted. I had assumed that people were valued for their educational qualifications and for doing their job well. In many ways I had kept to a 'stereotypical male script' up to this point in my career. I had been happy and productive there. However, my taken-for-granted assumptions were now undermined. I remembered those arguments with my mother and father in the small narrow kitchen in Walkinstown. I wondered if my father rather than my mother had been right: that it was who you knew rather than what you knew that was important.

Another blow ...

My father did not want to retire – and had a one-year reprieve due to confusion about his date of birth. In 1981, a year after his retirement, he was diagnosed with lung cancer and was given a year to live. He felt that it was a death sentence. It was the first time that I ever knew him to lose hope. I was working in London at that time and he told me of the terminal diagnosis – holding it back for several months from my mother and sister. In January 1982, he became confused – putting the lighted ends of the cigarettes into his mouth – and had to be hospitalised. It was the year of the big snow and no one was able to visit him. He felt abandoned. I felt dreadful. But he recovered his wits and went home.

I had gone to London for three years in 1973. Nine years later, and with the break-up of my relationship with Seán and my father's terminal diagnosis, it was time to come home. While I was sailing off the coast of Scotland on Joanna in July 1982, just before moving back permanently to Ireland, he had a heart attack. I only heard about it when I came back to London. (There were no mobile phones then). I packed up and flew straight home. I rented a car at the airport and went immediately to the hospital, bringing a bottle of whiskey, his favourite tipple. He was still alive. I wept with relief.

He died six weeks later on 17 October. I had driven to Dublin that weekend. He had been released from hospital and was at home in Walkinstown. I took him out to Dun Laoghaire in the car on Saturday. On Sunday afternoon, before I left, he was still in bed. He looked tired.

I asked 'How are you feeling?'

The cup in his hand was shaking. He shook his head wearily. He had fistfuls of tablets that he needed to take in a green kitchen bowl.

'I don't feel right', he said.

I had brought him some tea – Earl Grey. I could feel his despair.

'You must have something to live for Pop, even if it is only Earl Grey tea.'

The inevitable 'ay-yeh' as he settled his glasses to read the side of the box of tea.

'That must have been expensive', he said.

I read the side of the box aloud to him, afraid his eyesight might not be up to it. Not wanting to know how bad it was.

'I am sorry to see you so out-of-sorts Pop.'

'I know – I know you would do anything you could.'

'Oh Pop'. Recklessly I hung on to hope: 'You will come down to Dunmore East when you are feeling a bit better. You will. I know you'd love it. You'd only have to sit into the car.'

His eyes looked disinterested. 'Please God' – I said frantically. Reluctantly he repeated it: 'Please God.' I kissed him.

It was Sunday. I was teaching on Monday morning. It was raining hard. The road was flooded. The thud of the wipers. The radio in the car was not working. Swish, thud; swish thud. I rang when I got down to say that I was back safely. He did not come to the phone. That was strange. I did not ask why. Later that evening I got a message from my sister to say that he had died. I was distraught. I had only been living in the village for six weeks. I knew no one well. I rang Jane Nelson, an old friend in the UK, who was bewildered about what I wanted her to do. I went down to the harbour and looked at the sea. I decided to go to Dublin. With tears streaming down my face, I stopped in Waterford to buy petrol. I got as far as Thomastown, 65 kilometres away. Then I turned the car and came back to Dunmore. As long as I didn't go to Dublin, he was not dead. The following day I set off again and this time I got to Dublin. The sound that came out of my mouth when I saw him laid out was like an animal. I did not realise it was coming from me.

I was not there when he died. My mother and sister were there. I went through the funeral in a daze. There were few people I recognised. I had been away for nine years. It had all happened so fast in the end. That New Year's Eve my sister Stella wrote an account of his death in one of her children's copybooks. I appreciated that very much. Her youngest was only 8 months old when he died. She had three other children. It was years before I could open the copybook.

I was 32 years old.

The Grim Reaper

For much of the early 1980s, the lights, metaphorically were on, but there was no one at home. After my father died in 1982, my mother fell and broke both arms (osteoporosis was diagnosed) and lived with my sister for six months before going back to her own house. Then she was diagnosed with motor neurone disease, with her speech and swallowing affected. All her food had to be liquidised. Semolina featured prominently. To ease the pressure on my sister who was pregnant with her fifth child, I invited my mother down to visit several times in the year before she died.

Christmas 1983 was the only time I ever cooked a Christmas dinner. When I was young we never had more than the four of ourselves for Christmas dinner, but it was a worrying event which cast a long shadow. My mother's stuffing was wonderful and the roast potatoes were excellent. But the worry of the turkey dominated the day. After Stella married, my mother never cooked another Christmas dinner. Like my mother, I now worried about the turkey being undercooked. The day was spent checking it before eventually deciding it was done at 7 p.m. It had to be liquidised for her and it took her two hours to eat it. It was after 9 p.m. before we both, with a sigh of relief that it was all over, sat down with a Bailey's Cream – my mother's viciously anti-alcohol views forgotten by both of us.

She came down again for Easter 1984 and although her speech was bad and her difficulty in eating even liquidised food was awful, she was more herself. The weather was bright and sunny. I took her on a tour of Dunbrody and Tintern Abbey, both famous ecclesiastical sites:

'Not another ruin' she said.

On 4 July 1984, she was given two to three months to live. Without hesitation or discussing it with anyone she decided that she did not want any medical intervention to help her swallow. She knew that meant that she would starve to death. I had often seen her as a clinging vine. No more. I admired her courage in the face of death.

She stayed for three weeks in Dunmore that summer. I was glad that she did. She was terribly old and thin and the first week was very hard. I had difficulty understanding her and was afraid to leave her on her own. Then I began to relax and by week three it was nice to have her staying with me. Ever frugal, she joked that if she died, to save the cost of a hearse making the journey, I should pop her in the car:

'Put my hat on my head and drive me back to Dublin.'

With black humour, we laughed about what might happen if we were stopped by the Gardai. As my return to work loomed, I drove her back to Dublin. We stopped at a lay-by for a break. I lay down on the grass margin. I knew that she would never be back down again. It felt like I was abandoning her. A traitor. Pulling myself together, I got back in the car and drove on.

She died on the 1 October 1984. Unusually, she had gone to stay at my sister's house for the weekend because she was not well. I had been at the only local wedding I was ever invited to on Saturday and got up late. I was wearing an orange jumpsuit. I rang Stella on Sunday and also very unusually, she sounded worried. Her fifth child was only 2 months old and her husband was away for a few days for work. I got into the car and drove to Dublin. Mother was in bed. I sat with her and reminisced about nice things in the past. I did not think that she would die. By the following morning she was dead. We washed her ourselves. I went through the funeral in a daze in my orange jumpsuit. We found jars and jars of Nescafe Instant coffee and dozens of toilet rolls in the wardrobes in her house. Life's essentials.

Our parents had discussed their wills with us several years before. It was agreed then that their house would be sold and its contents divided between my sister and I. I had never liked the house but I found the dismantling of the props of my childhood very difficult. Even charities did not want most of the furniture as it had woodworm. My sister had to burn most of it. To my shame, I opted out. I could not even watch. We divided the rest amicably. Stella took the old dining room oak table. I took the 1950s fireside chairs, reeking of memories of those endless discussions on politics and religion. I still have those chairs. They have been recovered and repainted several times. They are old and not particularly comfortable, but I do not feel able to part with them. They are a link to positive memories of my mother.

I ended up with a choice between the large black and white studio portrait of my mother on her graduation day and a similarly sized picture of the Sacred Heart. I had no hesitation in choosing the studio portrait. It had hung in our formal sitting room, the room that was only really used at Christmas in the house in Walkinstown where my parents lived until their death. She sits there holding her parchment in her gloved hands in her graduation gown. Her eyes are calm and steady. Her mortar board is at a jaunty angle. It was a moment of triumph and of intense disappointment, one that she continued to talk about until her death at 71 years. The photo sits on top of the filing cabinet in the porch of my little house. Every time I go out the door, her eyes follow me.

Grief hollowed me out. The lights were on but there was nobody at home.

What can I do about me?

I have always read self-help books – feeling that I was never good enough – that I needed to improve. These feelings had many sources but they never reflected a sense that as a woman, I was not as good as a man or that I should be subordinate to my (male) 'betters' and be happy with that. When I was 23 years old, Seán described me as (amongst other things) a: 'fighter, frightened thinker, untrained woman and child feeble'. I thought then that it was a pretty perceptive assessment. If like me, despite appearing self-confident, you have underlying anxieties, the question: 'Is it me?' becomes increasingly difficult to avoid:

> 'Am I too confident/not confident enough? Do I say too much/too little? Do I look too feminine/not feminine enough?'

What to wear – especially at work – became a problem. In my 30s I neither knew nor cared about the professional or social conventions as regards what I wore. I saw it as a personal choice and unrelated to doing my job. I was far too busy finishing my (part-time) Masters and PhD, teaching, researching and publishing to think about clothes. Even more importantly perhaps I did not see why I should do so. My favourite outfit for work in the 1980s was a petrol-coloured jumpsuit and a well-worn black leather jacket whose rips on the sleeves I had mended with black insulating tape. I did not see what was wrong with it – nor how what I was wearing made any difference to my ability to teach and research. After my attempts to get support for a social work degree in Waterford Regional Technical College failed, despite the clear superiority of my academic performance to the man the director/president backed, I asked a colleague to tell me straight what I was doing wrong:

> 'Look at yourself', she said. 'You look dreadful. You need to wear smart casual to work – or at least to soften your image.'

My colleague was very clear: my outfits were unacceptable – too unconventional and not feminine enough. She dismissed my protestations about lack of time:

> 'Keep a pair of ear rings in the car. Put them on when you are driving. How much time will that take?'

I could do that even though I felt that I should not have to do it. Her other comments were more difficult to absorb:

'Management sees your area-child care – as trivial. That affects how they see you. No matter what you do, you are unlikely to be able to change that view.'

She said that the predominantly female area I worked in at that time (the National Diploma in Child Care) was not taken seriously and that, despite my PhD and publications, because I was seen to embody that area, I lacked intellectual credibility. Those in power did not identify with me, and so would not support or sponsor me. The earrings were easily sorted. But management's perception of me posed a more fundamental challenge. I realised that I had a lot to learn and that I probably would not have the opportunity to do so there.

When I moved to a new job in the 1990s, I made more of an effort. I always wore earrings and I dumped the petrol jumpsuit and the leather jacket. After a particularly gruelling period of job rejections and with some important interviews coming up, I decided I needed professional help. I went to *Colour Me Beautiful*. The lovely woman I met, Hilary, could not believe the extent of my ignorance. I had no idea of my body shape (I am an extreme version of a pear). I had no idea what shapes or colours suited me. I had never understood the concept of smart casual. I occasionally bought very dramatic outfits and pieces of jewellery – but these sat uneasily in a functional and unintegrated wardrobe. My weak ankles meant that black low-heeled boots were my default option with any outfit. She went through my wardrobe and culled it. She took me to shops I had never noticed and under her instruction I bought an entirely new wardrobe including a soft wool grey trouser suit for interviews and a dark red and black bouclé jacket and knee length skirt which (yielding to my love of the dramatic) she paired with a spectacular large chunky star-shaped piece of junk jewellery. I loved them and the other pieces that we bought together. They were comfortable and they looked good.

She insisted that I buy a whole set of new make-up and try it out for her. When I saw liner, I assumed that it was for my eyes. It was a kind of pink – and I did think, even without my glasses, that I looked a bit strange, a bit like Percy the pig in fact – but then this was a new image. I was willing to go outside my comfort zone. When I showed her my efforts, her jaw dropped. I had put lip liner on my eyes. I thought it was hilarious.

Her work alleviated one of my chronic worries about interviews: what to wear. I had some success in my new rig-outs – although there were still tricky moments such as when I only noticed just before going into one interview that the seam on my soft grey elegant trousers had given so that I had to back out of the room after the interview lest all be revealed.

I was very sad when she died unexpectedly and far too young. It had been fun and under her guidance I did look much better. It took me a long time to recognise that, as my colleague earlier recognised, there was a bigger problem and that no matter how I looked, I was not likely to be acceptable.

Not the only chancer ....

For the first time in my life, when I came back from London in 1982, I chose where to live. That choice was the little fishing and sailing village of Dunmore East. Since I was living there it seemed a pity not to sail. In the early 1980s I put up a sign in the sailing club saying: 'Experienced crew available.' This was strictly speaking accurate. I had sailed with very competent skippers on Joanna. I had done several sailing courses and short cruises organised by Glenans in Baltimore and Collinmore. Their philosophy involved each person doing a day's cooking during their holiday. I liked that ethos but put myself in the most unskilled jobs (i.e. chopping and cleaning) since I was still hopelessly inadequate on the domestic front. I found the sailing courses challenging. The essence of sailing is that you must adjust your position relative to the wind and the sea. For someone who had always listened to their own tune and did not adjust their metaphorical sails to the prevailing environment, this was a challenge. Going straight into the wind (my usual approach to life) was a way of stopping the boat. This forced me to challenge my reactions. 'Experienced' was not however a full description of my abilities. After a dreadful couple of days trying to handle a dingy in a force 5 wind during a course in Baltimore (when I was violently sick with anxiety every day before even getting into the boat) I had concluded that small dinghies were not my forte. I had failed the skipper's course on larger boats. Yet I was 'experienced'.

Two opportunities appeared. Des Greene and his wife and family had rented a house in Dunmore East for several years. He was an engineer who had built a wooden clinker boat which he sailed. Himself and his adolescent son and an elderly relative were taking the boat out on a sunny day in the 1980s and they asked if I would like to join them. Great. They were going to have a picnic over by the Hook lighthouse. Off we set with Des at the helm. We dropped anchor near the Hook and had the picnic. Then on the way back Des offered me the tiller and hence also control of the sails since in a dinghy both are the responsibility of the skipper. This was generous and unexpected since I was at best a crew member. All went well initially. Then it was necessary to negotiate a path between six rows of boats to get to their berth. I managed it with ease. Premature self-congratulation set in. His son stretched himself out on the front of the boat ready to pick up the anchor ball when I stopped the boat by bringing it straight into the wind. I failed and had to whip the boat around to try again. In doing that, his son, who fortunately could swim, shot off the bow of the boat. I tried again. Again, I failed to get the boat to stop. I shouted to Des to drop the sail so as to slow us down. In doing that the sails got tangled in the ropes and so we again failed to stop. After three failures, I asked for help. With Des at the tiller, we hit a rock in the inner harbour and waded to shore – to the amusement of the line of people outside the sailing club watching our undignified end. We saw the funny side of it and remained friends, although I never sailed with them again.

The next opportunity was an invitation to join two strangers who had seen my notice in the sailing club and who needed an extra person on their boat to sail to Kinsale in west Cork. I accepted with alacrity. We set off at dark which was a bit surprising. We were not long at sea when it became clear that a lack of competence was not only an issue on my side. The boat became tangled in fishing nets. The men were unable to drop anchor and so we were unable to stop until we reached a marina. The cooker was not on gimbals so every time the boat tilted the contents of the stove slid across the cabin. We eventually reached Kinsale without any loss of life. There was an excellent disco scene there. To my surprise the men, who had been so careless of my life at sea, looked after me there, making sure I got safely back to the boat after the discos. One of them even offered to clean my shoes-something no one had ever done for me since I was a child. During the day, I decided to get in some sailing experience and ended up trapezing out of reasonably big boats – exciting but not too nerve-wracking. The two men decided they had enough of sailing and went off on the ferry to the UK while I got the bus back to Dunmore.

I concluded that perhaps I should restrict my sailing to the Joanna where the skippers were fully aware of my inadequacies. However, that era too was coming to an end. By the mid-1980s everyone in the syndicate had either to pay for repairs to the boat or do the repairs themselves. Doing the repairs was out of the question: I was useless at that kind of thing. Ireland was in yet another recession and I was embarking on building a house. Money was tight. And so, I lost my share.

All the men I sailed with, like so many other men I met socially, were decent, honourable, kind men. In my naivete I never expected them to be anything else. I was well into my 60s before I fully appreciated that neither my expectations nor my experiences of men were shared by most of the women I knew.

Some of these men's competence, however, like my own sailing competence, was overstated. I was not the only chancer.

Building a house

When my parents died, their house in Walkinstown was sold and the proceeds divided amicably between my sister and myself. Unlike most Irish women of my generation, I had never been interested in owning property or discussing back boilers. I was then in my mid-30s and still renting. But now it was becoming clear that I needed a home base. I looked at a few houses in the Waterford area but none seemed right. I knew that I wanted to live within the ambit of a street light since I was still afraid of the dark. I wanted a sea view. I also wanted a house small enough to be filled by one person but sufficiently flexible to absorb a large number of visitors without feeling crowded. I decided that I would have to build and that I would do so in Dunmore East. At that time – in the mid-1980s – estate agents were not interested in selling sites there. One June bank holiday weekend I set out. I identified green spaces here and there around the village and knocked at the nearest door and introduced myself:

> 'Hello. My name is Pat O'Connor. I am renting a house in the village. I am looking for a site to build on. Would you be interested in selling me that one?'

They said no – but suggested other people I might contact and places I might look. Eventually I came to a garden with a part of it overlooking the sea – and the owners were interested in selling. It had outline planning permission. A price was agreed (£8,000 – all my inheritance from my share of the sale of my parental home). I lodged a cheque for that amount with the solicitor. I now just needed to build the house.

I was not practical and knew nothing about building. The most popular book at the time for those building a house was *Bungalow Bliss*,[27] which included a large number of standard plans. I approached a builder. On the standard plans, windows were to be at the front overlooking the road. It made sense to me to have the windows overlooking the sea side. The builder suggested that I get a draughtsman. The site had a slope on it and that was a problem for the draughtsman. He suggested that I get an architect. Following visits to a number of architect's offices it was clear that the cost was prohibitive. I approached Alan O'Neill, an unconventional architect who was then working in the department of architecture in the college where I worked. He was too busy challenging constructions of masculinity, something that became his life's work. He passed me on to a young inexperienced, eccentric architect-Oliver Dempsey. Over a cup of coffee, we agreed that he would design my house and supervise the works for £900 – less than a fifth of the going price for an architect. I could just about afford that.

I had thought of having an entire wall of glass on the sea side, but he said that was structurally problematic. He asked me to imagine each of the rooms and we talked about what preoccupied me. At that time there was a tension between my catholicism and my feminism. This became reflected in the basic structure of my house: conventional catholicism was reflected in

---

27   Fitzsimons, J. (1971). *Bungalow Bliss.* Meath: Kells Art Studios.

its overall rectangular structure, with small traditional windows. My feminism was reflected in the more avant-garde flamboyant square superimposed on part of that rectangle, creating glass-filled angles, a double height in the living room and a gallery with a floor-length window upstairs. The design showed that tensions create space and do not need to be resolved.

With all extras eliminated, the cost came in at just under £50,000: a substantial amount of money then. A colleague advised me that I would be able to get a mortgage to cover it. The architect did the drawings and I applied for planning permission. Then the problems started. A number of people objected. The most persistent was the owner of a large building on the sea side. He wanted me to put clotted glass on the window overlooking the sea. Every time I met him, the conversation would end with an invitation to meet again the following day. Years later, I wondered if he wanted a bribe. That thought had simply not occurred to me then. Meanwhile I marshalled my most persuasive arguments. Eventually I got planning permission and the build started.

My sister gave me a present of a book called *Building Your Own House*.[28] I read it closely. I followed its guidance. I got a number of building tenders and opted for the cheapest one. But when the start time came, that builder was not available and so I went to the next one: Gerry O'Higgins. That was one of my biggest pieces of luck. A gentleman in every sense of the word, his skills were totally different to mine – he was a practical man who had never read a book in his life. As recommended in *Building Your Own House*, I included a time clause in the contract so that when it over-ran (as nearly all building projects do) I was able to negotiate for free wardrobes, a shed, a patio etc. rather than impose a financial penalty. This suited both of us.

I liked the idea of having open fires. In the houses I had rented after I came back to Ireland, I had lit an open fire every day. There was to be one of them downstairs on the black tiled raised heart in the kitchen cum dining room that occupied half of the house and another one upstairs in the galleried studio. Then my ever-practical and equally diplomatic sister asked:

---

28 About 10 years ago I faced the fact that I was not going to build another house. I thought the paperback might be useful to someone else, so I gave it to a charity shop. I have failed to find a reference for it.

'Who is going to carry the coal up the stairs? Who is going to carry the hot ashes down?'

A good question. I got the builder to install a gas fire upstairs. The double-height dormer ceiling seemed an obvious place for a light and so a socket was placed there – prompting Stella to ask:

'Who is going to change the light bulb?'

She did not need to say that scaffolding would be required to do this. The light was abandoned and the builder put an S hook up. There were innumerable gulls in the area and they nested on the chimney. I had the idea of hanging a large timber seagull from the S hook which would float above the kitchen/living room area. I bought one in Cork, with a wing span of a metre, suspended from a timber hanger. It could (theoretically) be easily suspended from the S hook, just by leaning out from the gallery. The first one fell 15 metres to the ground and broke. With the builder's help, using a cherry picker, the next one flew happily there for thirty-three years. During COVID-19, I went to clean it. Now the gull rests on the gallery, waiting to be returned to his original perch when scaffolding is next erected in the house.

The process of building was not always smooth. The architect had vision but was unconcerned with details. Thus, the bath barely fitted in the bathroom and I ended up with six manholes in my very small garden – none of them for my own sewage. Never having had any interest in the details of house decoration, the myriad decisions to be made was a challenge. What kind of door handles did I want? I had barely registered that door handles existed. But once presented with a choice, the homework needed to be done. What colour did I want the walls painted? White I said – all white – except for the double-height chimney breast which I wanted painted midnight blue. But when I saw the white on the rounded dormer ceilings in the bare rooms upstairs, my courage failed me. Upstairs looked like an igloo. I rang Gerry, the builder, in a panic and said:

'Maybe I should go for magnolia?'

'It will be grand Pat' he said.

I suspect that he had already bought the white paint but that was not mentioned. I had no doubts about the colours of the internal doors. I wanted them to be in primary colours (maroon, dark green and blue). I had never seen this anywhere but I had loved the colours on the outside of the George Pompidou Centre in Paris and that may have influenced me – or perhaps it was children's bricks.

The triangular floor-length window in the room pretentiously described in the plans as the studio was vaguely gothic – the two side window openings giving access to a tiny triangular flat roof where one person could sit protected by two rails – not unlike the prow of a boat. Earlier, I had nearly bought a second-hand house because it had a spiral staircase. When I explained why I was tempted, the architect said

'Why don't you have a spiral staircase?'

'Could I really'? I asked.

And so, a spiral staircase was carefully lowered in by a crane before the roof was put on. I had no doubt about the colour of this either: it should be yellow – a bright primrosy cheerful yellow. Gerry's patience was again required as numerous shades were tried before we arrived at one that matched my imagination. There was no doubt either that the gallery in the double-height kitchen/living room should be the same colour. Many years later, when I began to be interested in eastern belief systems and meditation practices, I realised that, with the large purple wall – hanging that I had bought in 1970, all the colours of the chakra were in my little house.

One Monday morning in November, with three weeks to finish the building, the plumber's apprentice was soldering in the tiny attic, without a bucket of water, and a spark caught the tarry felt in the roof. I got a phone call at work from a stranger to say that my house was on fire. Momentarily confused I thought he was referring to the house I was then renting – but no. I arrived to find the fire brigade outside my new house and was told:

'Ma'am I wouldn't go in there: only upsetting yourself.'

When I went in there was smoke still coming from the attic. The firemen's water was running down the spiral staircase and the ceilings were saturated. The timbers in the roof and the slates were burnt and had to be replaced. If the apprentice had died in the attic, I might never have moved in. As it was, by panicking and running out of the house the damage was greater but no one was injured. There was a problem with the fire insurance but Gerry, the builder said:

> 'Don't worry Pat. We will be back on site as soon as possible. We can sort out the fire insurance later.'

I had given notice on the house I was renting and was under pressure to move out. The man who owned it took to following me round to reinforce his message that I needed to leave which totally unnerved me. I moved into my new house while the repairs were being done. I was not an early riser – much to the chagrin of the workmen who paced up and down the garden path at 7.30 a.m. waiting for me to get up so that they could start work. It was the 1980s. I was a woman living on her own: propriety had to be observed.

Although never good at celebrating, building the house was such a monumental achievement that I threw a housewarming party and invited friends and colleagues from the various parts of my life. Money was short so I brewed gallons of homemade wine. The builder Gerry O'Higgins and the architect, Oliver Dempsey were guests of honour and were found deep in conversation in the bathroom of the house that they had made. Such was my gratitude to them that screwing my courage and competence to its limit, I later hosted a dinner for themselves and their wives to thank them for their work.

The décor is much the same now – thirty-five years later – as it was then. The chimney breast was not quite midnight blue so I changed that a few years later. More recently I upgraded the kitchen, tiled the bathrooms and improved the insulation, but as for the rest? Perfection cannot be improved on.

I had a home at last. But with that bad timing which has been a feature of my life, I had simultaneously run out of road at Waterford Regional Technical College.

Trying to make a life

Unlike most women of my generation, relationships have not been at the heart of my life. There were times of course when I was very lonely. But a lot of the time, I was simply too busy. Moving around for work from Dublin, to London, to Waterford and later to Limerick and back to Waterford did not help. In my late 20s, I remember laughingly saying that I only needed a relationship for sex, food and holidays. The break-up with Seán had made me recognise my vulnerability. When I built my house, I was clear that I wanted it to be small enough so that one person – me – was not rattling around in it. The local butcher said that what I needed was a man to fill it. I had this image of flesh leaking down the stairs, a thigh here, an arm there. But I saw it as a place of refuge – a place to recharge, to relax and unwind, to move out from to various kinds of sociable activities.

Over the years I have been interested in a couple of men who were married, and so, by my standards, unavailable. I was interested in a man who came out as gay. A couple of men were interested in me – but the feelings were not reciprocated. I don't think I ever decided to be single. Even yet I am sometimes surprised that an extrovert like me lives alone. Work was the heart of my life: it was what I enjoyed doing, what I was good at, what gave me meaning and satisfaction. But after coming back from London, and particularly after the death of my parents, I recognised that I needed to get involved in the local community if I was to survive. Although I had never been a joiner, I joined the church choir, the village drama group, a social justice group, a running group and the film society, in addition to my occasional involvement with the sailing club. This was all very welcome distraction, although it became clear in the 1980s that my views on the abortion and divorce referenda were not exactly shared by the rest of those singing in the church choir.

But I needed to finish the PhD. I had published an article with my PhD supervisor in 1984, but nothing else from it.[29] So, in the mid-1980s I cut back a bit on my group activities in Dunmore East and pushed myself

29   O'Connor, P. and Brown, G. W. (1984). 'Supportive Relationships: Fact or Fancy?', *Journal of Social and Personal Relationships*, 1, 159–76.

to finish it. I was still unable to type and this 100,000-word thesis ended up being typed by seven people who managed to cope with my handwritten maverick script. My internal supervisor was still not encouraging its submission. But then the university's rules changed. Only external examiners appointed by the university -and not internal supervisors – were allowed to evaluate PhD theses. Remembering how my supervisor's closest female senior collaborator had not got a PhD when I worked there, I decided to submit. What had I to lose? At worst it could be failed – but that at least would be a result. I submitted it and Professor David Morgan, from the University of Manchester, was appointed as external examiner. I flew over for the viva. My PhD thesis was passed with no corrections and champagne was produced. A friend in Waterford, with a black sense of humour, suggested that if I passed the Viva, I should tell him by texting the code words: 'Ulster says yes', that is, the improbable has happened. I did. My dominant feeling was one of relieved disbelief.

The conferring was to be at the Royal Albert Hall in December 1987. I had not gone to my M.Soc.Sc. conferring in University College Dublin and in retrospect I felt that it had been a mistake to miss that rite of passage. I had decided that no matter what happened, I would go to this one. I invited my sister, Stella and my friend, Jane Nelson, the mature student who had worked with me in the 1970s, to it. Money was very tight. My sister who had five small children at this stage went by boat and I flew and we arranged to meet in Euston Station a few hours before the actual ceremony. The fall-out from the fire in my new house was still in train and I was paged in the tiny train station in Waterford before I left because of problems with the fire insurance. After my sister and I met, we seemed to have so much time that we went to buy a special cream, available only at Boots in Oxford Street, for one of her daughters. Although I had lived in London for nine years and had used the tube extensively, I was addled and we got the Circle Line tube in the wrong direction. We tried to rectify this by getting a taxi to the Royal Albert Hall, which of course got stuck in traffic. We ended up running along beside the lines of traffic and arrived with minutes to spare at the entrance.

I wore a simple white silk blouse, black trousers, black and white earrings, over the black conferring gown with its red satin hood with gold trim, hired at the Albert Hall. Years later, when I bought my own academic gown, I realised that my conferring gown was not the correct one (it should have been all maroon). At the time, I was just relieved to make the ceremony. Princess Anne, then chancellor of the University of London, wearing gold and black robes was seated on the stage and those of us who were being conferred moved slowly across in front of her. I drew the line at making a courtesy but did a kind of discrete bow.

Of the four people in my life when I had started out on the PhD – my parents, Seán and Stella – only my sister remained. She never referred to the logistics involved in sorting out her five children so that she could be there. To my shame, I never asked. I was just so glad that she was at the ceremony that marked the long overdue end of my PhD.

With the PhD awarded, I set about getting a book contract. Yet again, strangers were very helpful: particularly Professor Graham Allan, a UK academic and Professor Barry Wellman, a US academic – neither of whom I knew personally. Eventually (after twelve unsuccessful submissions to other publishers) I got a contract from Harvester Wheatsheaf in the UK and Guildford in the US to write a book on *Friendships Between Women*,[30] drawing on but transcending my PhD thesis which had focused entirely on married women's friendships. It was to include other work I had done on such relationships involving elderly men and women as well as reflections on the nature of friendship; its characteristics at different life stages; the conditions facilitating it and its future as a relationship of choice in increasingly fluid and less structured societies. I set about writing the book.

Diary: 28 August 1990

It has been a wonderful summer – peaceful, quiet; its best times (90%) disciplined work (on a book); listening to the radio; swimming every day; planting in the garden. After the dreadful storms and ice of April/May I went on holidays – to Switzerland – alone (marvellous) and to Oxford (to a conference) where I was amazed to discover how popular I was ... I was over-awed and excited by the eminence of the people I met there – a daft child-like self is still astonished that I could meet, talk to and be liked by people who write BOOKS. Then home to Dunmore and days of quiet work.

30 O'Connor, P. (1992/2002). *Friendships Between Women*. New York: Guildford; and Hemel Hempstead: Harvester Wheatsheaf.

It has been a summer like my childhood in the Kerry Gaeltacht -endless, peaceful, punctuated by sociability – but easy somehow.

Meanwhile, in autumn 1990 Mary Robinson declared her candidacy as president of Ireland. I had never met her. But she represented hope. In the world of the 1950s and 1960s where I grew up, women had no place in politics or the public arena. The idea that a woman, a young attractive, left-leaning feminist, a wife and mother could become president of Ireland was unthinkable. The assumption then was that women's place was in the home. If women were not married, they were suspected socially and sexually. If they were married, they had to be neglecting their homes and families. This was unstated until, during the presidential campaign, the larger-than-life Fianna Fáil TD, Pádraig Flynn, accused Mary Robinson of 'having a new-found interest in her family' – the implication being that she was a bad mother and was only using her status as a mother to increase her election chances. Hearing it spelt out like that was a turning point in the campaign. She was also helped by Brian Lenihan, the Fianna Fail candidate, effectively shooting himself in the foot through his own hubris – but that is another story. In a country where left-wing politics had been notoriously weak, Mary Robinson, nominated by the Labour Party, but standing as an independent was elected president of Ireland. Out of the chaos of powerlessness and oppression that was Ireland in the 1980s Mary Robinson emerged.

My mother was dead six years – my father eight. It was the sale of their home that had enabled me to buy the site for my little house. I now had a home of my own. But a really satisfying public life still eluded me. And so, I sat in the little house that I had built and watched the inauguration of Mary Robinson as president of Ireland on TV on 3 December 1990. She said that she was elected by the women of Ireland who instead of rocking the cradle rocked the system. She was dressed in purple with a torque of gold – like an Irish chieftain. She stood out among all the old grey men in suits and said: 'I am of Ireland … come dance with me in Ireland.' I was coming up to 40 years old. It seemed to be a new dawn for Ireland, for women and for me. If Mary Robinson could do it, then maybe somehow it could be done. Maybe women could have a place in the public arena.

Maybe we were as good as men. Maybe we could be treated fairly and be given a chance to contribute.

A chance my mother never had. A chance that I wanted. Just a chance ... The tears ran down my cheeks.

CHAPTER 4

Success?

Context

The 1990s was a period of increased national awareness around gender equality. For a short time (1993–97) there was a separate Department of Equality and Law Reform, with a minister responsible for moving that agenda forward. That department worked their way through the actions recommended in the Second Report on the Commission on the Status of Women (1993)[31] and produced a series of annual progress reports. During this period, time-specific targets for women in senior positions were used in the Civil Service, although this was not widely known. Most universities in Ireland in the 1990s taught women's studies. The course directors of such courses all knew each other, frequently collaborating on conferences; sharing international speakers and external examining on each other's programmes. From 1992 to 1997 I was one of these course directors. We formed a loose and almost entirely virtual national network.

The late 1990s also saw the beginning of unprecedented economic success in Ireland – described as the Celtic Tiger (1997–2007), although much of it was driven by women's employment and hence might more appropriately have been labelled the Celtic Tigress. Ireland became a model to be emulated internationally, with economic growth rates (1994–2000) in excess of 9 per cent per annum.

In this changing context, might there be opportunities for people like me?

31   Government of Ireland. (1993). *Second Commission on the Status of Women: Report to the Government*. Dublin: Government Publications.

Out of the frying pan into the fire ...

From a spectacularly promising undergraduate degree and first job, I had been very slow to make the transition to a permanent job. Meanwhile, the occasional men among my PhD group in London had got permanent jobs in academia, some very prestigious indeed. After twelve years on research contracts, I had managed to get a permanent job in Ireland, at the bottom rung of the career ladder in what was then Waterford Regional Technical College (later SETU), an institution that was seen as much lower in status than the Economic and Social Research Institute where I had begun my career.

My CV in the 1980s could be framed either in terms of social policy or sociology. I had long wanted to work in University College Cork – closing the circle of my parent's lives and my early experiences in Cork. I applied for a job in social policy/social administration there in 1989. I was not successful. I applied for a junior lectureship in sociology there in 1991. I was not successful. I cast my net wider. I applied for a junior lectureship in sociology in what was then NUI Galway in 1990 and again in 1991 – with the same result. Every job that was advertised from 1989 on, I applied for and always with the same result. In some cases, I got to interview; in others, not. Frequently the jobs went to internal candidates, but whether internal or not, overwhelmingly they went to men.

I rewarded myself for putting myself through the recurrent torture of job applications. There was a craft centre in Salthill in Galway that produced beautiful purple handwoven wraps and, over time, I acquired quite a selection. But there were dark days.

Diary: 1 July 1991

I didn't get the job in Galway. I've known really since the [Sociological Association of Ireland] Conference in May but kept hoping that somehow, something would give. I feel dead inside. Tired. My life force seems to be going out. I don't know who I am or what I want. I seem unable to direct my life. Yesterday I held despair at bay. The day before not. It is a beautiful day and I should be working. ... What is the point? Where do I go from here? Why bother? ... How long more can I keep up the pace of the past two years? Why should I? What will it achieve? I have tried. I feel lonely and empty. What has it all been about?

I developed the ability to forget about the rejection letters as soon as I received them. Many years later, when I was clearing out the files, I could not believe how many times University College Cork had rejected me. And yet I had continued relentlessly applying there and elsewhere.

To move from a lower status institution to a higher status one is difficult for anyone. But if you are a woman, over 40, whose only lecturing experience is in an area that is applied and female-dominated, it is even more so. I had drifted away from the educational and work-based networks I had in Dublin. When my kindly Master's thesis supervisor introduced me, he always referred to my affiliation with the Economic and Social Research Institute rather than to my position in what was then Waterford Regional Technical College. I wondered about this. I maintained personal ties in Dublin and London, but these did not translate into work-related social or cultural capital. In any event I would have felt uncomfortable using them to promote my career.

Eventually, in late 1991, I got offered a job as lecturer in sociology in the University of Limerick (UL). At the same time, a permanent position as head of the College of Business came up in Waterford Regional Technical College. I was called in by the then director there and encouraged to apply for the latter: this was the same man who had favoured the degree led by my footballing colleague over my proposal for a degree in social work. He must have seen something in me, but I had no background in business and was not even working in the College of Business. I found it hard to see how I could be a credible candidate. But I did not want to leave the little house I had just built in Dunmore East. I applied for the job – but told no one, and changed into my interview clothes in the toilets. I was interviewed for that post the same week as I had my heart-warming leaving 'do', where I was presented with a huge card, and a little stuffed toy with 'Being Boss is Best' on it from the students and an oil painting of water hitting off rocks from the staff. It was surreal. I did not get the job as head of Business. I accepted the job in UL and by 2 January 1992, I had started work there.

The vacancy there had been created by the departure of Dr Evelyn Mahon to take up a position in Trinity College Dublin. I knew her from

the Sociological Association of Ireland. I did not really know anyone else
there. I rented a room in a Hansel and Gretel style house outside Murroe, a
then very small village about 14 kilometres from the University of Limerick.
The house was very pretty and there were other lodgers there. However, the
landlady treated us all like children. I found myself being scolded for not
wearing my slippers coming down to breakfast and other minor personal
misdemeanours. This irritated me. When I mentioned this to my sister,
she recalled that I was not willing to take this kind of direction from my
mother at 15 years old: 'so it is not surprising that you won't take it from a
stranger in your forties'. I was going to have to move again.

As a lecturer in sociology in the University of Limerick, part of my job
involved administrative responsibility for women's studies. This was the
most difficult assignment in my entire forty-six-year career. It shaped me
irrevocably. As course director for the MA in women's studies, I could no
longer avoid the reality of misogyny. During my first job at the Economic
and Social Research Institute in the 1970s, I had struggled with that un-
named force. Later at Waterford Regional Technical College, I had survived by creating a bubble that allowed me to ignore the devaluation of
my area and myself. By taking responsibility for women's studies, I became
an open target. At lunch time I used to like to sit anywhere in the main
restaurant and fall into conversation with those around me. Now, every
interaction became a goading session based on the assumption that I was a
'ball-breaker' who hated all men. I found this bewildering. I gave up going
for coffee. My assumption that everyone was good and kind was challenged
by the grinding day-to-day evidence to the contrary.

It was normal for all academic staff to have a research day in the
University of Limerick, that is, one free from teaching and meetings where
they could focus on their research. I decided that mine would be Friday –
thus giving me three days – that is, including the weekend – to recover from
this incessant negativity. It was unbelievably cheeky and assertive of me –
but I instinctively knew that if I did not get that head space I would be in
difficulty. So, I simply said to the head of department and those compiling
the timetables that 'it was not possible for me to be in the university on
a Friday'. Intriguingly, over the next twenty-four years, no one ever asked
why this was not possible. By offering no explanation it was impossible for

others to 'solve the problem'. It did mean that in order to clear my desk, I often did not leave the office until 10pm on a Thursday evening. I had no problem with that. But I needed the solitude and head space to do research that a run of three days provided. It allowed me to go back to my bolt hole in Dunmore and to regain my energy for the following week. I was astonished to find that people adjust to a pattern so that as the years went on, if, for example, there was a conferring ceremony on a Friday and I attended it people would say: 'How come you are here – it is a Friday.' To which my response was: 'No worries: I won't be here on Monday' – thus enabling me to still have three days together.

Dedicated staffing in women's studies was limited at that time and was mostly part-time and temporary. Very few of the academic men in the faculty were even vaguely interested in gender-related issues, nor were management interested in increasing gender expertise in the faculty. Yet students in the 1990s were interested in gender inequality – creating a pool of unmet needs. The 'convenient' solution was that these would be met by me – the only permanent appointment with an explicitly gendered brief, albeit with other non-gender-related responsibilities as well. As long as this extra work was invisible, any arguments about increased resources in the gender area could be avoided.

Undergraduate students' final year projects (a major independent piece of work) became a flashpoint for these issues. Students were encouraged to choose a topic that interested them, and to seek out a supervisor who would be officially responsible for directing their work: reading drafts, recommending literature and evaluating what was effectively a mini-thesis. Many of the students were interested in gender-inequality-related issues and the men identified themselves as their official supervisors, but proceeded to delegate the day-to-day work of supervision to the 'expert', that is, me. This dramatically increased my invisible workload: I was not their official supervisor, but I was doing the work. A long queue of students formed outside the door of my small office in a side corridor: the students having been told by my male colleagues to 'talk to me'. There was no question of me becoming their co-supervisor: their male supervisors simply wanted me to 'help' the students. When I tackled the men involved, they protested that they were doing me a favour by recognising my area of expertise. Their explanation appeared logical but I began to feel overwhelmed by this extra, invisible work. Never blessed with equanimity, I began to get irritable with the students. This was counterproductive since as a woman, particularly one in women's studies, I was expected to be the 'great breast' who nurtured all women. In my calmer moments I recognised that this situation was not the students' fault. The underlying problem, given most of the men's disinterest in the topic, was the imbalance between the gender profile of staff and students. In desperation, having failed to get action on this at any level, I put a notice on my door:

> 'BEFORE YOU KNOCK: Please note: More than half of the students are women, but only 15 per cent of the academic staff are women. Please draw this fact to the attention of the Dean of the Faculty and the head of the Students' Union.
>
> If having done so, you still need to knock, please do so.
>
> Thank you
>
> Dr Pat O'Connor'

That seemed to me to be very reasonable. Academics diverting from the main corridor to look at the notice suggested an alternative interpretation. I was summoned to a meeting with the then dean. He saw the notice as implying that he was not concerned with gender equality and asked me to remove it. He did not propose solving what I saw as the underlying problem involving the inadequacy of staffing in the area and so I refused to do so, although I did agree to modify it. I was surprised by the fuss. It seemed to me that my action was entirely logical and I was frustrated at the absence of any attempt to solve what I saw as the underlying problem.

As course director in women's studies, I was (metaphorically) continuously sitting at the end of a branch that someone, somewhere was trying to cut down. I had to be familiar with every nuance of the rules in academic grading meetings since every decision and non-decision in women's studies was challenged by academic colleagues. There were constant attempts by management to close down women's studies. My predecessor, Dr Evelyn Mahon, had very astutely got European funding for the MA in women's studies. As the possibility that this funding would be withdrawn increased, the course was continually under threat. I remember standing on a railway station in Paris on my summer holidays in the 1990s, arguing with the then dean about the value of the course on a public phone, in an attempt to stave off another such attempt.

Issues related to women were a lightning conductor, but so were those related to children. In the late 1990s, I invited Nuala O'Faolain to speak in the seminar series I organised as part of my responsibilities as course director in women's studies. I did not know her but I loved her weekly pieces in the *Irish Times* – one of which happened to be about parents' beating their children, although that was not the topic of her lecture. Before her talk, I was berated and ridiculed at lunch by academic men I didn't know for inviting her. Ostensibly perfectly reasonable men asserted that she had no right to challenge this practice since their children belonged to them and they were entitled to do what they wanted to them:

'They are my children and I will beat them if I want.'

Their hostility to her, their misogyny and their perception of women and children as 'theirs' to do what they wanted with, astonished and appalled me. Her lecture was a tour de force: she spoke without notes, for 1.5 hours to 150 people (mainly women) crammed into the elegant green room in the genteel building housing the president's office (the biggest attendance ever in those series). Their appreciation, admiration and affection for her was as striking as the opposite had been shocking in those lunchtime conversations with the men in the university restaurant.

My research interests had up to then (unconsciously) avoided public power. A colleague in engineering, Dr (now Professor) Ita Richardson, asked if she could use the students and staff involved in women's studies to pilot a decision-making tool she was developing for her PhD. I agreed with alacrity. The position of women in the university emerged as one of the top issues that concerned them. I was amazed. I had never really thought about it. While I was rebellious and 'difficult', up to then, I had never thought of this as an issue (maybe I saw it as too dangerous?). However, as course director in women's studies, if it was seen as a key issue by those in the area, I felt that it was my duty to take it on and to champion the position of women in the university system. From then on, I monitored the gender profile of academic staff in UL. A man in Human Resources, who was the husband of a former student of mine on the National Diploma in Child Care in Waterford Regional Technical College, compiled the data for me: imitating I wryly noted, the kind of informal ties that are so often used by men in organisations.

At that time Atlantic Philanthropies, founded by Chuck Feeney, an American of Irish extraction, was a major funder of Irish higher education but worked secretly so that anyone who received funding from them was obligated, under threat of losing the funding, from ever referring to the source. The nature of the funding was such that it required long-term buy-in by management since the posts they funded were five-year contract ones which they expected to be made permanent by the university. It seems possible that they influenced the Higher Education Authority. In any event to our considerable surprise each of the leaders in women's studies in all the universities were invited by their respective registrars to attend a meeting with the Higher Educational Authority in 1995 to discuss funding for women's studies. This was an extraordinary development. Most of us were at best at lecturer level and so far down the 'food chain' that we were unknown to the registrars. At the meeting, it became clear that a budget line was to be identified by the HEA specifically to promote women's studies in each university. £20,000 per year was agreed for the University of Limerick with similar amounts for the other universities. This might seem quite a small amount – and it was clearly insufficient to create a post. But accustomed as we were to having no control whatsoever over resources to organise conferences, seminar series etc. it seemed a fortune. It reduced our dependence on the male-dominated management structure (which was often less than enthusiastic about funding women's studies events). Furthermore, since budget lines are slow to change, we thought that it might potentially increase in the future. We came out from the meeting giddily triumphant.

As course director of women's studies, the allocation of this money was my responsibility. In the interests of transparency, bids were asked for, allocations agreed and progress monitored through a public newsletter. It was revealing how little money women asked for and how conscientious they were in discharging their commitments. This money continued to arrive every year for several years to the amusement of the finance officers. We all quietly chuckled over it.

My new job revealed the face of misogyny in my own university. It was impossible for me to continue to believe that everyone was good and kind. I mourned the loss of innocence. At the end of every week, I travelled back to my bolt hole in Dunmore East and celebrated my survival with a mad combination of my then favourite treats: paté; ice cream with chocolate sauce and whiskey.

It was an opportunity. But it was hard.

Gender equality in the health services

During the 1990s there was active concern about the under-representation of women in senior positions in the civil service, in local authorities and in other Irish state and semi-state structures. Under pressure from Europe, the mainstreaming of gender equality in the National Development Plan was very much on the agenda and most government reports referred to gender equality. Denis Doherty, health services chief executive officer (CEO) in the Midland and Midwestern areas, invited tenders for research on the barriers to women's promotion in these services. I put in a tender and got the work. Over the next 18 months I did focus groups with 162 women in administration, nursing and therapies. As I listened to them, I had a series of light bulb moments. The report – the *Barriers to Women's Promotion in the Midland and MidWestern Health Boards*[32] – was published in 1995; and an article focusing on organisational culture was subsequently published in the *Economic and Social Review* in 1996.[33]

In the predominantly female nursing area women's chances of promotion from permanent staff nurse to matron were very low (28:1). Although

---

32 O'Connor, P. (1995). *Barriers to Women's Promotion in the Health Boards*. Limerick: MWHB.

33 O'Connor, P. (1996). 'Organisational Culture as a Barrier to Women's Promotion', *The Economic and Social Review*, 27(3), 205–34.

the area was predominantly female, men had double the chance that women had of promotion (14:1 for men). The women in the nursing focus groups felt bewildered and angry because those very characteristics and ways of behaving, which had been positively valued and encouraged in them as women, now seemed to be working against them individually and collectively. They blamed themselves for putting up with things, for accepting that there was always someone more important. They berated themselves for not being willing to stir things up: as they saw it when they were asked to jump 'we'll say: how high'. The societally valued 'feminine qualities' which had brought them into nursing were, as they saw it, not really valued when it came to pay or promotional opportunities. Individually they felt they lacked information, confidence and education. They pinned their hopes on additional training. Collectively they noticed the scarcity of senior posts in nursing. They stressed the importance of targets and of the employment of an equality officer: structural things that (as they said) would: 'boost women's confidence'; 'make them [management] encourage women' and reduce the chance that they would be 'squeezed out'.

Within the administrative area (i.e. the bureaucratic organisational and management structure), women were competing in what was still then, especially at senior level, a male world. Chances of promotion were much better there, but there was still a gender difference. Thus, men's chance of promotion was roughly 1:2 whereas women's was 1:8. As the majority of the women saw it, the organisational culture was not conducive to the promotion of women:

> 'You get the impression of so many cliques and black suits … – at present the women are outside it'. [It was] 'assumed that a man will go further'; 'If a woman is pushy, she's aggressive'.

They felt that women were taken 'less seriously' by management and that:

> 'The thing about it is that there are jobs for the boys – years in advance you know that they are going to get that job.'

They noted that there were frequently informal 'routes' to senior positions whereby a man was selected (without interview) as an assistant to the person in the senior post. This was commonly seen as a signal that this was to be the next senior position holder ('men cloning the clones'). They drew attention to the subtle ways in which, as they saw it, management 'up and down' put them under pressure to prove themselves, for example, by drawing attention to any mistake they made and saying (laughing):

> 'What do you expect? It was a woman who did that.'

They noted that when a woman stepped into a job that had 'always' been done by a man, there were attempts to undermine her by so-called 'humourous comments – a kind of a dig'. They felt that men at senior level still had very traditional views about women, and saw employing them as a 'total hassle': If women were married, they anticipated the costs and inconveniences of maternity leave, and if there were not, they wondered: 'What was wrong with her.' Those who had been in management settings noted that typically they were the only women there and that:

> 'It was nearly automatic that the "old boys" would go off together. If I were a man, it would be "would you like to come for a drink" but because we are not men it does not happen.'

They felt that management positions in the administrative structure would be a lot more attractive

> 'if there were enough females there to give you back up – you would have more confidence if more were in the same boat'.

There were different issues in the therapies area where there were only two points on the career path (basic and senior). Although theoretically, there was a 1:3 chance of promotion for both men and women, in practice the number of senior positions was fixed, so that for any individual, there was little possibility of achieving promotion in their own hierarchy for fifteen to twenty years. In addition, therapists were typically working in outlying offices, away from senior management, and lacked information, visibility and sponsors.

The launch of my report on 10 April 1995 was organised by Denis Doherty, the chief executive officer (CEO) of the health boards in those areas and a man who understood gender inequality. My sister came down from Dublin to support me, but it was friendly, low key and uncontroversial. The report got quite a lot of coverage in the media 'Men monopolising management jobs in health' (*Irish Press*, 11 April 1995), and a year later, with a nursing strike in the offing, the report was still being quoted: 'Angels prepare to test their wings' (*Irish Times*, 20 January 1996). Many research reports, especially regional ones, are ignored. However, this research influenced the *National Plan for Women's Health*.[34] In June 1996, the then secretary general of the Department of Health indicated that he was discussing its findings both with the CEOs of the other health boards and key people in his own department. He also suggested that once the then current dispute with the nurses was resolved, I might consider doing some research on the underlying causes of the dispute. This strike did not occur until October 1999. In the meantime, I was invited to make a presentation to the Joint Oireachtas Committee on the report which was well-received. Listening to 162 women talk about things that had been inchoate in my own mind was transformative for me. I began to think about whether the issues they talked about were peculiar to the health services.

The invitation from Denis Doherty to write 800 words for an internal publication in the Office of Health Management provoked me to reflect on what I had learned about men, power and organisations.[35] I was then 46 years old and had been in paid work for twenty-seven years. Although I was a sociologist, it had taken me more than twenty years to realise that people do not get promoted for doing their own jobs well. I still believed in a meritocratic world where educational credentials were the key to career success. Like many women, I assumed that if I increased my qualifications I would be 'discovered' and rewarded. On a day-to-day basis I got absorbed by the job in hand, and although I was occasionally irritated by lack of recognition, I was too busy to dwell on it – and anyway, fighting

34 Department of Health. (1997). *A Plan for Women's Health*. Dublin: Stationery Office.

35 O'Connor, P. (1997). 'What I Didn't Learn in College', *Facilitating Management Development for the Health Services*. Office for Health Management Newsletter, https://healthmanagement.org/c/hospital/issuearticle/office-for-health-man agement-ireland, accessed 18 May 2002.

for myself somehow seemed all wrong. In other words, I had ignored the realities of power and prejudice in organisations. Indeed, for many years I had chosen to teach and to do research on topics where I did not have to face these issues.

I realised then that I needed to rethink my assumptions about my own area of employment – higher education. I needed to wake up to public power.

Firing on all cylinders ...

The 1990s as I experienced them were characterised by a range of research projects as well as conference activity, particularly with other academic staff involved in women's studies and/or gender equality. Most of this activity involved collaborating with women who were outside line management structures. It was energising.

There was a very active programme of seminars and conferences in women's studies in the University of Limerick. We invited numerous women as speakers including Professor Sylvia Walby, then a major figure in the UK because of her book on *Theorising Patriarchy*,[36] and Ailbhe Smyth, a pioneer of women's studies and research on women in academia[37] and an abortion activist. Dr Ronit Lentin came to the University of Limerick for a short period and edited several collections of student and staff research, under the title *In from the Shadows*,[38] with the ultimate hope of developing a University of Limerick Press, in collaboration with the then director of the library. These events and publications were covered widely in the local and regional press.

36 Walby, S. (1990). *Theorising Patriarchy*. Oxford: Basil Blackwell.
37 Smyth, A. (1984). *Breaking the Circle: The Position of Women Academics in Third Level Education in Ireland*. Dublin: Irish National Advisory Group for EEC Action Programme on the Promotion of Equal Opportunities for Women.
38 For example, Lentin, R. (ed.) (1995). *In From the Shadows: The UL Women's Studies Collection*, Vols 1 and 2. Limerick: University of Limerick Women's Studies; Aniagolu, C. (ed.) (1997). *In From the Shadows: The UL Women's Studies Collection*, Vol. III. Limerick: University of Limerick Women's Studies.

My first sole-authored book, *Friendships Between Women*,[39] published by Harvester Wheatsheaf in the UK and by Guildford in the United States, challenged the lack of importance attached by society to such ties. It suggested that the idea that women cannot trust, work with or be friends with other women is simply a device to strengthen their dependence on men. However, since friendships are usually between those who are similar in many ways (e.g. in terms of gender, age, class, ethnicity) it raised questions about whether they could bring about societal transformation. It came out just a few months after I started work in UL, where, as course director in women's studies, I was perpetually under siege. It was nominated by *Choice* in the US as an outstanding academic book, but I had neither the time nor the energy to celebrate its publication. Reflecting many years later, I wondered whether the ways men sponsor other men in academia, by supporting and advocating for them, could be understood as a kind of friendship that not only brings individual benefits but that also perpetuates the status quo.

I had long been interested in what used to be called B & Bs (Bed and Breakfast accommodation) as a site for women's economic independence. In the 1990s, I did some research on women in the rural tourist industry with Susan Liddy a former Master's student (now Dr Susan Liddy, president of Women in Film and Television International). We focused on an EU-funded Leader project in Ballyhoura in North Cork in 1995. Although the women involved in such tourism initiatives were well-educated and articulate and had lots of ideas, the overwhelming majority of them did not recognise that their ideas differed substantially from those of the men in charge. They were unaware of power as well as of their interests and priorities as women. They had not 'noticed' that one board had funds to allocate and the other had not. The majority were unaware of the committee structures and of women's very low representation on them. They assumed that women's interests would be looked after. They assumed that because they knew one or two women at the top table that there must be more women there.[40] It seemed that I was not the only one who was naive about power. It was another light bulb moment.

39   O'Connor, P. (1992/2002). *Friendships Between Women* New York: Guildford; Hemel Hempstead: Harvester Wheatsheaf.

40   O'Connor, P. (1996). *Invisible Players? Women, Tourism and Development in Ballyhoura*. Limerick: Women's Studies; see also O'Connor, P. (1995). 'Tourism and Development in Ballyhoura: Women's Business?', *The Economic and Social Review*, 26 (4), 369–401.

In the 1990s, I also did research on the position of women in Údarás na Gaeltachta, a regional state agency responsible for the economic, social and cultural development of Irish-speaking regions, located in Galway.[41] This research was part of an EU-funded project. Although the final report could be written in English, the data had to be collected through the medium of Irish. I had used very little Irish since my oral examination at Waterford Regional Technical College almost fifteen years earlier. There was the additional complication that my Irish was Munster Irish and that most of these were speaking Connaught or Ulster Irish. But I really wanted to do the work– not least to see how similar/different the patterns there might be to other structures. No problem I said. And then frantically rang everyone I knew to ask them to speak Irish to me.

In Údarás na Gaeltachta, women were concentrated at the bottom of the hierarchy, making up almost 90 per cent of those there, with men making up 93 per cent of those at the top. Four-fifths of the women then employed in the Údarás spoke to me in focus groups. As they saw it, senior management was 'kind of afraid of women'. Most of the women were interested in promotion. Overwhelmingly they thought in terms of moving up just one or two steps. As they saw it, they had been doing the same job for years and were not allowed to take on any new responsibilities or given a chance to develop themselves within the Údarás: 'We are only qualified as secretaries: that is what they say to us.'

During this decade, I also had the opportunity to evaluate what was known locally as a Community Mother's Programme, that is, a community-based peer-led support programme for new mothers in disadvantaged areas funded by The Van Leer Foundation and the MidWestern Health Board.[42] It involved up to thirteen visits by

41 O'Connor, P. (1999). *The Glass Ceiling: Report on the Position of Women in Údarás Na Gaeltachta*. EU: ADAPT report; see also O'Connor, P. (2000). 'Structure, Culture and Passivity: A Case Study of Women in a Semi-state Organisation', *Public Administration and Development*, 20 (3), 265–75.

42 O'Connor, P. (1999). *Parents Supporting Parents: An Evaluative Report on the National Parent Support Programme*. Limerick: Van Leer Foundation and MWHB; see also O'Connor, P. (2001). 'Supporting Mothers: Issues in a Community Mother's Programme', *Community, Work and Family*, 4 (1), 63–85.

experienced local mothers to disadvantaged mothers after they came home from hospital with the new baby. Although in most cases, the mothers were in their 20s and this was not their first child, with the majority having a husband or partner at the time of the birth as well as other relatives living nearby, more than half of the recipients described the period immediately after they came home from hospital with the baby as 'terrible', 'very hard, very stressful' and 'felt tied down, terrible'. Over four-fifths of them identified positive effects of this Community Mother's programme on themselves and/or on the way they handled their children. Their knowledge about the supports available in the community also increased. It illustrated the need for this kind of programme – and implicitly challenged assumptions that women do not need, and experienced local mothers cannot provide, this kind of support immediately after a birth.

On the 1 July 1996, Professor Eddie Moxon-Browne, a quiet, gentle, political scientist whom I did not know well (and who later described me as the 'only one with balls in the faculty', a gendered but well-intentioned compliment) nominated me for the Research Excellence award in the university. In his nomination he referred to my research output; its impact on public policy; my profile as a public intellectual; my networking nationally and internationally – and commented that I had:

> 'Striven tirelessly, and often against considerable odds, to establish, defend and promote the salience of gender in the teaching, research and the administration of the University.'

I was amazed and delighted. His nomination led to a letter of support from the then dean, who described me as 'the most productive and inspiring researcher in the College at the present moment' and echoed the points made in the nomination. I was at the time at lecturer level and had crossed swords with the dean on gender inequality, so I was even more surprised to read his comment that:

> 'At any other university I have worked, she would by now have been in very strong contention for a personal chair.'

In my maroon University of London academic gown, with its red satin panels and cream trim and tasselled soft black velvet hat cocked at a jaunty angle I was presented with the (less prestigious) Award for Special Achievement in Research by the university president. It was years before I noticed that I had not got the first prize which was for Excellence.

The swirl of research productivity and visibility that characterised my life in the 1990s continued with my next sole-authored book, *Emerging Voices: Women in Contemporary Irish Society*.[43] I had noticed a strange paradox when I came back from London to work in Ireland: on the one hand women were undervalued by Irish society, not only in female-dominated areas such as nursing, but in also in male-dominated ones such as higher education; but on the other hand, there was a sneaking admiration for them as strong, capable people. This book took me over five years to write, driven by an attempt to understand how and to what extent the position of women in the home and workplace was changing. The Marriage Bar had ended in the 1970s, but married women in their 40s and 50s, many of whom had been forced out of paid employment by that Marriage Bar were finding it difficult to get access to accredited courses and qualifications that would facilitate their re-entry into the labour force. The machinery of the state still did not seem to understand the concept of indirect discrimination. Thus, the European Court of Justice found that the treatment of job sharers in the revenue commission was illegal; as were the payments to married men, introduced as part of the state's attempt to implement the EU Directive on equal treatment. Although more than two-fifths of mothers with one or two children were in paid employment, child care was still seen as a woman's problem, with very little support from the state. Girls were doing very well in the educational system and women made up two-thirds of those in the professions, but they were not accessing positions of authority in the civil service, in local authorities, in the health services or in the private sector (making up only a quarter of those in management positions – and mostly at the lower levels).

---

43 O'Connor, P. (1998/99) *Emerging Voices: Women in Contemporary Irish Society*. Dublin: IPA.

Mary Wallace, Minister of State at the Dept of Justice and Law Reform launched the book in the Round Room of the Mansion House in Dublin on the 7 October 1998. I spoke about male privilege – but there was no real perceived threat to it at that time and my comments could be indulged and ignored. The cover of the book beautifully captured the complexities of women's lives: a purple and green-clad woman, half of her face in shadow, half in light, her arms wrapped around a very large brown book while her finger moved across a PC screen, a frying pan at her side, a baby in a pram embedded in her head, washing drying on the line and red, green and yellow structures (maybe office buildings?) to her right with a church in the distance (the image also used in the cover of this book). It was published by the Institute of Public Administration, which was surprising, since women at the time made up only seven per cent of those at the higher echelons of the Civil Service and only 14 per cent of those in the Dáil. The then commissioning editor Jim O'Donnell had the vision to see it as appropriate, and Professor John Jackson from Trinity College Dublin supported its publication. This time I had caught the tide. It was reprinted in 1999, and I gave numerous talks on it.

Then in the late 1990s I was invited by an all-female, cross-national EU consortium to become part of an EU project on the reconciliation of Work and Family among young people. I only knew one of the members from my work in London in the 1970s – Professor Julia Brannen. The Project was led by Professor Suzan Lewis, with colleagues from Portugal and Sweden. We each were responsible for collecting interview data on young people aged 18–30 in our own countries and analysing and writing up that data. My interest was on these young people's gender awareness in social contexts where gender inequality existed but was obscured by ideologies such as individual choice.[44] We met in various cities – but Lisbon was our unanimous favourite. I heard fado music there for the first time, in a tiny little restaurant in a back street: the aching, yearning song sung by a

44   O'Connor, P., Smithson, J. and Das Dores Guerreiro, M. (2002). 'Young People's Awareness of Gendered Realities'. In J. Brannen, S. Lewis, A. Nielsen and J. Smithson (eds), *Young Europeans, Work and Family*, pp. 89–115. London: Routledge.

tiny woman dressed all in black. The cheapness of the food, the delicious wine and the friendly easiness of the culture drew us back time and again.

We were at that time mostly in our 40s and all had our usual share of relationship troubles. I can remember our laughter after long productive days as we ate together in cheap but atmospheric restaurants in the evenings. One night, in a tiny restaurant off the beaten track in Lisbon, a real live cock hid underneath our table, concealed by the heavy tablecloth. Banished from there by the proprietor, he strutted up and down the restaurant, and finally, crowing loudly, proceeded to survey us from the top of the dresser. We laughed hysterically at this manifestation of male dominance.

Looking back, I am impressed by the efficiency of this all-women team – and the fun we had. Certainly, that experience (and subsequent ones) belied the idea that women cannot trust or work with other women, the topic of my first sole-authored book.

Being useful inside the university

In 1996, I was invited to address the governing authority in the University of Limerick on the topic of women's studies. This was an opportunity. I grasped it and highlighted the 'disappearing woman' phenomenon in the staff academic hierarchy in the University of Limerick.

Diary: 25 September 1996

Extraordinary day yesterday. Presented to governing authority [on the Disappearing Woman in UL]. It went very well. I know I was good – passionate, factual, controlled, practical. Good on my feet. Strong. The part of me that is wonderful is still there. ... Felt completely in control. Amazing. When I think of the days that I have felt alone. The nights I have cried.

In UL at that time, there were no women at dean or full professorial level and only four per cent of those at senior lecturer level were women, although almost half of the undergraduate students were women. I compared this profile to Maynooth University whose main claim to fame

at that time was its role in the training of catholic priests. The founding
president of UL, Dr Ed Walsh, prided himself on having founded a secular
university. I hit a nerve. Within a week I got a handwritten note from him
asking me for a one-page document on 'The most effective practical steps
the university can take within the law to address the matter of recruiting
and promoting a greater proportion of females'. I identified fifteen short-
term actions to be taken within a year including the appointment of an
equal opportunities manager at senior level; the formulation of action
plans by line managers; gender awareness workshops for all line management (including executive committee); gender auditing of training and
travel budgets; gender monitoring of those applying/shortlisted/pro-
moted; monitoring the wording of advertisements and the fine-tuning
of interview and search procedures; mechanisms to sanction breaches of
procedure and/or to reward compliance; as well as annual gender audits
of appointments by governing authority. I also recommended the creation of gender equality and promotion policies and related structures
as well as lobbying around the Equality Section of the Universities Bill
(then in draft). It was an ambitious agenda – and one that is still relevant
in many higher educational institutions twenty-seven years later.

My analysis of the data on the academic staff in UL showed that a
considerably higher proportion of them were at senior lecturer level and
above in male-dominated faculties such as Engineering than in ones such
as Humanities where there were more likely to be women. This seemed
to reflect the greater availability of senior posts in these male-dominated
areas since these areas were seen as strategically important. In addition,
since they were overwhelmingly staffed by men, there was internal pressure to facilitate men's progression since they (apparently unlike women)
'needed' a career path.

I also identified a number of medium-term actions to be undertaken
within five years: the clarification of the basis for allocating senior posts to
faculties; the identification of SMART gender targets (specific, measurable,
achievable, relevant and time bound) at faculty level; the achievement of
such gender targets to be used as a criterion for evaluating line management;
gender awareness workshops for all members of interview boards and the
creation of career development opportunities for women who were 'high

fliers' (involving visibility, responsibility etc.). Many of these ideas eventually found their way into the expert report on gender equality in Irish higher educational institutions (HEA, 2016[45]).

I had invited the then secretary general of the short-lived Civil Service Department of Equality and Law Reform to speak at a women's studies seminar in the university and invited the president of the university, Dr Ed Walsh, to chair it. Given the eminence of the speaker, he was hosted in the president's office before the seminar. The secretary general was not a socially radical man. But he was astonished at the president's views on gender and after their meeting, he wryly noted that he now understood my problems.

Nevertheless, after my address to governing authority, gender quotas for search committees were put in place by Dr Ed Walsh, and all-male competitions were not allowed to proceed without his express permission. In addition, he initiated a gender awareness workshop for executive committee (obviously led by an external man ...). The programme for this workshop was not radical – but that it happened at all in the late 1990s was an achievement. It was not repeated for another fifteen years.

During the 1990s I participated in two management training courses. One of these was specifically for women, and this meant that Human Resources had to go beyond the 'usual suspects' in looking for participants. At this time, I was course director in women's studies and so was very visible, and hence was invited to participate. The course was held in Dublin City University and was led by Professor Pat Barker. It included twelve other women in their 30s and 40s from various universities. There were two revealing moments during it. The first occurred in a session which was being led by a dapper young man with a business background who talked about the factors which had helped him to advance his career. Quite unselfconsciously he tapped his address book and said that he had 'lots of friends': the implication being that friends were defined as those who were useful and it was entirely legitimate to use them in advancing your career, since that this was what friends were for. This provoked visceral shock in

---

45   HEA. (2016). *National Review of Gender Equality in Irish Higher Educational Institutions.* Dublin: https://hea.ie/assets/uploads/2016/06/hea_review_of_ gender_equality_in_irish_higher_education.pdf, accessed 15 Janury 2018.

all the women, including myself. Babysitting and children's birthday presents were traded, but friends were relationships that were valued in themselves. The idea that they were valued because of their usefulness struck us as crass and exploitative. The young business trainer was equally puzzled by the groups' reaction.

The second moment of illumination came during a presentation on negotiation. The same trainer went around the class and asked everyone when they used negotiation as a strategy. When it came to my turn, I said that I used it as a last resort, when I had exhausted all the usual strategies (including charm, persuasion, advocacy, negative comparisons etc.). It was his turn to look puzzled. He could not understand why negotiation, with its clear rules about offers and counter offers would not be the first approach adopted. But this kind of strategy presupposed a rough power equality between those involved, with the expectation of give and take in reaching an outcome acceptable to both parties. To me, like the other women there, these were unrealistic assumptions, given our positioning as female academics at the middle and lower levels of the predominantly male academic hierarchy.

The course illustrated our very different worlds and positioning. Although it was helpful in showing us that we were not alone in struggling with masculinist constructions of leadership and male-dominated structures, we were unclear how we could move forward except by becoming effectively pseudo-male business entrepreneurs, which was a stretch too far for most of us. Many years later, I noticed that Irish leadership and management courses still seem to embed these assumptions.

The other management course I attended was led by Maynooth University. It was held in a charming off-site location: a country house with a lovely restaurant. Again, we were a small group of academic women. This time, part of the experience involved meeting and mingling with powerful men in a social location. Each of us was allocated a senior officer in the university (typically a man) as a dinner companion. My companion was the then bursar in Maynooth University, a layman. Conversation flowed easily. We talked about the position of women in universities; the religious ethos of Maynooth and the impact of this on staff and students. It was obvious that the bursar was far more conservative than I on such matters. However, when it came to ordering the meal, he ordered oyster and pigeon, while I went for mushroom soup and lamb chops. We both laughed heartily at the reversal of our conservative positions. It was a heart-warming moment. Courses can be helpful in bringing people together, helping them to learn the informal rules of the game and to recognise the structural barriers they face. This course was unusual in facilitating exposure to those at the top of the organisation – predominantly men. However, such one-off experiences do not compensate for ongoing informal sponsorship where those in power recommend and open metaphorical promotional doors for their protégés – a 'normal' part of many men's experiences.

There were indications in the 1990s that changes were occurring in the position of women in higher education. However, in, for example, UL at this time, the number of professorial chairs increased by 40 per cent, with most of these being located in male-dominated areas so that it was almost inevitable that they were going to be filled by men. Targets at that time were being used in the Civil Service but were viewed as legally problematic by the then (male) chair of the equality committee. The request by the (male) registrar asking line management to identify specific SMART objectives to promote gender equality was largely ignored. These included targets related to the gender profile of academic staff; targets related to changing the organisational culture through workshops challenging negative and stereotypical gender attitudes; and targets related to fostering a management style that valued diversity. By the beginning of 2000 the attempt to identify such SMART targets had been abandoned.

For individuals, there was the possibility of treading an uneasy line between compliance and commitment by becoming a 'tempered radical',[46] committed to the organisation but also committed to gender equality which necessitated change in that organisation. As I saw it there was no shame in earning a living while being a 'tempered radical'. I could see that some women 'kept their head down', focusing on their own students and lectures; while others (as I had done in Waterford Regional Technical College) created a 'bubble' which shut out negative evaluations of themselves and

46 Meyerson, D. E. and Scully, M. A. (1995). 'Tempered Radicalism and the Politics of Ambivalence and Change', *Organization Science*, 6 (5), 585–600.

their areas. It was not clear whether these strategies could really be seen as resistance. However, others were challenging their own acceptance of the situation; while yet others were openly naming aspects of the organisational culture, procedures and career paths that were not 'women friendly'. Some were creating/mobilising allies and identifying key structures and sites that needed to change. These strategies offered real possibilities for resistance. Very very few were thinking about whistle-blowing and industrial action: actions that were likely to effectively end an academic career.[47]

Activity related to the promotion of gender equality in the university was not part of my job. The head of department saw it as a distraction from the core activity of the department. The Universities Act, which was being drafted in the 1990s, became law in 1997[48] and obliged all higher educational institutions to develop a gender equality policy. Implicit in these legal obligations was the idea that 'this gender businesses' was a legitimate and necessary focus. Suddenly, people like me who had been an irritant, became useful. I was asked to take a lead in developing a gender equality policy for UL. As long as my activity was limited to dealing with this, it was valued by senior management. More fundamental change was not on the agenda.

I was frustrated and disappointed and, as with so many of these experiences, I poured it all out to my sister. She stitched a sampler, which showed ducks paddling on the top half, with their heads submerged in the water while feeding in the bottom half. The words 'Life has its ups and downs' were stitched on it. The message was clear. I put it on the window in my bedroom.

47   O'Connor, P. (2000). 'Resistance amongst Faculty Women in Academia', *Higher Education in Europe*, 25 (2), 213–19.

48   Universities Act. (1997). https://data.oireachtas.ie/ie/oireachtas/act/1997/24/eng/enacted/a2497.pdf, accessed 1 June 2023.

Becoming an overnight success after almost thirty years

I had wanted to be a professor since I was a teenager. I did not know what professors did, nor even the difference between a professor and someone with a PhD. I don't know where the idea came from but as I saw it, a particular advantage was that it obscured marital status (the only alternatives then were Miss or Mrs: MS had not been invented). Twelve years of contract work, some with less than helpful bosses, obliterated that ambition. My energies became focused on surviving – personally and professionally.

I was now in my mid-40s and, after twenty-five years of teaching and research, I was still at lecturer level: the first step on the academic career hierarchy, albeit that I was now permanent. There was no woman at full professorial level in the University of Limerick. It was unconceivable to me that I would get to senior lecturer, then associate professor and then full professor before I had to retire at 65 years. I was a diligent and responsible lecturer and a member of the union so management could not sack me. They seemed highly unlikely to promote me. A stone rolled off my back. I realised that they had no hold on me. Using the data I compiled annually, I started to present it in various fora. I used my own case history as an example and joked that if I were a horse, you would not back me.

Then, quite suddenly, a professorship in sociology and social policy was advertised which did not require applicants to be at senior lecturer or associate professor level. What had I to lose? I had extensive experience of job rejections: one more would not kill me. I applied. However, this time I looked for help in presenting my CV from a former male colleague outside the university and followed his advice. Since I was irritated by claims that women did not want to move up, and was determined to show that some women (like me) did, I emailed the members of the department of sociology, indicating that I was going to put in an application.

The process involved a presentation and interview. I remember nothing about either. To my surprise I was offered the position. Given my skirmishes on gender I suspected that my departmental colleagues might not necessarily be pleased. So, I left a bottle of wine in the departmental office for them to celebrate or not in my absence. I went back to my little house in

Dunmore East. Then I was (unexpectedly) torpedoed by feelings of guilt and unworthiness. I felt that I did not know enough to be a professor: that the shoes were too big. There were women who were better qualified than I who, I felt, should have got a professorship before me – although none of these had applied for this position. I rang then Dr (now Professor) Kathleen Lynch, University College Dublin, who was one of those whom I felt should have got a professorship before I did (she had not applied for the job). She reassured me and that helped but I still felt that the shoes were too big.

I remembered my mother and her unfulfilled ambitions. To make peace with the past, I created two annual fellowships for high-achieving young undergraduate women who had chosen to do the then new degree in History, Politics, Sociology and Social Studies in UL (initially at £500 each, and then a few years later I increased them until they were eventually €1,500 each (the euro came in in 2002)). These were based on their Leaving Certificate results so as to eliminate any perceived favouritism by myself that might create difficulties for the young women. I named them the SOCs (after my mother – Sheila O'Connor). For the next thirteen years they were funded by me, but the cheques and certificates were presented by the president of UL or one of the vice-presidents, mostly in the elegant green room in the university White House, with its gilt-framed paintings and Georgian windows overlooking the rolling green campus.

I made a speech every year referring to the many false dawns as regards gender equality in higher education: in my mother's time in the 1930s and in my own time in the 1960s – asking the young recipients to remember this day thirty years hence and to do something to advance the position of women in the academy. Very few of my academic colleagues attended these 'do's' and some of those who did complained that the SOCs were only available to women. Others complained that they did nothing to improve the position of working-class students. Since they were funded by me, there was little they could do. The administrators, initially in the Admissions office, and later Ann Ryan in the dean's office were unfailingly helpful. Senior management were astonished that I would invite them to give away my money. To me, it was an opportunity to gain profile for gender equality, to make peace with the past and to try to shape the future. It was well worth the money.

When I look back now, I am surprised at the university's lack of interest in recognising my professorial appointment as a symbolic mould breaker, although I was the first woman to be appointed at full professorial level in that university (and the first female professor of sociology in Ireland). I still felt overwhelmed and unworthy but it was important to me to have a rite of passage. There were no procedures for an inaugural address in the university at that time. I decided to give mine through the Sociological Association of Ireland in February 1999. As one door opened, another closed. My inaugural coincided with very heavy menopausal bleeding, signalling the end of my periods. The Inaugural went well and was well attended. Later, as dean, I institutionalised inaugural professorial addresses in our own faculty.

Before I had come to the University of Limerick as lecturer in 1992, I had been shown a very nice light airy office and promised that it would be mine. When I arrived, a male colleague was already ensconced in it and no-one showed any interest in persuading him to move. Not wanting to cause a fuss, I accepted the situation. I was assigned a very small – and in the summer an extremely hot – office (so hot that I had to sit in the corridor to work). After my professorial appointment, there was still no interest in moving me. This time I decided to take the law into my own hands. I had noticed that Professor Mícheál Ó Súilleabháin was moving from a nice office in the Foundation Building to an entirely new building dedicated to music. His office was much further away from the power corridor where the dean was located but it offered a view of trees beyond the car park, and there were some sociology colleagues already in that area. He was a man who was both gender aware and willing to break rules. I laid my problem before him and asked him to ring me when he was actually moving. In this way, I acquired a professorial office. I was happy and productive there – not least, I suspect, because it represented my refusal to be endlessly ignored. Sometimes a woman can be pushed too far.

With my appointment as a professor, it was possible to think in terms of buying somewhere to live near UL. I had moved several times from the room I had started off renting in Murroe, first to a bed -sit in Shannon Banks (which was painted bright pink and had a fridge which revved beside the bed) to a lovely little 'Granny Flat' attached to Des and Mary

Greene's house in Corbally, and then house sitting (organised by them) in what was to me a scarily big house in the area. I had made considerable inroads into paying off the mortgage on my little house in Dunmore East and reckoned that I could just about afford another mortgage. I thought about building again but was daunted by the amount of work involved. I started to go round the estate agents, and meanwhile stayed in bed and breakfast accommodation. The only thing I was clear on initially was that a mortgage of £50,000 was my limit – with one estate agent remarking in exacerbation:

> 'What you want ma'am? Do you want a holiday home? Do you want a suburban family house? Do you want a town house? Do you want an apartment? What do you want?'

I looked at all of them. It gradually became clear to me that I was still fixated on small villages – possibly reflecting my happier childhood memories of Mogeely, in East Cork. I almost bought a thatched holiday home in Murroe – but was deterred by my sister's rhetorical question: 'Would there be much light there?' Its traditional small windows gave a very clear answer to that question. I eventually realised that I wanted to be near water. So, I settled on a tiny one-bedroom apartment with big windows overlooking the street in Killaloe on one side and the canal beside the river Shannon on the other, within sight of the beautiful eighteenth-century bridge with its thirteen arches. It was at my price limit. I had spent over five months living out of a suitcase in bed and breakfast accommodation in Limerick. I signed the contract and moved in.

At 47 years old, while in my probationary year at professorial level, I learned of an interview board which appeared to breach the newly approved university policy requiring gender balance (at the appropriate level) on appointment boards: a policy which had taken two years to draft and get approved. The post was in history – a male-dominated department. I knew none of the candidates and had no personal or professional interest in the appointment. The shortlisting process had produced seven men and no women for interview. The president's permission to continue with the interviews appeared not to have been sought: possibly because he was due to resign as president in 1998. I attempted unsuccessfully to contact those in line management – all men – who had signed off on this board to raise my concerns. There was no structure or mechanism for monitoring/sanctioning breaches of this policy, so I emailed all the members of the department of history and of the equality committee who had drafted the policy, outlining my concern about whether a female disciplinary expert at a similar level to the male experts had been included on the board as required.

In response I received a letter from personnel summoning me to a formal hearing involving the three levels of line management who had signed off on this board (i.e. the then head of department, the dean of the faculty and the registrar) as well the chair of the equality committee and the personnel manager (all men) to 'explain the actions I took during the course of the competition'. To underline the gravity of the situation, I was advised to bring a union representative. I was shocked and afraid. Despite my skirmishing, it was the first time I had ever been the subject of what looked to me like a disciplinary hearing (although it was not described as such). I rang a senior colleague in the university to ask for advice. He suggested that I apologise but said he could do no more as he might be involved in the process.

I had been a long-standing member of the union but it was difficult to get a union representative to accompany me. I knew instinctively that it had to be a man. I was turned down by several. Dr Tom Turner, with whom I had co-authored a paper on equal opportunities in Africa,[49] agreed to do it. On the morning of the hearing, he rang to say he was ill but he still came with me. The men were all there when I arrived. I explained the reasons for my action. It was all over in 30 minutes. Its purpose was to indicate disapproval and to generate fear in me. It seemed breaches of policy could not safely be challenged by employees-even senior ones.

Becoming an overnight success after almost thirty years had its limitations it appeared ...

49   Turner, T. and O'Connor, P. (1994). 'Women in the Zambian Civil Service: A Case of Equal Opportunities?' *Public Administration and Development*, 14 (1), 79–92.

Feminist, 40s, seeks ballroom dancing partner

I have always loved dancing, particularly dancing when you are held in a man's arms. Although I had done Irish céilí dancing, and particularly Irish set dancing since I was a teenager, I was well into my 40s before I went to ballroom dancing classes. I went because I felt that I was becoming a grey, dull, bureaucratic person, the same sort of motivation that drove me to a creative writing class after I had submitted my PhD.

The classes were initially held in a hall in the student residences on the university campus. The first teacher had a mathematical bent. She spoke about angles and orientation. My approach to dancing has always been intuitive. Aged 15, I scored 25 out of 100 on spatial ability and if anything, I had disimproved since then. I had serious difficulty doing three-point turns when I was learning to drive because I could never envisage my future spatial location. The teacher could not imagine anyone having that kind of problem. This was a challenge to both of us.

Although the ads for the course stressed that you did not need a partner, most people came with one. Thus, I was dependent on the generosity of my neighbours and the ingenuity of the teacher in bringing along 'spare' men or in encouraging couples to split up for a few dances. There were excellent waltzers among them with whom I could spin and spin into infinity. I loved the tango too, the dramatic solo spin and spin and spin before I threw myself back into a partner's arms. Always confident that I would be held.

The classes were attended by students and staff and moved, over time, from the student hall to the main university building and then to a local hotel. I had a reputation at work for being tough, direct, taking no prisoners, someone who was opinionated and combative: endlessly bringing up 'the woman business'. I vaguely recognised that my alternate persona would seem a bit strange to some of my male colleagues. However, I had long developed the uncanny habit of caring little about what other people thought of me at work, not least because I was busy thinking what I thought of them ... When the director of computing marvelled that I had no problem with him leading in a quick step, I simply laughed.

Ballroom dancing was my attempt to create balance in my life. Doing like Ginger Rodgers, everything that Fred Astaire did, but backwards and in high heels. Well, not quite in high heels. Having always had weak ankles and a tendency to fall over, high heels were out of the question. I compromised with my default pair of low-heeled black ankle boots, just about feminine enough to pass muster. The foxtrot, the quickstep, the tango were all wonderful, particularly if your partner was a good dancer. Then, my feet skimmed the floor. I felt I was flying. The lack of such a consistent partner was a bit of a problem. I considered putting an ad in the *Limerick Leader* saying: 'Feminist, 40s, seeks ballroom dancing partner.' I discussed it with a friend at the time and her response dissuaded me: 'No market' she said. Could she have been wrong?

I vaguely regret that I never tested that market, but I did continue to dance.

CHAPTER 5

Ten years in Management

Context

The 2000–10 decade was one of contrasting fortunes in Ireland. The 'Celtic Tiger' which continued until 2007, was characterised by dramatic increases in women's paid employment and economic growth rates that were the envy of the world. It was followed by economic collapse, created by a reckless construction sector; ineffective state regulation and a clientelistic male-dominated culture in the political system, the construction industry and the banking system. The state guaranteed all bank debts, however reckless and unsecured. In November 2010 Ireland lost its economic sovereignty to the 'troika' of representatives from the International Monetary Fund, The European Central Bank and the European Commission. There were worries about whether the currency, and even the country, could survive.

The public sector was the first target for cuts in expenditure. These included dramatic cuts to state support for higher education and a simultaneous substantial increase in student numbers because of very high levels of unemployment. There was pressure on higher education to increase research output to improve university rankings in a landscape increasingly dominated by managerialist, private sector practices. In the University of Limerick, there were additional problems arising from the earlier knock-on effects of the impact of the dot.com bubble on the information technology area, and the expectation that this area would be subsidised by other areas.

This was the setting for my line management experiences.

Getting a line management position

I never wanted to be in management. Suits I thought. Doing no real work. Just looking important. When a female colleague in another department said that she wanted to be dean (an academic line management and leadership position) of what was then the College of Humanities, I had no hesitation in supporting her. In June 2000 there was no indication that the position would be available for quite some time. But it was good to think ahead. She had just got a sabbatical after waiting for it for twenty-seven years and had made arrangements to let her house in Ireland, organised a university affiliation for herself in the United States, as well as schooling there for her children and accommodation for herself and her family.

Then, on 10 July 2000, the unthinkable happened. The current incumbent unexpectedly stood down as dean and left the university. The procedure for appointing a dean was more complicated than it is today. The first step laid down by the then president, Professor Roger Downer, was a call for nominations. Since her plans were already made, my female colleague decided to go ahead with her sabbatical. Another woman, Dr Bernadette Whelan, a women's studies colleague in the department of history, nominated all women at lecturer level and above for the position. Thus, as a lecturer, I had a nomination.

As a former course director in women's studies who had been in trouble with management over breaches of procedure in the gender equality area, I was a very unlikely candidate. I had never been head of any department nor had I held any management position. Reflecting my valorisation of knowledge over power and my dismissive attitude towards management, I was not daunted by the size of the dean's shoes. I reckoned that I had a better chance of setting future agendas if I was seen to be a contender. I decided to stand as a voice for change. I was one of thirteen people to do so: seven men and six women. Most were not currently in management. The sheer number of people contending clearly indicated that there was no appetite for the appointment of a current head of department as dean.

The next step laid down by Professor Roger Downer was to produce a vision statement. This required work, but I had no problem with that. That requirement reduced the field to six candidates: four men and two women. My vision reflected the fact that I was uneasy with the lack of criteria in appointment and promotion competitions. I was uncomfortable with references to candidates being 'team players', seeing it as a coded reference to cronyism as a rationale for appointing them. Recruitment procedures at that time typically included a presentation to the host department. I felt that much more difficult questions were often asked of female than male applicants, with internal male candidates appearing to be given a pass by predominantly male departments. Thus, I focused on accountability and also on what I saw as the invisibility and marginality of humanities and social sciences in the university.

The next step involved the president taking soundings from academics across the university. I knew instinctively that I needed the support of senior men outside my own faculty. I set about looking for it. I had never done this kind of thing before and was struggling when I got a detailed email from a woman in another department whom I barely knew. She made clear that she would not be supporting me but proceeded to give me two pages of advice about what I should do to increase my chances. I was amazed. The idea that someone would take all this trouble to advise me was astonishing. I proceeded to follow her advice.

The last stage was an interview by the president. It was now early august. I always left the university at this time to rest in my little house in Dunmore East: swimming and eating ice cream every day. It was not clear when the president would interview potential candidates. There was a network of women in secretarial positions around the university: people who could not speak truth to power themselves but who appreciated those who did. I found out that the last possible day before a decision had to be made by the president was 5 September. I got my interview pencilled in for the day before that and went off on my summer holidays.

At the interview on 4 September 2000, I was not nervous. I was quite sure that I was not going to be appointed. Professor Roger Downer questioned whether I was a single-issue candidate (i.e. only concerned with gender equality). I drew an analogy between discrimination on the basis of gender and on the basis of religion, a salient issue for him since he was from Northern Ireland. Suddenly I realised that he identified with me. I could well be appointed. Somewhat shaken I left the room.

The president was to contact all candidates on 5 September 2000 to inform them of the outcome, beginning with the successful person. I was so sure that this was not going to be me that I popped out to put letters in the post. He was waiting in my room on my return and he offered me the deanship. The term of appointment was three years. I had been happy in my (illicitly acquired) office and asked him if I could return to it when I had done my stint. I also repeated my mantra that 'it was not possible for me to be in the university on a Friday' and asked if that was a problem? He brushed these concerns aside and said that he was quite sure I could organise things so that these things were possible.

Within two days I was giving the dean's address to the new students in the university concert hall. I was not the least daunted by that. Neither was I daunted by giving the conferring address a short time later to those who had just graduated. There I stressed the contribution of all of those who had supported them during their academic careers, not only their parents and teachers, but all of those in the university, including those in the cleaning and catering departments, in admissions and finance, all of whom took pleasure in their success. I could feel the emotion in the conferring hall. I loved that.

I was troubled by the idea of moving to the dean's office. It was all dark mahogany furniture. I could not justify throwing out this expensive furniture but it was a symbolic indication that I did not fit there. I was also uneasy about moving to the 'power corridor'. For six weeks, I 'commuted' between my old office and the dean's office. Then since I could not justify occupying two offices, I moved. However, I took the plywood pale circular table from my old office and installed it incongruously among the dark mahogany furniture as a reminder of who I was and where I had come from.

At that time women made up roughly 10 per cent (9/83) of the deans in all Irish universities. I was touched by the supportive emails I got from inside and outside the university, welcoming my appointment. I did not know it then but it was the beginning of a ten-year adventure.

Fitting and not fitting in

I was initially appointed dean for three years by the then president, Professor Roger Downer, and then was asked by him to continue for a further three years. After he retired prematurely due to ill health, John O'Connor, formerly chief financial officer in the university, was appointed by governing authority as acting president, the first non-academic ever appointed in an Irish university. He had been very close to the founding president, Dr Ed Walsh, and was an extremely shrewd, visionary and re- putedly ruthless man. I liked him. Much later reflecting on my tenacity in advancing gender equality issues in the university, he commented that: 'You have an extraordinary skill for breaking through all bureau- cracy. No bureaucracy is safe with entrepeneurs (or is it entrepreneuses) like you.' I interpreted this as a compliment. He did not wish to make academic appointments, so all deans were run on for roughly a year until the next president, Professor Don Barry was appointed in 2007.

The name of the faculty was Humanities when I became Dean. I was not happy with this since as I saw it, it did not reflect the disciplines in the faculty. I eventually succeeded in getting agreement in the faculty on a change in title: and it was renamed the Faculty of Arts, Humanities and Social Science. A completely unintended consequence of this was that much later, it was possible for me to be re-appointed dean of this 'new' faculty. At that stage, I competed for and got a further three-year appointment. This meant that I was dean for over ten years – a very long period. In retrospect I think it was too long, not least because it closed off other options later.

To my very considerable surprise, I enjoyed being dean. I had never played group sports and it was only then, at 50 years old, that I began to understand and really appreciate the joy and satisfaction to be got from leading and working as a member of a team. I had got some insight into this when I was sailing, but I had never led in that context. I wish more women realised that making things happen can be fun. Suddenly too, many of the qualities which had been liabilities all my life became assets. I remained the impatient, warm, blunt woman that I had always been, but somehow the evaluation of these qualities changed. I found that whereas my irreverent attitude to authority had been a problem before, now as an authority figure, the same attitude was perceived very differently. As a woman, my gender was not a problem at faculty level since as dean I embodied authority and so my presence effectively changed the norm.

Women frequently assume that the more senior the job, the more difficult it is. In my experience, it can be the opposite. Any job normally done by men comes with a lot of back-up in terms of resources, including personnel. In the case of the deanship, such resources included a secretary, a faculty manager, assistant deans and heads of department. It seemed to me that unless you were unable to tie your own shoelaces, it would be possible to do the job with such infrastructural supports. In jobs mostly held by women there are frequently few if any supports, as I had discovered when I was course director in women's studies.

I have always had an instinctively authoritative presence. Thus, I was not daunted by being chair of the Management Group and of the Faculty Board. I now had a tiny possibility, but still a possibility, of making changes. Some of these coincided with institutional developments. Thus, for example, although initially I was very much on my own in insisting on changes in the recruitment processes, within a few years many of the changes I wanted were normal practice in the university. Others remained less common. Thus, for example, I was unhappy with the idea that management committee at faculty level would consist largely of senior (male) academics. Hence, I made it clear that anyone at any level could be nominated/nominate themselves to serve as head of department or assistant dean, and encouraged them to consider doing this as a service to their department/faculty for a period of three years. This increased the chance that those in these positions would be diverse in terms of gender, age, and nationality. I was pleased that the thirty people who served on the faculty management group over the ten years of my deanship reflected that diversity. Departments for the most part still nominated their own heads so that most of the people on the management team were not of my choosing. I enjoyed understanding and supporting them. The permanent faculty manager had a totally different style to mine, but for ten years we worked together very productively and harmoniously. I found the pace of change frustratingly slow, but my impatience meant that things did happen. My tenacity too was now an asset, not a liability.

I always presumed that the higher up you went, as a woman, the more you would be hated or resented by men. Not true. I found that most men defer to those who occupy positions of authority, since they expect that in such predominantly male structures they will be 'looked after', sponsored and given opportunities, with the hope that they will ultimately occupy these positions themselves. That is how such male-dominated structures reproduce themselves. I found that most men were reluctant to take on a person in authority. When I was course director in women's studies, they had no such reservations.

During the first seven years, I was one of six deans (and the only woman). As such I was a member of an (internal) university structure called deans' council, although it in fact included a wide range of heads of function as well as deans. Because I had spent so much of my working life up to that time in largely female settings (albeit under an ultimate male authority), I was initially dismayed by a work situation where women were very much in a minority. At the very first meeting of dean's council when I saw the composition of the group (twenty-eight men and two women, apart from myself), I backed out of the room. 'I must be in the wrong place' was my immediate and entirely unconscious response. Confident and outspoken though I was, this response was visceral. Having checked my folder: date, time, location I realised that I was in the correct place. That first meeting was difficult. After it, I confided in Dr (now Professor) Sarah Moore, one of the two other women there:

'That was dreadful, absolutely dreadful. I don't know what I am going to do. The only two roles on offer are the dutiful daughter and I don't fit that and the harridan and I don't want to fit that. What am I going to do?'

'Look to your supporters', she said.

That was helpful. I managed to carve out a role that I was comfortable with: a disruptive, challenging presence that by combining humour and warmth, managed to stay just inside the bounds of acceptability. I learnt that there is nothing as persuasive as enthusiasm, except perhaps persistence and the combination of the two are very effective. An awful lot of men are unaccustomed to emotion, passion, enthusiasm and authenticity combined with a good logical argument. I often threw in humorous phrases so that people dissolved in laughter and that disrupted the formal dance that so often happens at meetings. I recognised that if you keep (metaphorically) hitting people over the head you are seen as tiresome, but if people can get a good laugh, you can escape this. There was little real power in those settings. So, using that kind of strategy to lobby and advocate worked.

I had much greater difficulties later, when deans were included in executive committee, the most senior management group in the university, chaired by the president. This was a nine-person group in the University of Limerick, including the president, vice-presidents and from 2008 onwards, the four executive deans. It was unclear whether it was simply an advisory group to the president or an actual decision-making body. Two (and for a short period three) of the nine people on this group were women. But power was embodied in the men. In that context as a woman, I was defined relative to the male norm. There were subtle exclusionary strategies. Pre-meeting 'bonding' conversations were frequently about male sport, a central theme in creating male solidarity in Irish society, and one that I had no interest in. I was very interested in national politics, also a 'male' subject, but this was almost never discussed. Before meetings, the men either huddled in a corner and talked exclusively to each other or they sat at the table and buried themselves in their lap-tops, occasionally raising their heads to comment on some match or other, whether soccer, rugby, Gaelic football or hurling. The conflation of informal ways of 'doing men' with 'doing power' irritated me. I tried various strategies including humour in this forum but none worked. It was a gendered, extremely political arena. I was neither comfortable with, nor adept at these games.

My personal relationship with the then president remained positive, and privately he admitted that he found me difficult to handle in these fora. He had extended the composition of executive committee to include the deans but had simultaneously weakened our position by creating a recruitment committee where the vice-presidents assessed the dean's recruitment plans for their faculties, but without any reciprocal structure where we could assess theirs. On one occasion they deleted a focus on gender in an advertisement for a post in the faculty I led. This infuriated me but there was nothing I could do about it except complain at executive committee, where it was eventually agreed that this was an abuse of their power. However, the absence of a structure to allow the deans to evaluate the vice-presidents' recruitment plans reflected and reinforced their differential power within executive committee. For the second time in my forty-six-year career (the first was in 1972 at the ESRI), I found myself crying (privately) before and after executive committee meetings. Eventually at an off-campus training and development day for the executive, chaired by external facilitators, I spelt out that I felt marginalised, devalued, and isolated at executive committee meetings. This was greeted by an uncomfortable silence. Things did not improve.

As many women have done in similar situations, I wondered if I was the problem – if there was something wrong with me. I found a group, Through the Glass Ceiling (TTGC), in the UK and flew over to a meeting organised by Professor Sally Brown, then Pro-Vice Chancellor of Leeds Metropolitan University. The most moving and extraordinary session was one called *Dealing with Professional Disasters*. In it four very high profile, very strong women spoke with heart-rending honesty about times in their careers when they had experienced professional disasters, involving termination of employment and in some cases legal action. They openly discussed how they felt; what they did; what supports they had; what signals had been there beforehand; and how they felt now. There was no self-pity in their accounts – but every other emotion was there. I felt privileged to listen to them and simultaneously terrified of a system that could attempt to destroy women of such intelligence, ability, integrity and character. I realised that it was not just Ireland. It was not just me.

In the university, I saw just how complicated women's relationship with public power is. Women who want to 'pass' as pseudo-males will not challenge male power, and often that is exactly why such women are allowed access to those spaces. Many women at middle and senior level withdraw, seeing these male-dominated power arenas as unfamiliar, dangerous, problematic. As course director in women's studies, I had worked closely with women across the campus for over six years. Now many of them withdrew from me, seeing me as having 'gone over to the other side', whether in terms of management and/or gender. I found this hard. It increased the isolation of those women, like me, who were in positions of power. It was very different to the easy relationships that many men enjoyed with men in senior positions, where the legitimacy of being one of the 'club' and having almost filial relationships with those in power was unquestioned.

I was surprised to find that I found resistance by women to the enactment of power much more unsettling than similar behaviour by men. During the restructuring of the faculty, there was sustained opposition from several women. It provoked me, only for the second time in my ten years as dean, to consider resigning (the first time was four months into my deanship when an unsuccessful attempt was made to impose a research agenda on the faculty I led). I had a visceral feeling that if I did not have the support of the women, my legitimacy was undermined, at least in my own eyes. Eventually the matter was resolved but it was a disquieting indication to me of my political vulnerability.

In retrospect I can see that I was marginal to both the world of powerful academic men and less powerful academic women: occupying an uneasy and liminal position, personally and professionally. Many of my difficulties, I also subsequently realised, reflected the experiences of other women in positions of public power in higher education.

Successes and failures as faculty dean

My priorities as dean included providing academic leadership; creating transparent and gender-sensitive procedures/audits; developing programmes; increasing the research profile of the faculty; improving/consolidating its resources; and restructuring/renaming it. Like many women I looked down to those I served rather than up to those I was accountable to for the sources of my satisfaction and affirmation. I know I made mistakes and that I fell short in different ways but it was certainly not for the want of trying. I learned that access to power is very useful in getting things done. I kept a rough list of my achievements pinned to the back of the door, a very important exercise since the nature of management is such that successes are everyone's, but the failures are your own.

The thing that gave me most satisfaction was the change in the gender profile in the faculty and in the university during my deanship. In the Faculty of Arts, Humanities and Social Sciences, the proportion of women increased at all levels, with women constituting 50 per cent of those at full professorial level when I completed my term. In the University of Limerick, in 2012 women made up 34 per cent of the full professors, the highest in the country at that time and considerably above both the Irish (18 per cent) and the EU average (20 per cent).[50] It was zero before I was appointed as the first woman at that level in the university in 1997. As a woman, a professor, researcher and dean, I took a quiet pride in the contribution that I made to this change.

Trying to create fair, transparent processes for recruitment and promotion was an important focus of my deanship. There were constant struggles around the composition of recruitment and promotion boards, with women frequently being the last people to be selected and being required to fit into the disciplinary and time slots chosen to suit the male majority on the board. The procedures at that time included presentations by candidates to the department, who could ask questions and send their comments on the candidates to the chair of the board. Standardising the questions did not eliminate the bias, nor did dropping the practice of departmental feedback.

I had earlier been on a university promotion board where, as I saw it, there were a couple of women who on any objective criterion were better than their male counterparts. The board was not minded to consider them. I tried to argue their case. Unusually, I was supported by a senior male colleague, Professor Don Barry, then Professor of Mathematics and Statistics. I did not really know him at this time. He was also over-ruled. It was not fair. It was not right. I emailed him after the board to try and see what we could do. I became a firm advocate of clear pre-defined criteria before advertising,

50 O'Connor, P. (2014). 'Understanding success: A Case Study of Gendered Change in the Professoriate', *Journal of Higher Education Policy and Management*, 36(2), 212–24.

linked to clear indicators and marking schemes. On the boards I chaired as dean I insisted that each candidate was scored by each person on the board, on each criterion immediately after each candidate's interview. At the end of the interviewing period scores were agreed for each indicator on each candidate before the overall pattern became clear.

But I continued to feel uneasy: something was still not right. Much later, on listening to a paper at a conference, I realised where the problem lay. Applications were circulated to each member of the board well before the interview. On the day of the interview the board met and it could 'tweak' the marking schemas. If candidate A was strong on work experience but weak on publications, and if there was a desire for whatever reason to select him, the criteria and the weightings could be adjusted so that candidate A looked the stronger candidate on the day. It was very subtle; the process looked objective, but the outcome still reflected global judgements, which were frequently influenced by less than objective factors.

Many women do additional courses, take on extra administrative and teaching responsibilities in the naive hope of increasing their chances. Few women at that time were senior enough to be actually involved in promotion processes, and hence many of them did not realise that these activities are not valued in these fora. They continued to believe that the processes were gender neutral: that women needed to try harder; that they/ we were just not good enough. They did not see that academia is created by and for men; that the structures and criteria implicitly or explicitly favour men. Most men find it much easier to notice, identify with, sponsor and favour other men; so male privilege is reproduced and legitimated.[51] Those women who are promoted are frequently those who accept that system: frequently from the same class, with the same ethnicity, networks and ethos as the men in power. They are also expected to favour men and are criticised if they favour women, reflecting an observation made many years ago by Elizabeth Moss Kanter that when women are in a minority

---

51   O'Connor, P. (2020). 'Why Is It So Difficult to Reduce Gender Inequality in Male Dominated Higher Education Organisations? A Feminist Institutional Perspective', *Interdisciplinary Science Reviews*, 45 (2), 207–28.

in organisations: 'The price of being "one of the boys" was a willingness to occasionally turn against "the girls".'[52]

I had been dean of the faculty for almost seven years before I went to a European Conference on Gender Equality in Higher Education in Berlin in 2007. There I met Barbara Bagilhole and Kate White, the founders of a loose network of academics called the Women in Higher Education Management (WHEM) Network. This was a feminist research consortium with a vision to analyse the challenges for women in university management and to develop strategies to empower them to apply for and succeed in senior management roles. I was invited to become a member, that invitation being conditional on a willingness to collect data on those in management positions in Irish universities. There was no funding available to support such a project: the idea was that it would be done for free in my spare time. It was an offer that I could not refuse, despite its ostensible unattractiveness. Thus, began a co-operation that has lasted over sixteen years to date. It has produced four books published by Palgrave Macmillan,[53] several comparative articles, lots of fun and work. Initially there was some funding from Swedish sources, but for the most part the network has managed to continue without funding, with the co-ordination being done initially by Kate White and more recently by Angela Wroblewski, on a voluntary basis. It is striking that, in the absence of positions or resources, there is little politicking, and the general tenor of the group is collaborative and efficient.

Once a year as dean I had the chance to address the university management committee, a very large (predominantly male) structure consisting of heads of academic departments and functions, as well as those in more senior management positions. I relished these opportunities and

52   Kanter, E. M. (1977/93). *Men and Women of the Corporation*, p. 228. New York: Basic Books.

53   Bagilhole, B. and White, K. (eds) (2011). *Gender, Power and Management: A Cross Cultural Analysis*. London: Palgrave Macmillan; Bagilhole, B. and White, K. (eds) (2013). *Gender and Generation*. London: Palgrave Macmillan; White, K. and O'Connor, P. (eds) (2017). *Gendered Success in Higher Education: Global Perspectives*. London: Palgrave Macmillan; O'Connor, P. and White, K. (eds) (2021). *Gender, Power and Higher Education in a Globalised World*. Cham: Palgrave MacMillan.

used them to highlight gender inequalities. Thus, for example in 2004, I highlighted the relationship between the gender profile of staff in the then six faculties and the level of internal resources they received; their staff/student ratios and their publications per faculty post. I showed that the more male-dominated faculties in terms of staffing (such as Engineering and Information Communications Technology) received substantially more funding per student; had substantially better staff/student ratios and also had a much lower number of publications per academic post than those areas that had a higher proportion of women on the academic staff (such as Humanities and Business). This provoked an outcry and culminated in a vote proposing that I be prevented from presenting comparative data in future, on the grounds that such comparisons were misleading. The fact that the data was provided by the faculties themselves and compiled by Human Resources was conveniently ignored. The vote was passed, which I saw as an extraordinary exercise of male dominance and an abuse of power. However, by the following year their vote silencing me had been forgotten so that I could continue to raise issues.

The faculty I led was dynamic and innovatory. By 2006, the undergraduate intake of students had increased by 50 per cent in five years and the number of full-time PhD students had doubled. It has long been recognised that the particular metrics used in evaluating research output are key: with a focus on peer-reviewed journals favouring particular areas in hard science. The then vice-president research, Professor Vincent Cunnane, who was supportive of the humanities and social sciences, developed the concept of first-class publications, which included books, chapters in books as well as refereed journal articles. This metric reflected our publication output much more accurately, and the number of such publications doubled over five years so that by 2006 although the faculty had only 19 per cent of the university's posts, it had 25 per cent of the university's first-class publications. This facilitated the inclusion of the faculty in a successful funding bid by the university under the fourth Programme for Research in Third Level (PRTLI 4): one of five fully funded projects in the university.

Because Arts, Humanities and Social Science were not seen as a national priority, there was little possibility of getting funding for a new building large enough to include all its academic staff (although we did manage to get a new building for languages). Hence, at that time the academic staff in that faculty were scattered all around the university campus. This made casual conversations difficult: conversations which are important in creating a sense of belonging, facilitating exchange of ideas and building research co-operation. In a context where the numbers of junior staff were expanding, we began a process of interim partial spatial consolidation: using retirements or departures as opportunities to bring members of departments spatially closer.

Just before I was appointed dean, Atlantic Philanthropies evinced interest in funding women's studies as part of their social justice initiative. They indicated that they would be receptive to a five-year funding proposal of €1.5 million. This application was successful after I became dean. It facilitated the creation of two posts specifically in women's studies: one in sociology and one in English, with a view to developing the interdisciplinary nature of women's studies. They also funded postdocs in other departments, with varying success as regards embedding women's studies in those departments.

Atlantic Philanthropies subsequently invited a university submission to tackle the under-representation of women in senior positions in the university. This required that 'the problem be named'. There was considerable reluctance by the university to do this. Eventually a small proposal (half a million euros) was submitted and funded which mostly focused on changing ('fixing') the women, for example, increasing their confidence; improving their time management skills: the underlying assumption being that the reason why women were under-represented in senior positions was because of these deficiencies. This proposal did identify targets at senior lecturer level (which were subsequently achieved). The dedicated post in gender equality funded by Atlantic Philanthropies was later subsumed within Human Resources, and disappeared after its three-year funding ended. It was several years before I learned the implicit salutary lesson. Gender equality is a disruptive agenda involving as it does a challenge to male-dominated power structures. The brief of Human Resources, particularly in universities which are being run like private corporations (which is the case for most universities in the western world today) is to make the university look good. Highlighting a university's inadequacies in dealing with gender equality is thus virtually impossible for those who work in Human Resources. That lesson has not still been learned in many Irish universities.

It is very tricky claiming achievements as dean. However, the impetus to create a chair in creative writing was mine and I started the process of putting funding in place for it, although it did not come to fruition until after my time. Equally the development of journalism as an area, as well as the initiation of psychology as a discipline and the diversification of the existing suite of undergraduate degrees were my initiatives. I noticed that even people who were opposed to change, once it seemed inevitable, came on board, and frequently became some of its most vociferous champions.

I developed a reputation for being very energetic, combative, passionate and relentlessly persistent. This meant that opposing me was very tiring. Other staff and management eventually also realised that the more obstacles I encountered, the more relentless I became, and this too helped to see off opposition. But I did fail sometimes. Thus, for example, the faculty was initially included, but at the last minute was dropped from a university-wide funding application under the second Programme for Research in Third Level (PRTLI5) during my tenure. Occasionally too my initiatives were subsequently dismantled. Thus, although I had worked hard to get the faculty committed to and willing to fund a broadly based research institute to provide an umbrella for our research activities, my successor appointed as its director a man who had rarely collaborated internally with anyone, and under whom the institute did not thrive and was subsequently disbanded. (It has recently been reinstated).

I had thought that senior management would be extremely fraught and awesomely responsible, but to my surprise, overwhelmingly this was not so. Even more surprisingly, at times, for example, around the development of new programmes, new research areas or new research metrics, there were opportunities for intellectual and organisational creativity and fun. I loved the feeling of leading a team working together for a common objective, where we worked hard, but laughed a lot, at ourselves and at life. I wonder why these kinds of experiences are not more widely discussed, and whether this might influence women's willingness to take on such positions. Ignoring these elements, as well as the extensive supports available to women in jobs previously held by men, presents a very limited picture, and in effect discourages women from considering such positions.

Elephants and human beings

In an attempt to maintain my academic credibility, I continued to do research (on Fridays) and presented a research paper at an international conference every year. In 2006, the conference was in Durban in South Africa. I flew to Cape Town, a beautifully located and pretty city where I spent a day on my own. A week-long pre-conference tour using small mini-vans was organised from Cape Town to Durban, where the conference was to be held. My fellow travellers in that mini-van were two middle-aged male American academics and their wives and an Indian driver, none of whom I had met previously. They were great company especially Ian and Adelaide Coulter. We went to Kruger National Park and Adoo Elephant Park. I used to think that if I was going to be re-incarnated, I would like to be a lion. It was probably the Metro Goldwyn Mayer Image at the start of every film that did it. The magnificent mane, that throaty roar, the reputation for courage, strength and majesty. But in Kruger National Park I learned that one in four lion cubs die of hunger because the lion is too lazy and greedy to move off the prey to let the cubs eat. I saw elephants, magnificent vegetarians and such messy eaters that other animals followed to pick up what they pulled down and didn't eat. The African elephants' life expectancy is sixty to seventy years, in comparison to the lions' average of sixteen years. Elephants only die when their sixth set of teeth wear down so much that they can no longer eat. This is endearingly human if tragic. The herds are run by elderly females. Yet although the males are early expelled from the herd and live solitary lives, they have their uses. When as part of a culling exercise the old bulls were taken out, the keepers noticed a dramatic rise in the aggression of young male elephants towards other animals, a pattern that had never ex-isted before. Even the solitary bull elephants it seemed had a role to play. But they did not run the herd.

One evening as dusk was falling the guide took four of us out in an open-topped jeep to see the wild life at dusk in Kruger National Park. I was in the back seat with an American who had his camera perpetually glued to his eye. We were driving up a narrow dirt track when, coming over the crest of the hill, we saw the outlines of a herd of elephants and heard their trumpeting. The guide, a man in his 30s, who had turned from poacher to gamekeeper, reversed the four-by-four jeep rapidly down the hill into an adjoining cul-de-sac. He turned off the engine. We sat there nervously listening as the trumpeting came closer. The herd turned into our cul-de-sac. The guide started to talk to them in a low calm voice: saying over and over: 'we mean you no harm'. It was obvious that they were upset, angry even. The leading female elephant came up to the side of the jeep, her ears pinned back and her trunk down. We thought that she was going to over-turn the jeep with her trunk. She was so close to the man with the camera sitting beside me that his hands shook in the open-topped jeep and he could not focus the camera while inches away from her. Meanwhile the guide continued to reassure them of our intentions, saying over and over 'we mean you no harm'. After what seemed like an eternity, the old matriarch trumpeted loudly and led the herd out of the cul-de-sac. Just one young elephant raced back, scooped up the dirt from the track and blew it in the air and throwing up his trunk hit the front of the jeep before racing back to the herd. A mock display of adolescent aggression. The real danger was past. We sat there in silence: stunned and relieved. The guide lit a cigarette. I noticed that his hands were shaking. These powerful wild creatures, led by an aged matriarch, had been tamed by a calm reassuring voice. I knew then that if reincarnation existed, I wanted to be an elephant.

The Drakensberg mountains were magnificent. In many of the vil-lages and towns we visited in the interior we seemed to be the only white people, a disconcerting experience. The conference attendance was huge, about 3,000 participants, mostly white. At that time, there were extremely high levels of unemployment in Durban and no social welfare. On the first night 150 of the participants were mugged and/or robbed. We were warned not to leave our hotels in the evening and were escorted to the conference venue during the day by police mounted on horseback. This felt completely bizarre. The Indian Ocean was opposite our hotel. Two women from the conference went there for a morning swim, leaving their rings and money in the hotel, and taking it in turns to swim so as to mind their jeans, tops and underwear. These ended up being stolen. I did go for a swim there with a group of other participants, and even went to a party on the beach at the end of the conference without any mishap. However, the experience revealed the naivete of locating international, mainly white, conferences in areas of severe inequality and deprivation. But the nature reserves, although they were of course tourist traps, were fascinating. And those elephants raised fundamental questions about power and social structures that just might be equally relevant to humans ....

Trying to move up

I have always been irritated by assertions that women do not apply for senior positions because they do not want to get and use power to improve things in organisations or in the wider society. Some women, like some men, do want to do this. Many read the signs and recognise that they are not the 'favoured one' and so do not apply. Then the men in power claim that women are the problem, referring to lack of ambition, lack of confidence, unwillingness to compete, fear of failure etc. I was not willing to play that game. I had found to my surprise that I enjoyed mobilising support for creating organisational change to better serve the students and the staff. I was good at it. It created none of the anxieties in me that being a professor did. Why not try and move up?

In 2004, I participated in a management development course in University College Cork. I felt very comfortable among the participants who were all at senior management level, some from Ireland, but mostly from the UK and elsewhere in Europe. My personality profile was very similar to the then vice-president for research in the University of Limerick, Professor Vincent Cunnane, a man I liked (who went on to unsuccessfully apply for the presidency of the University of Limerick, and later became president of the new Technological University of the Shannon). I was 53 years old. I had completed my first three-year period as dean, and had been re-appointed for a further three years. It appeared that I was doing a good job and, to my own surprise, I was enjoying it. The position of vice-president academic and registrar came up in my own university. There were two elements to the job: an innovative academic leadership element and a bureaucratic administrative element. I figured that I would be good at the former and that the other element just might become part of a new position. My colleagues encouraged me to go for it. I applied. I was not successful.

I wanted a new challenge and I reckoned that I needed to get it in the next four or five years (given a mandatory retirement age of 65, and five-to-ten-year appointment periods). With what in retrospect looks like extraordinary courage or stupidity I applied for five positions: some at my own level, some higher up, inside or outside UL over the next four years. My dream of a return to Cork drove me to apply for a five-year (temporary) position as dean of the Faculty of Social Sciences in University College Cork in 2005. The application involved a presentation to the academics in the faculty, as well as being interviewed by an extremely large board of fifteen or sixteen people chaired by the then president of University College Cork, Professor Gerry Wrixon. The presentation went well: the stillness in the lecture hall told me that I had understood the university and the faculty. The interview was much less successful. The chair found it difficult to believe that the research output in the faculty I led in the University of Limerick had doubled in the previous five years, to the considerable embarrassment of the rest of the board. I calmly repeated the figures to support my assertion. The interview ended shortly after. I was rattled: upset, angry, frustrated. The job went to an internal candidate, who had previously indicated that he was not interested in it. Walking down the Western Road in Cork after the interview, my sister rang telling me that she had just been diagnosed with a serious health issue. I could not take it in.

I unsuccessfully applied for a position in University College Dublin. When in 2007, Professor Roger Downer, the then president of the University of Limerick resigned unexpectedly due to ill health I applied for the job. At that time no woman had ever held the position of president of an Irish public university. I made my application public: explaining why I was doing that and giving an interview to the student magazine because I wanted to see off the idea that women are not interested in such positions. The question of whether this might be misinterpreted by the men in power simply did not occur to me. I was not shortlisted. Later it emerged that, for various reasons, the interview board had been entirely male, to the considerable chagrin of the sole (external) female candidate who had been given an interview.

With the encouragement of colleagues, I applied for the position of vice-president academic in the University of Limerick for a second time in 2007. The then president of the University of Limerick, the man who had defeated me for that post in 2004, was now chair of the appointment board. This time I got to interview. Again, I was unsuccessful. I asked for and got an appointment with him so as to get some feedback. He knew me well since we had worked together for three years: he as vice-president academic and registrar and me as dean of the faculty of Arts, Humanities and Social Sciences. At a personal level, we got on well. We shared a zany sense of humour and I embodied his more radical aspects. Both of us could be direct, with little time for small talk:

> 'Thank you for seeing me', I said. 'I would like to know what scores the appointment board gave me.'

> 'I can give you your scores', he said 'but they will tell you nothing.'

I looked straight at him, a puzzled expression on my face. He lifted a piece of paper from the low table between us, the second and third fingers of his right hand stained dark brown from years of smoking. I reached out for the sheet saying as I did:

> 'I'd like to see them all the same.'

> 'Of course', he said. 'But it came down to a choice between you and Paul.'

Paul was one of the five heads of department who reported to me. The president continued after a short pause:

> 'I had to choose between politics and principles and I chose politics.'

I looked at the scores the board had given me: 85 per cent (26/30) for leadership; 85 per cent (17/20) for interpersonal and communication skills; 80 per cent (12/15) for academic credibility; but 66 per cent (10/15) for understanding the system and 65 per cent (13/20) for judgement and decision-making. It was not immediately obvious how my scores on leadership could be so high if I didn't understand the system and was a poor decision-maker. The president's comment as regards his choice between principles and politics provided a much-needed clue.

There was nothing more to be said. Nowhere had there been any reference to a criterion which asked the board to choose between politics and principles. The irregularities which had always been denied were confirmed. He was being honest. I was defeated but vindicated. I got to my feet. He smiled. He knew I would not hang him. He extended his hand. I took it. I closed the door quietly.

There was one more internal defeat to come: a small but significant one. I had been elected as a member of the university's governing authority a number of years before and had established that real power lay in the finance sub-committee. Hence, I went forward for membership of that committee. A rule suddenly appeared that deans could not be on that committee. There was no point attempting to challenge it. The message was clear. My face did not fit.

Between 2004 and 2007, I had applied unsuccessfully for five positions. I was exhausted from failure. I spoke on the phone to my sister every Saturday and confided freely in her about my professional frustrations and failures. Our lives were completely different: she had left paid employment when the second of their five daughters got scarlet fever as a child more than thirty years before. I knew that she was totally discreet and that she had my back. She sent me a sampler that she had made. It said 'Believe in your dreams'. I no longer knew what they were. I grieved for my lost hopes. I felt no sense of excitement about future possibilities. I saw only loneliness and closed doors. I needed achievements and a sense of contributing. I felt diminished and de-energised. A friend bluntly pointed out that my strategy of wanting to move up did not square with pointing out 'that the king had no clothes'[54] saying:

---

54   From a children's story, *The Emperor's New Clothes* by Hans Christian Andersen.

'Most people want to work with people who agree with them, who don't want to rock the boat. They cannot be bothered with inequality, seeing it as a fact of life.'

When people benefit from a system, why should they want change? I could see the logic of her argument, but emotionally I could not accept it. In 2008 I applied for a further three years as dean of the faculty in UL since I felt I could still make a difference there. I was the only one of the outgoing deans to be re-appointed, one of two women and two men appointed. I was acceptable, it appeared, coming up to the elbows of the men in power, but not to their shoulders. This was my limit. I was pleased and disappointed, and got on with the job. I recognised that I was very unlikely to be even eligible to apply for other senior management positions because the time window before my retirement was narrowing. In the meantime, I embarked on a research project on management and gender in higher education. Knowledge, it appeared, was more accessible than power.

If I could not change the system, I could at least try to understand it.

The end of my management career

On 3 July 2010, on a first visit to Odense, Southern Denmark to explore the possibility of our two universities collaborating on an EU project funding bid, an email came through from the then president of the University of Limerick. It asked me to meet him to discuss my future in the context of my current deanship term ending in December 2010. My heart sank. I had been thinking about this for six months. I knew that I would have to resign as Dean, that it was time to go. I had tried unsuccessfully to move up. Like several women in other universities at that time, these applications were unsuccessful. I had also tried to make sideways moves to other Irish universities. To no avail.

I was going to be 60 in December 2010. I had no clear plan for the future apart from finishing the book that I was writing. Standing down as dean was not only the end of an era: it was the end of a hope – a hope of moving on to bigger challenges, of starting something new. This was it: I was going no further. The official retirement age for all university employees, like those in the public sector, was then 65 years. Indeed, I had signed a contract with that date on it when I got a job there in 1992. I assumed that I would have to retire then. A few years later I discovered that Professor Des Fitzgerald, who subsequently became president of UL, and senior men in other Irish universities, had been appointed for ten-year terms when they were near the retirement age of 65 years. Indeed it emerged that men in my own university had never got/did not sign the paperwork and so continued working after 65 years if this was what they wanted to do.

I did not want to retire. But I also did not want to leave Ireland again. This limited my options. I had no problem with the idea of going back to teaching since I had always enjoyed it. There was the possibility of an EU project on gender equality starting in 2012 and I knew that I would enjoy that. I would go back to my old room which was good. I knew that it would be wise to take a sabbatical, to give my successor, whoever they were, a chance to settle in. A sabbatical would be a kind of prelude to my actual retirement, and a portent. I was still afraid that a lack of structure would again generate the self-doubt that had characterised the beginning of my career. I had learned then that full-time research did not suit me. Now that was what lay ahead in my retirement. In the intervening period, I was not sure how I would be received by my colleagues. I had been a strong dean who had not worried about who my decisions offended. Sitting on the bed in Odense, I sent a holding email and putting a determined smile on my face, I got ready for the next meeting there.

The day after I came back from Denmark, I met the president. I had sent on a detailed agenda. The last item on it was my own future. I was totally calm. I suspect that he anticipated that I would not go without a struggle. In any event he was taken aback when we came to that item and I said that I would be standing down in December 2010 and would be notifying the faculty that day of my decision. I was glad of the element of surprise. I just wished that I could disappear in the intervening period.

Immediately after that I met the faculty manager who was calm and practical. I was now almost tearful. I dreaded becoming a 'lame duck' dean. I knew that as soon as my stepping down was announced, power, such as it was, would begin to leak away. The only way I could exercise any agency was to announce my departure myself. On 6 July 2010, I drafted the email resigning as dean with effect from 31 December 2010 and sent it out.

There is a small earthy path beside the River Shannon in O'Brien's Bridge. It leads out of the village and along by the side of the river. From it you can hear the sound of oars dipping in the water as the rowers move rhythmically up and down the river, with occasional shouts from those in the training boat. The path winds beside the water with dappled light underneath the trees. As I walked along it, the tears streamed down my face. I felt pain. Sharp white pain. End of a secret hope. A great dream. I had to face it. I had got as far as I was going to go. The miracle was that I had got this far. But it was not as far as I had hoped. I walked on.

On 8 September 2010 after a particularly depressing meeting of executive committee when it was clear that radical action was needed but was not going to be taken, I felt a glimmer of gladness that I was stepping down as dean in three months' time. By 21 September 2010 as the plans started to become more concrete for my sabbatical, I began to feel excited. The last three months were, as I had anticipated, the most difficult in my entire deanship. Power was seeping away and a couple of people smelt blood and wanted to settle scores. I was unsettled and anxious anyway as I coped with the waves of despair and meaninglessness that this ending evoked as a portent of my retirement. I started the depressing process of clearing out the dean's office.

There was to be a presentation to me to mark the end of my ten-year period as dean. The faculty manager suggested that I might like to choose a painting, which would be presented to me at the last faculty board that I was to chair. On 24 November 2010 heavy snow started falling in Ireland, the heaviest for years. I had decided that I would choose a painting from an exhibition to be held in Waterford at the beginning of December, just days before that last Faculty Board. Driving conditions were difficult but I got there. The painting I initially picked out had been sold. Exhaustion, emotional stress and a heavy cold made me feel weak. I sat down on the floor of the gallery, sweating and dizzy, as I tried to choose an alternative. It came down to a choice between a yellow and grey painting of what looked vaguely like a space craft and an elegant white still life painting of a jug. I settled on the space craft since I was truly being launched to an unknown destination. Later, I was amused to find that it was called *Utopia and Enigma: All that is Solid Floats in the Air* by Angela Fewer. The incoming dean, Professor Tom Lodge, made the valedictory speech. It was a nice occasion.

I came back to Dunmore before Christmas, where, in a weird twist of fate, I was invited by search consultants to apply for the Presidency of Maynooth (a ten-year assignment), with a closing date in January 2011. I had turned down several such invitations before on the grounds of age. With my future so uncertain, I decided to ignore the question of age. I applied. I was not successful.

It really was the end of my career in management.

A sabbatical

To most people the idea of a sabbatical is fantastic – a year to research what you want, to meet interesting people, to be free of routine meetings and administrative responsibilities – what more could you want? I did not want it. I had eventually recognised that I like and need structure – even if only to react against it. I had plenty of freedom given my life style. I needed roots. My work and my little house in Dunmore East provided that. Although I had always travelled, it was for short periods, two to three weeks at most. The thought of a year on my own in a rootless, unstructured context was very scary. I remembered how lonely and anxious I had been in London in the 1970s. I needed the day-to-day stimulation, human contact and feedback that teaching provided. The sabbatical was a foretaste of what I might experience in five years' time in retirement and that only added to my anxiety. Retirement to me presaged death. My courage, which had sustained me in difficult situations in the past was at a low ebb. My dreams were in ashes. I was feeling anxious, tired and defeated.

I knew it would be unfair to my successor to have me hanging around like a dead fish. I booked accommodation in a student-type large old-fashioned building, the William Goodenough House, near Russell Square in a lovely safe, central area of London. The rest of my sabbatical began to fall into place. I planned to go to the University of Aveiro in Portugal to work with Dr (now Professor) Teresa Carvalho; to Linkoping in Sweden working with Dr Anita Goransson and to Deakin and Melbourne in Australia, working with, among others, Dr Kate White and Professor Jill Blackmore. Several of these were members of WHEM and during my sabbatical I got to know them better. None of them were particularly close relationships, but there was a sense of shared vision and trust.

The sabbatical started well. I had applied for and got a desk space for three months in the Thomas Coram Research Unit in the Institute of Education in the University of London, where Professor Julia Brannen, a friend and colleague from the 1970s, worked. Unfortunately, she ended up on sick leave for most of that period. I continued to work on various publications. I gave papers to two seminar series there. I had some other friends from when I had worked in London in the 1970s, including Jane Nelson and Maggie Coster and Steve Scarlett and I met up with them from time to time. I had always loved the sheer buzz of London. I was not under any immediate work pressure now and was able to finish work by 5.30 pm. I went to the theatre/musicals/opera at least once a week. I loved going down to Covent Garden or the National Theatre after work and having a glass of wine and a simple bite to eat before a performance. I mostly went on my own and I was happy. It felt like a little holiday. After years in my little house by the sea with very little formal cultural stimulation, I relished these experiences. I saw twenty-two performances over the three months in London: everything from the Barber of Seville, the Magic Flute, Aida, Madame Butterfly to Les Miserables, Chicago, to War Horse, Mogadishu, Children's Hour, Knot in her Heart. If cheap tickets were not available for what I was hoping to see, I simply went for whatever was available. The venues were beautiful: the Cottesloe, the Littleton, the Old Vic, The Royal Opera House. Because of cheap Ryanair flights to Waterford airport, I was able to come back to Dunmore East frequently. Perfect.

However, when it came to going to Aveiro, my anxiety returned. Aveiro is a lovely place, a kind of Little Venice, but I spoke no Portuguese. I had been there before, but I knew only one person there, Professor Teresa

Carvalho, a colleague whom I really liked, but who had a heavy workload and family responsibilities. I stayed in a lovely old-fashioned residence, but felt uneasy somehow. One of Teresa's colleagues, Professor Rui De Santiago, took me under his wing and showed me round the old university city of Coimbra. I invited my youngest niece, Lizzie, then in her 20s, to join me for a long weekend. At the start I ran her into the ground showing her the gondolas and the azuelos and all the sights, but then she suggested:

> 'Let's get a train to Geminares and have lunch there.'

We did, and by chance came across a colourful, zany art exhibition in the castle and saw the local Easter procession led by the children in their white holy communion dresses. The message was clear. Sometimes just taking it easy and letting things happen is a very good idea. I relaxed and thoroughly enjoyed her visit. I began to feel fine again.

When I look back at the photos from that year, I am amazed at how much I travelled and all the places I saw. I went to Linkoping, a new university, like the University of Limerick, with rolling campus views from the little office where I worked with Dr Anita Goransson. At the weekends I was a tourist and saw the remnants of the original convent and monastery at Vastena, with the grilles through which the nuns and monks talked and passed notes and books on their walks. I gave a seminar in the Samuel Johnson building in Oxford University, and stayed overnight on campus, dreaming of spires and had breakfast in Christchurch College (which was used I was told in the filming of Harry Potter). As I was in the UK, it seemed a pity not to go to Stratford to see some theatre, and a friend came over to join me for a very enjoyable weekend there. For the first time ever, two of my first cousins, Clare and Ita (Mary's sisters) were going to the Kerry Gaeltacht and invited me to join them for a weeks' holiday. It was a trip down memory lane. We even went to Maire Breathnach's house in An Graigh near Dunquin where I had spent such free and happy summers in my teens, walking, swimming and dancing. Then in June it was straight on to give a paper at a conference in Amsterdam and to meet up with Dr Kate White with whom I was to work later in Australia. While there we took in the Van Gough Museum and marvelled again at the disturbing beauty of his paintings.

In July 2011, the Women in Higher Education Management Network launched our first book, *Gender, Power and Management: A Cross Cultural Analysis* of Higher Education[55] at a Women's Worlds conference in Ottawa, a very British city but calm, peaceful and green. We saw the statues of the five women, with their cups of tea, commemorating their success in the 1929 case allowing women to sit on juries, holding the journal headed 'Women are persons'. I had never been to Canada and with a friend, stayed on for a holiday in the Laurentians: a stunningly beautiful wooded area of Canada. We stayed at a lovely house, where the choice for breakfast was between sweet and savoury pancakes. We cycled on the Petit Train du Nord cycle track and swam in the artificially created beach at the Lac Mount Tremblant, before moving on to Montreal, a busy truly bilingual city where even the poorest of the poor spoke two languages. We visited the museum of a Huron settlement near Quebec. These north American Indians traced their lineage through the female line and the men lived with their wives' extended family. It seemed to not only have been matrilineal and matrilocal but also matriarchal. The Huron lived in a world in which everything that existed, including man-made things, possessed souls. Remembering my stripey orange marble and the black Ford car ZB7239, I could relate to that. Small pox, the inroads of western civilisation, including Christianity and conflict with other tribes, eventually led to the disappearance of their way of life. But the fact that they existed showed that social arrangements other than patriarchy were possible.

In the autumn of 2011, I went to Australia; with an academic link to both the Centre for the Study of Higher Education at Melbourne University and to Professor Jill Blackmore at Deakin University. Australia was a mental stretch for me, not least because I realised that unconsciously, I saw it as a black hole into which people disappeared (two of my mother's people, nuns, had gone to Australia and 'had never been heard of again'). The fact that a WHEM colleague, Dr Kate White was living not far from Melbourne was very helpful in helping me to settle in. I worked during the days but again took the evenings and weekends off. I had a room in a lovely, central,

55   Bagilhole, B. and White, K. (eds) (2011). *Gender, Power and Management: A Cross Cultural Analysis*. London: Palgrave Macmillan.

Italian part of Melbourne, a city that felt like a town, had a spectacularly modern attractive Federation Square and was easy to navigate. Perfect.

My Irish accent made me feel totally at home in Melbourne: standing in bus queues people hearing that accent talked about their Irish ancestors. I went to Sydney for several weekends and loved the glamour of the Opera house, the water taxis and the sandy beaches. I had one contact there, Celeste, a friend of Deirdre O'Toole's, and I visited her, but I was mostly on my own. I had often watched the New Year being rung in with fireworks going off round Sydney Opera House. I was thrilled and excited to be there.

I had decided that I would try and see some of Australia before I came home. More than forty years earlier I had taken the greyhound bus across America. Now I set out to see some of Australia. Again, I was on my own and I was anxious. I flew up the coast to see the Great Barrier Reef off Cairns. Screwing my courage to sticking point (since I am afraid of swimming out of my depth) I went snorkelling off a boat. I also took a helicopter trip over the reef but the multicoloured stunning fish corals that I had seen in the aquarium in Sydney were no longer there due to pollution. I saw one white fish. However, the urgent vitality of the tropical rainforest around the Aboriginal Centre outside Cairns was extraordinary. I was simultaneously fascinated and appalled by the spectre of hundreds of bats hanging like rectangular black cloths from the trees outside my hotel in Cairns.

I wanted to see Uluru so I flew there from Cairns. It was very hot. It was possible to walk six kilometres into Kings Canyon in that blistering heat. A few people were doing it, all much younger and thinner than I. We had to get up before dawn to have any chance of avoiding the relentless heat. I was fearful that I might become dehydrated. I carried five litres of water in my rucksack. They were heavy, but were soon gone. The orange rock, the bright blue sky, the windblown trees, the occasional rock pools reflecting the blue sky and the grey green vegetation were spectacular.

After a windy helicopter ride over the canyon, there was barely time for a rapid shower before a seven-hour bus ride to the hotel. I began to feel very unwell in the overheated hotel room. I opened the sliding door to the patio area, but that turned off the cooling system. For the first time since I had arrived in Australia, I felt so unwell that I thought I was going to die. While the hotel was trying to sort out the air conditioning, I went and sat in the cool reception area; drank yet more water; read emails from home and chatted to one of the other women who had been on the trek through Kings Canyon. Eventually I got back into a now cool hotel room. I was still tired when I woke up 13 hours later. It had been a bit too much for me. But I had managed it.

I went on to Alice Springs. I had read Nevil Shute's book of that name[56] when I was a teenager. It was nothing like I had imagined it. It was suburban and yet different. Aborigines were much more in evidence there than in any other part of Australia where I had been. Seeing those working in the hotel reception and in shops and other services in their bare feet, made me realise how I took wearing shoes in these places for granted and how surprisingly unnerved I was by their absence there. The Ghan railway brought me to Adelaide, where I had a longer stop than planned due to an airline strike. There I met British 1950s men with handlebar moustaches in the museums, lamenting the fact that little Irish colonial labour had been available there. I was not impressed.

It was an extraordinary year. Although there were a few periods of intense anxiety, to my surprise I enjoyed meeting new people, seeing new places and having fun. I got some work done and contacts made, but the most important thing I learned was that I could survive without a structure or even a base. Retirement seemed a tiny bit less scary.

56   Shute, N. (1950). *A Town like Alice*. London: Heinemann.

Back to being a full-time professor again ...

Context

Ireland, like Portugal, Spain and Greece (the PIGS) was traumatised by the loss of sovereignty in 2010 consequent on the need for an economic bailout. The numbers employed in the public sector were cut, which exacerbated unemployment levels (they rose from 4.5 per cent in 2007 to 15 per cent in 2012). Salaries were cut; hours increased and the public services cut in an attempt to bring the public finances into line. By the end of 2013 economic sovereignty was restored but society was reeling from the cuts.

In Ireland, this was the beginning of a political realignment in a context where the two opposing Civil War parties (Fianna Fáil and Fianna Gael) had long dominated. Despite or maybe because of this loss of trust in the political and economic establishments, other social changes moved on apace, with Ireland being the first country in the world to approve same-sex marriage by a popular vote in 2015 (with 62 per cent of the electorate in favour). In 2014 gender equality in higher education began to publicly resurface as an issue.

I stood down as dean in December 2010, knowing that I would have to retire (because of compulsory age-related retirement) by September 2016. In the intervening period, I returned to the department I had left in September 2000. It was a challenge.

Going back to teaching ...

I returned to teaching in January 2012. I was glad to do so. There is an immediacy about teaching that I enjoy. Even if a lecture does not go well, or a class is not engaged, there will always be another lecture, and another class. Teaching involves an endless series of new chances, where, particularly at undergraduate level, the students never grow old.

The technology had of course moved on in the intervening period. I sweated profusely trying to get to grips with the online platform, terrified that my comments on an individual student's piece of work would inadvertently go to the entire class. Opening and closing technological gates for the submission of written work was another stressor. I got the hang of the basics with the help of Dr Martin Power, a generous (male) next-door colleague; while a perceptive female colleague-Dr Amanda Haynes – recognised that I would love Twitter (now X) and set me up on it. I recognised that the students were never going to be impressed by my techie ability: I had voice and presence and that would have to be enough. Meanwhile I worked hard to keep the content of my lectures up to date and relevant. Even people who disliked me personally saw me as a passionate and inspirational lecturer. I just enjoyed what to me, is an exciting form of love and service.

Many universities (including at that time the University of Limerick) actively encouraged the involvement of senior academics in first year undergraduate lecturing, not least to expose students to experienced teachers and researchers. Lecturing large groups of undergraduate students is typically seen as low status work, with post graduate teaching being seen as much more prestigious, and of course opening up opportunities as regards PhD supervision. I noticed but ignored the fact that on my return, I was only allocated undergraduate teaching by the then male head of department.

I like lecturing to large groups. It is rather like a theatrical performance. I love to hear silence descend on the lecture hall and to feel that kind of stillness that happens when the students are listening with anticipation. An authoritative approach and clear expectations are critical. The only downside of such large lectures is the high level of student absenteeism, a common problem in Irish universities. It is inadvertently facilitated by the expectation that lectures will be put up on the web, so that students who cannot attend physically can follow the lectures online. Theoretically this is a good idea. In practice, most students who miss lectures do not get around to listening to online lectures until near the exams, thus frustrating the whole idea of a gradual growth in knowledge and understanding. The limitations of online lecturing have of course emerged very clearly during the COVID-19 pandemic.

The University of Limerick also encouraged academic staff to collaborate on teaching courses, partly to expose students to a variety of styles and approaches, partly to enable students to benefit from academics' in-depth knowledge of a particular area, and partly to increase academics' knowledge of each other's areas and potentially stimulate cross-fertilisation of ideas and research. I enjoyed this experience too. One of my responsibilities was to input into the large first year introduction to sociology module by providing lectures on gender. Gender is one of those topics that most young people understand in relation to identity (as men/women/trans/intersex/ asexual etc.). My input aimed at getting the students to think about how our day-to-day interactions, the structure and culture of organisations and the policies of the state reflect and reinforce binary constructions of gender (one where non-hegemonic actions and activities are devalued), and to ask whose interests are served by these constructions. I loved hearing the watchful silence in the lecture hall as light bulb moments happened.

Third and fourth year undergraduate students were encouraged to select optional courses of particular interest and with classes of thirty or forty students, it was possible to do a kind of small group teaching, where the focus was on getting the students to think about their own intellectual positions and to challenge each other. I taught a shared course in the sociology of the family with Dr Carmel Hannan which we renamed *Love and Its Dark Side*. My input was to implicitly challenge assumptions about love and family, drawing on research in the area. In my lectures I looked at the importance of support from extended family and very close friends, challenging assumptions that such ties are unimportant. I explored how gendered expectations and ways of behaving continue to be reproduced in families and in schools, despite assertions in the educational area that gender is irrelevant. I provided evidence on the disproportionate allocation of caring and domestic work to women in western societies, including Ireland (with implications for women's free time, paid work and pensions); as well as looking the reality of domestic violence, the most overt manifestation of the exercise of power within families. The course also underlined the fact that families exist in societies and are supported in various ways by states, which typically reflect and reinforce taken for granted, 'natural' and 'inevitable' gendered inequalities. We had great fun seeing the students, many of whom came from very conventional Irish backgrounds, wrestling with the questions that the course raised.

I taught other modules at undergraduate level including one on higher education, which tended to be taken by international students. In that module, I looked at the nature and purpose of higher education; the impact on it of neo-liberalism and globalisation; the transition from an elite system to what has at least technically been defined as universal access; the gendering of its organisational structure, culture and micropolitical processes and the masculinisation of its leadership; the similarities and differences in higher educational institutions cross-nationally, shaped by states, private industry and other key stakeholders. This course enabled challenging questions to be asked about universities as meritocratic institutions at the level of academic staff recruitment and promotion; and the extent to which they remain middle-class bastions, premised on the assumption that students and staff do not have caring responsibilities. The limits and possibilities of individual change agents in bringing about organisational transformation were also explored– and the institutional resistance and foot dragging that often occurs, despite rhetorical statements about the need for change and the importance of gender equality.

One of the wonderful things about teaching sociology is that you have to keep learning all the time because societies change. New research is carried out reflecting new ideas and new evidence is produced. Preparation is essential. Boredom is impossible. The one element I did not like was correcting exam scripts, with its echoes of my mother's distress over the results of her BA degree. But I enjoyed the preparation and the delivery, whether in large lecture halls or small groups.

We are all born into families and other structures in societies that are not of our making and yet we all have some power to accept, reject or evade those constraints and opportunities. Teaching was, to me, a meaningful and enjoyable way of highlighting those options for the students.

Coming back to the department ...

When I returned to the department of sociology after my sabbatical, I decided to keep a low profile after my ten years as dean, except on one issue: the future, after my retirement, of the professorial post I held. In retrospect I think that decision was a mistake since it effectively disempowered me. However, to do otherwise seemed to be attempting to cling to a power and authority that I no longer had.

I was lucky to be involved, with Dr Ita Richardson and Dr Clare O'Hagan, in a cross-national research project which won five years of EU funding for research on Female Empowerment in Science and Technology in Academia (FESTA, 2012– 17). From mid-way through the funding period, we started to publish articles drawing on the Irish data, exploring how excellence was defined and measured, ideas about masculinities/feminities and career paths in STEM, and later exploring micropolitical and leadership practices.[57] It was wonderful to have a new focus and context for my energy. With colleagues in Sweden, Portugal and Australia I also published comparative articles and chapters based on the cross-national

---

57 O'Connor, P., O'Hagan, C. and Brannen, J. (2015). 'Exploration of Masculinities in Academic Organisations; A Tentative Typology', *Current Sociology*, 63 (4), 528–46; O'Connor, P. and O'Hagan, C. (2016). 'Excellence in University Academic Staff Evaluation: A Problematic Reality?', *Studies in Higher Education*, 41 (11), 1943–57; O'Connor, P., O'Hagan, C. and Gray, B. (2018). 'Femininities in STEM: Outsiders Within', *Work, Employment and Society*, 32 (2), 312–329; O'Hagan, C., et al. (2019). 'Perpetuating Academic Capitalism and Maintaining Gender Orders through Career Practices in STEM', *Critical Studies in Education*, 60 (2), 205–25; O'Connor, P., et al. (2020). 'Micro-political Practices in Higher Education: A Challenge to Excellence as a Rationalising Myth?', *Critical Studies in Education*, 61 (2), 195–211; O'Connor, P., et al. (2019). 'Leadership Practices by Senior Position Holders in HERIs: Stealth Power in Action?', *Leadership*, 15 (6), 722–43.

study of management in higher education undertaken by the Women in Higher Education Management (WHEM) Network.[58] Thamar Heijstra from Iceland[59] and Estrella Montez Lopez[60] from Spain came to work with me as PhD students and in both cases, we subsequently collaborated on publications. I loved this.

Following from an opportunity created by Professor Pat Clancy, University College Dublin, I was invited to be a member of the International Research Evaluation Panel funded by Linnaeus in Stockholm, and chaired by the eminent Professor Guy Neave. The following year I was invited to chair that panel. This led to an invitation to collaborate with Antoinette Fauve-Chamoux and Staffan Wahlén in evaluating a large Nordic research project and making recommendations to the funding agency, the Swedish Foundation for Humanities and Social Sciences. This in turn led to an article on the research project, co-authored with Antoinette Fauve-Chamoux[61] which was nominated by *Policy and Politics* as article of the month. This experience illustrates the importance of small opportunities being provided to women by senior men– because such opportunities frequently mushroom: with molehills becoming mountains in Valian's words.[62] Various Irish universities invited me to give presentations on my work including

58   For example: O'Connor, P., Carvalho, T. and White, K. (2014). 'The Experiences of Senior Positional Leaders in Australian, Irish and Portuguese Universities: Universal or Contingent?', *Higher Education Research and Development*, 33 (1), 5–18; O'Connor, P. and Goransson, A. (2015). 'Constructing or Rejecting the Notion of 'Other' in Senior University Management: The Cases of Ireland and Sweden', *EMAL*, 43 (2), 323–40; O'Connor, P. and Carvalho, T. (2015). 'Different or Similar: Constructions of Leadership by Senior Managers in Irish and Portuguese Universities', *Studies in Higher Education*, 40 (9), 1679–93.

59   Heijstra, T., O'Connor, P. and Rafnsdottir, L. G. (2013). 'Explaining Gender Inequality in Iceland: What Makes the Difference?', *European Journal of Higher Education*, 3 (4), 324–41.

60   Montes Lopez, E. and O'Connor, P. (2019). 'Micropolitics and Meritocracy: Improbable Bedfellows?', *EMAL*, 47 (5), 678–93.

61   O'Connor, P. and Fauve-Chamoux, A. (2016). 'European Policies and Research Funding: A Case Study of Gender Inequality and Lack of Diversity in a Nordic Research Programme', *Policy and Politics*, 44 (4), 627–43.

62   Valian, V. (1998). *Why So Slow? The Advancement of Women*. Massachusetts: MIT Press.

University College Cork, University of Galway, Maynooth University and University College Dublin. I presented papers internationally at the University of Reykjavik, at Lancaster, Cranfield and Durham Universities and at a Summit of Senior Leaders at a Women in the World (WOW) Conference in Cambridge. This was all good.

My resolution to keep a low profile internally in the University of Limerick was tested by the results emerging from the internal promotion competitions where overall, across the university, men at the early career stage were more than twice as likely as women to be successful (43 per cent of the men versus 19 per cent of the women who applied at this level were recommended for promotion). The situation was particularly bad for women in my faculty (Arts, Humanities and Social Science) with no woman promoted, as compared with two-fifths of the men. The following year, although the overall picture improved for women in the university, in my own faculty, four out of five of the men who applied at this early career stage, but only one in ten of the women, were promoted. In the more senior promotions, which were chaired by the president, the trends were different, with roughly similar proportions of men and women being promoted.

I felt that I could not remain silent about these trends in early career promotions. I asked for a meeting with the then vice-president academic and registrar, who chaired the early career promotion boards. It took several months for a meeting to be arranged. In the meantime, a number of us started to meet to create a grassroots response. But at this stage my internal influence was waning. I was increasingly preoccupied with the FESTA project and anticipating my retirement.

My sister sewed a sampler for me: an orange cat clinging to a grill in a window, a yellow cat calmly surveying the scene and the black one relaxing on the window sill with a ball of wool. I identified with the orange cat. The caption was *Hang in There*. She had understood.

Revenge?

For women of my generation, modesty about achievements was expected: anything else was setting yourself up for a fall. I had had a very
productive period in terms of research output after the ending of my
deanship. Encouraged by Gobnait O'Riordan, Director of the Library,
a quiet but highly effective woman, in 2014, with two years to go to my
dreaded retirement, I decided on a high-profile launch of my fourth major
sole-authored book: *Management and Gender in Higher Education*.[63]
In retrospect, I suspect that I saw this as my swan song: marking my
own achievements and simultaneously raising the issue of the under-
representation of women in senior positions, the topic of the book and
a focus of my energy since before my own promotion to a professorship
in 1997.

Screwing my courage to sticking point, I invited the then president of
the university to speak. He accepted the invitation. Since the topic of my
book was the position of women in higher education, I also invited the
then president of the Royal Irish Academy, Professor Mary Daly, the first
woman ever to be appointed to that position, to speak. She too accepted the
invitation. Part of my agenda in 2014 was getting the Higher Educational
Authority to tackle the issue of gender inequality in Irish higher education.
Hence, I invited its chief executive officer (CEO) to speak about how the
organisation he headed was proposing to do this. I had known this man,
albeit not well, for over eight years. As far as I knew, our relationship was
cordial. He agreed to my brief (in writing). I was delighted. I dared to hope
that my achievements would be recognised and celebrated.

Dark blue and white invitations were printed, with a picture of the
cover of the book on them and sent to 150 people including my extended
family, friends, work colleagues from various times in my life; the three
presidents of Irish universities whom I knew and the most senior civil servant in the Department of Education. I booked a lovely room in the Royal

63   Published by Manchester: MUP in 2014.

Irish Academy in Dublin for 18.00–20.30 on 14 April 2014 and organised nibbles, wine, tea and coffee. I booked a restaurant for a meal with family and close friends afterwards.

I wore green, the colour of the heart in the chakra system. The book lined room at the Royal Irish Academy with its gilded portraits and long Georgian windows marked the status of the occasion. My family turned out in force: my sister was there in her smart black and white outfit with contrasting pink scarf with my brother-in-law discreetly taking photos. All five of my nieces, Emma, Suzanne, Mags, Claire and Lizzie and their children were there. Ann and Seán Maguire and Tom and Catherine Sheedy, couples I had hiked with in the 1960s and who had remained friends, came and laughingly recalled my unwillingness to compromise on my principles forty years before. Deirdre O'Toole from the book circle in Waterford came in a stunning mustard and black outfit. Dr Evelyn Mahon, my predecessor as course director in women's studies in the University of Limerick came, as did work colleagues from there and elsewhere. It felt like all the parts of my life were coming together. I could hardly believe it.

I stood behind the mahogany podium and talked about a university culture that was male-dominated and masculinist, a system that militated against women. Women made up half of the academics at lecturer level nationally, but held less than a quarter of the top academic professorial positions, with no woman since 1592 (at that time) having ever been president of an Irish public university. I felt relaxed and confident. The president of the University of Limerick spoke next. He complimented me on the publication of the book and on bringing about change in the position of women in his university over the previous fifteen years:

> 'Pat always kept the issue of gender at the top of her agenda', he said.

The president of the Royal Irish Academy, a female historian, was less effusive but still complimentary. Then the CEO of the Higher Educational Authority got up to speak. He briefly praised the book but then launched into an attack on me:

'Pat says here [tapping the book] that "girls are brighter, more hard working and hence academically more meritorious than boys, and so more entitled to positions in society that reflect that".'

With these kinds of biological essentialist views, who was I to be critical of discrimination in the universities he asked rhetorically? There was no element of jousting in his speech. The clear objective was to discredit me. I was devastated. There is evidence that girls work harder at school, spend more time on homework, but the idea that they are naturally brighter? I couldn't have written that? or could I? I felt numb.

Quite unconsciously, I adopted the stereotypically feminine way of smoothing over an awkward situation. I was determinedly cheerful and gracious. I thanked him and the other speakers. A woman whom I did not know introduced herself and said that she had written the CEO's speech and apologised for it. I have never seen any point in blaming subordinates, so I brushed off the apology. Dr Evelyn Mahon asked me if I was angry. I brushed that off too. Meanwhile, the children launched into the nibbles and scoffed glasses of orange. The atmosphere in the restaurant after the launch was strange and eerily unjolly. Eventually the evening came to an end. I was staying overnight at my sister's house. I woke early. I went down to the kitchen. The fog had cleared.

'I was shafted' I said to my sister. 'Yes', she said.

There was no more to be said. I went back to my little house in Dunmore East. I was angry and humiliated. I cried on and off for three days. My moment of triumph had turned to ashes. A week later, it occurred to me to check the sentence. The CEO had omitted the first part of it which said:

'In Ireland, access to higher education varies between different social class groups, and this has been explained in terms of meritocratic individualism. Gender differentiated patterns (in which girls outperform boys academically) in state examinations, in access to, and graduation from universities, are less often explained in this way. Thus, if an explanation similar to that in the case of class is used (i.e., one involving individual merit), then girls are brighter, more hard working and hence academically more meritorious than boys, and so more entitled to positions in society that reflect that.'[64]

64   ibid, p. 148.

I had hit a nerve. I had juxtaposed the assumption that middle-class children were 'naturally' brighter than their working-class counterparts with boys' academic underachievement relative to girls. I endorsed neither of these assumptions. I had repeatedly made the point that I did not accept the idea that 'natural' or biological explanations could explain gender inequality. I had gone on to say there (and in several other places in the book) that 'variation between Irish universities in the proportion of women in senior management (and indeed also in the professoriate) suggests that individual essentialist explanations ... are not sufficient'.

I could not let it go. A month later, on 16 May, I emailed the CEO and he accepted that he had quoted me inaccurately. I clarified this for those professional colleagues who had been at the launch. I could not bear to contact friends and family and had to trust that their opinion of me was not affected by my public humiliation. Fighting for my professional reputation in the only way I knew, through my tears I started to load up 25 years of publications on *Researchgate*, an internet network used by academics through which they can make their research available to researchers in over 190 countries.

> 'Let others judge me on the basis of what I have written', I thought.

It took six months before I felt able to invite the CEO to speak at a conference that I was organising on gender inequality. A year after that he invited me to be a member of the expert group to explore the position of women in higher education nationally. I accepted without hesitation. Over the year the report was being formulated, we met frequently at dinners and day-long meetings. It seemed petty to bring up the book launch. I had to rise above it.

In 2016, before I retired from the University of Limerick, there was an opportunity for policy stakeholders to assess the impact of research on policy. Taking my courage in my hands, I asked the same CEO of the Higher Educational Authority if he would assess the impact of my work on gender equality in higher education. In a written testimonial and on video on the University of Limerick website,[65] he publicly acknowledged my 'singular' contribution to gender equality in that context and my:

65   *Setting Agendas on Gender Equality in the Higher Education Sector in Ireland: Getting in but not getting on.* https://www.ul.ie/research/setting-agendas-gender-equality-higher-education-sector-ireland, accessed 16 May 2023.

'Powerful combination of scholarship, expertise, experience and commitment.'

I felt vindicated. But I still could not look at the photos of the book launch without reliving the devastation of my public humiliation before family, friends and colleagues. Seven years later I can at last look at them.

Did his action exemplify the kind of microaggressions that keep women down: the very ones that my book was challenging? Perhaps he thought that I needed to be cut down to size? The event fuelled seven more years of my research and publications on gender inequality in higher education.

Maybe the ultimate revenge was mine?

Advancing gender equality nationally

The year 2014 can be seen as the start of a new era in gender equality in higher education in Ireland. Projects on gender equality were funded at that time by the EU in three Irish universities, each pushing for change: FESTA at the University of Limerick; GENOVATE at University College Cork, and INTEGER at Trinity College Dublin. In 2014, Micheline Sheehy Skeffington won her gender discrimination case against NUI Galway (now University of Galway)[66] and was awarded E70,000 which she gave to the five other women who had been shortlisted but not promoted there in the 2008–09 competition. The president of NUI Galway, Professor Jimmy Browne, stressed that gender inequality

---

66   Equality Tribunal Report. 2014 https://www.workplacerelations.ie/en/Cases/
       2014/November/DEC-E2014-078.html, accessed 5 October 2022. Foley, R. and
       Sheehy Skeffington, M. (2023) *Micheline's Three Conditions* Galway: M3C Press;
       and Bosek, J. and O'Connor, P. (2023). 'Gender and Academic Careers in Ireland'.
       In J. Briscoe, M. Dickman, D. Hall, W. Mayhofer and E. Parry (eds), *Understanding
       Careers around the globe*, pp. 172–81. Cheltenham: Elgar Publishing.

was not peculiar to his university. The CEO of the Higher Educational Authority was retiring in the autumn of 2016 and in 2015 he set up an Expert Group to undertake a *National Review of Gender Equality in Irish Higher Education Institutions.*

I was invited to join this five-person Expert Group, chaired by Máire Geoghegan-Quinn (the first woman, since Countess Markiewicz in 1919, to hold a cabinet post in Ireland (in 1979); and a former European Commissioner for Research, Innovation and Science 2010–2014). She understood the issue of gender inequality. The other members were Professor Paul Walton of York University; Dr Helen Peterson, Uppsala University and Ryan Shanks, from Accenture. The secretariat was led by Dr Gemma Irvine then of the Higher Educational Authority (now vice-president, Equality and Diversity at Maynooth University). Professor Jane Grimson's report on NUI Galway in 2016[67] which was set in train by the Micheline Sheehy Skeffington case there, raised the bar for the HEA Expert Report by recommending that the proportion of women promoted at each level should reflect the proportion of women at the level below that (i.e. the flexible cascade model, a soft quota).

Being part of this Expert Group in 2015–16 was a great experience. We met the presidents/directors of all of the higher educational institutions, senior civil servants, leaders of the trade unions and student unions and other stakeholders to assess their commitment to ending gender inequality in higher education and their understanding of it. The Expert Group Report[68] also gathered quantitative evidence of gender inequality in Irish higher educational institutions. The majority of those who completed a national online survey (c.4,800) saw gender inequality as existing in them. However, men were much less likely than women to see it as existing or

---

67   Grimson, J. (2016). *Promoting Excellence through Gender Equality: Final Report of the Gender Equality Task Force NUI Galway,* http://www.nuigalway.ie/media/ equality/files/Final-Report-Gender-Equality-Task-Force-260516.pdf, accessed 15 September 2022.

68   HEA (2016). *HEA Expert Report: National Review of Gender Equality in Irish Higher Educational Institutions.* https://hea.ie/assets/uploads/2016/06/ hea_review_of_gender_equality_in_irish_higher_education.pdf, accessed 20 November 2022.

as extremely important: with obvious consequences as regards tackling it, since the majority of those in senior positions were men. Both men and women mentioned a 'macho misogynistic culture', a 'boys club', reflecting 'attitudes of the alpha male' and noted that 'residual sexist attitudes were rife throughout the system'. This culture was seen as 'often masked by the success of a small number of very accomplished women'.

The sixty-six recommendations made in the *HEA Expert Report* (2016) were detailed, time specific and targeted at all the main stakeholders (and not just the higher educational institutions). They included the linking of state funding to progress by the higher educational institutions in addressing the gender profile of those in senior academic and management positions. Given the institutional importance of full professors (the most senior academic position) in driving organisational change, it recommended that a minimum of 40 per cent of full professors on the appropriate pay scale should be women by 2024 (a quota). It also recommended the introduction of the flexible cascade model (a soft quota); the creation of a vice-presidential post for equality at executive committee level in each institution to drive developments in the area, with demonstrable experience of advancing gender equality being a requirement for all line management appointments up to and including the president. The purpose of these recommendations was to be disruptive of the status quo.

The Higher Educational Authority committed to publishing annual data on the gender profile of academia, thus enabling progress to be systematically tracked. Under the influence of the EU-funded INTEGER project led by Trinity College Dublin, Athena SWAN, a gender equality mark for higher education institutions had been introduced to Ireland in 2015. Building on, but going beyond the UK experience, the HEA Expert Report in 2016 recommended that these awards be linked to entitlement to apply for research funding. This recommendation was immediately implemented by the three main research funding bodies (Science Foundation Ireland, the Irish Research Council and the Health Research Board). The Task Force Report in 2018 reiterated the key recommendations in the HEA 2016 Expert Report. To expedite change in the gender profile of senior positions, a Senior Leadership initiative, involving forty-five such positions in areas where women were under-represented, was launched in 2019 by the then Minister for Higher Education, Mary Mitchell O'Connor. More recently there have been initiatives led by the Minister, Simon Harris to deal with sexual harassment and gender-based violence in higher education.[69]

Although there were a couple of recommendations where I wished for a more radical approach (such as those tackling the overwhelmingly male gender profile of the tax-payer subsidised Royal Irish Academy) overall, I was very pleased with the final shape of the report. To have been part of an initiative that attempted to move forward gender equality in higher education gave me considerable pleasure and satisfaction. To have been part of this initiative at the very end of a long academic career that had come to be dominated by the issue was doubly satisfying. It was hard work, but fun.

The date of my retirement arrives

Although retirement at 65 years was compulsory in higher education, as in the wider public sector, people's ages (and hence their retirement date) did not tend to be widely known by colleagues. Against my own desires and personal interest, I announced my retirement two years ahead in order to give ample time for the professorial post that I would be vacating to be filled. I had a written promise from the then dean that, following other developments in the department, the next post, which as it happened was my professorial post, would be advertised with a focus on gender. Such a focus would mean that research, teaching and activism on gender inequality would continue, driven by the person occupying that position. The then dean, the head of department (both men) and several members of the department were not enthusiastic about this focus. However, I argued that a promise, especially a written one, had to be honoured. There was a lot of foot dragging. Eventually the post was

69   O'Connor, P. and Irvine, G. (2020). 'Multi-level State Interventions and Gender Equality in Higher Education Institutions: The Irish Case', *Administrative Sciences*, 10, 98, https://doi.org/10.3390/admsci10040098.

advertised in November 2015, with a closing date in January 2016, but the interviews did not occur until May 2016. Not surprisingly, the applicants had found other things to do with their lives in the intervening period. I had made enemies arguing about the focus of the professorial post, and yet I could not deliver on it. I was angry, frustrated and disappointed. Despite my best efforts my replacement had not been appointed before my retirement in September 2016. Some years after, the focus on gender in the advertisement was diluted and the post was advertised and filled as a generic chair in sociology. The possibility of the appointee having both the expertise and the responsibility to continue teaching and research in the area of gender inequality was lost. The leadership that the department of sociology had given in the area for twenty years was at an end.

I had to retire by the September after my 65th Birthday. There was no way out. Struggling to come to terms with this, I attended the university's preparatory retirement day in May 2016. There we were asked to respond to a series of written questions and to discuss our answers. The first question was:

> 'What does retirement mean to you?' Grimly I wrote: 'End of the road, close to death; end of productive life'. Trying to be positive, I added 'A Challenge (BIG!)'.

My stomach, never my strongest organ, was not happy with the greasy sausages that I nervously gobbled at lunch. My 'take-away' at the end of the day was a pain in my stomach, partly created by the stress of contemplating retirement, and partly by too much fatty food. I went for a walk after which I vomited violently. Clearly the day had not agreed with me.

Friends and acquaintances found it hard to understand my fear and my fury. Several of them had taken early retirement. They offered me congrats on my retirement. When I scowled, they told me that I would be able to do what I wanted. That I would be free. That I could travel. I tried to explain that, although I was at times stressed and frustrated by work, I enjoyed it. I loved teaching, enjoyed research and (to my surprise) had been a competent manager. More than anything else perhaps, after forty-six years, it was who I was. My work was my world. I did not want to have to deal with the deconstruction of an identity that had taken me so long to craft. And now, for no objective reason, as I saw it, I was being forced to retire. On 31 August I was a respected employee. On 1 September I had to retire: theoretically apparently unfit for work. Age, not gender, was the basis for discrimination this time.

The Oireachtas Joint Committee on Justice, Defence and Inequality was beginning to consider the question of mandatory retirement on the grounds of age. It invited public submissions on the Employment Equality (Abolition of Mandatory Retirement Age) Bill in October 2015. I made an individual written submission to them, using myself as an example of someone who wanted to continue working, who was fit and able and was not being allowed to do so. I did an interview with the *Limerick Leader* highlighting my situation (headed graphically but a bit too starkly for my liking: 'I'm not married, don't have kids, don't play golf'). By 2020, compulsory retirement in the universities and the public sector was extended from 65 to 70 years. Discrimination on the grounds of age was still legally intact, although the age limit was now extended. But it was too late for me.

Retirement created practical problems. I would have to give up my lovely office. The contents of my six large filing cabinets would have to go somewhere, as would the books on the shelves. Some of them dated back to my undergraduate days in the 1960s. There was no way that all this would fit in my small minimalist house in Dunmore East. I had started to do a bit of clearing after I stood down as dean: every semester putting twenty or thirty books outside my door for students and staff to browse and take. But this had made little impression on the sheer quantity. I began to cull more ruthlessly now and initiated a daily black bag regime for the filing cabinets. I hired a carpenter to make more book shelves in Dunmore East. I had got used to spending my weekends in Dunmore East and my weeks in my one-bedroom apartment in Killaloe (which contained the duplicate essentials and work clothes that had enabled me to survive as a weekly commuter for over twenty-four years). That would need to be cleared out. My little house in Dunmore East began to resemble a second-hand clothes shop and book store.

There were other inconveniences. For years I had eaten lunch and tea at work. The main canteen had a good selection of nutritious inexpensive meals and simple teas. For a while there was an excellent vegetarian restaurant on campus. I hated cooking/thinking about food. That would have to be tackled. There were other challenges. I was going to be 24/7 in the same place. Somehow that unnerved me. Dropping into the office, or the canteen, would not be a viable option. I had never thought of creating an office in my little house in Dunmore East. Now that seemed an obvious omission. Since work had been my life, books and papers leaked into every room.

This confusion, aggravation and sheer disruption was to my mind all so unnecessary. My work competence was not an issue for anyone. I was quite happy working. I did not want to retire. Going on seemed to me to be an entirely satisfactory way of living. My pension was good but I wanted to earn it by continuing to write and teach. Some of my colleagues were invited to stay on to teach occasional courses. These opportunities were not offered to me. I had never curried favour with the powerful and they were not minded to facilitate me now. A female colleague in another university successfully applied for research funding that would continue after her compulsory age-related retirement and played hard ball by threatening to move the grant elsewhere. I lacked the stomach for that kind of fight at this late stage. The months before my retirement were difficult. I found it was impossible to avoid questions like:

'What has it all been about? Has it been worth it? What have I to show for it?'

I could see my life very clearly, too clearly. I felt vulnerable, alone, lost.

All that remained was to organise my leaving 'do'. After my book launch debacle two years before, that was a challenge. I knew that I wanted to have the 'do' before the summer break. I knew that I wanted to speak. I wanted the president of the university and the current dean to speak. I hoped that my family would be there. I also hoped that some people would turn up. I had the reputation of being a fighter, a straight talker, someone who took no prisoners, not necessarily a popular image in academia, and certainly not for a woman. I knew that some people would be very glad to see the back of me and would not come to my leaving 'do'. I just did not know how many.

There is an unspoken etiquette around public celebratory events which had been unexpectedly breached at my book launch. Could something happen at my retirement 'do'? Maybe it might manifest itself not in aggression but in no one turning up? With the memory of my book launch still fresh, I worried that I would be torpedoed again. I bought two new outfits: a magnificent taupe opera coat with a lime green top and a more sober winter white jacket and top. In the end, I did not have the nerve to wear either of them. I settled for a red jacket and purple top from my existing wardrobe. Red in the chakra system signifies being safe and grounded, with purple reflecting spirituality and higher states of consciousness. These were colours I liked. For the first time in my life, I had my make-up done professionally for the occasion. If I was going to be humiliated, I was going to look good being done in.

It went well. My sister and brother-in-law and three of my nieces (Lizzie with her infant son Art, Mags and Suzanne) came down from Dublin; as did Dr Evelyn Mahon whom I had replaced when I started in UL in 1992. Deirdre O'Toole again came from the Waterford book circle; Professor Linda McKie came from Edinburgh and Dr Patricia Kelleher whose friendship went back to UCD in the 1960s came up from Allihies. I could not face inviting those hiking companions from the 1960s who had seen me publicly humiliated at my book launch just two years previously. I kept my composure, with my voice only wobbling once when I spoke of my sister's support for me over the years. The president of the university struck exactly the right note. The dean, Professor Tom Lodge, had done his homework and was generous. There was an excellent turn out. I went out for a meal with my family and friends in Killaloe. My dominant feeling was one of relief that I had not been publicly humiliated again. After twenty-four years in the University of Limerick and a career that had spanned forty-six years it was a low bar to set.

Retirement, it appeared, was already grinding me down ...

Is there life after retirement?

The early months of my retirement were dominated by transitional tasks. A lifetime of problems with my teeth culminated in the need to have an implant (the dentist asked if I wanted the source to be animal, manufactured or deceased, which was not a good start). Six months of antibiotics later it was still infected and had to be removed. The Preparatory

Retirement Course had suggested that I make a will. I had never managed to do this. Death to my mind was a very bad idea. Like most bad ideas it was best not to focus on it. I took myself to the solicitor to get a form and some advice about what I needed to do if I was going to die. It still did not strike me as an inevitability. I found it almost impossible to complete the form so high was my level of anxiety. I managed to do so only by thinking that it was provisional: just for the next five years, after which time I would revisit it. I had a panic attack when returning it to the bemused solicitor. All this I fumed was caused by my entirely unnecessary retirement.

I had read some books to prepare for retirement. One of them said that you should do things that you enjoyed; things you were good at and things that had meaning. I then (unconsciously) mislaid the book. But that seemed good advice. I enjoyed a glass of wine. I was in a book circle that met once a month. I loved travelling, often combining it with conferences or other academic work. But I needed structured weekly enjoyable activities. My sailing career had ended in the 1980s, and I could not envisage re-invigorating it. I had always liked dancing and singing. Eighteen months earlier when passing Fisherman's Hall in Dunmore East, I had heard the sound of set dancing music drifting out. On impulse I went in. The teacher, Brona asked me if I could do set dancing. 'Absolutely' I said. I had done the Kerry set when I was a teenager in the Gaeltacht. I had also gone to Irish dancing sessions on Monday nights in Waterford in the 1980s with a group of women before an injury to my ankle and my departure to Limerick had literally put a stop to my gallop. I could not remember if we had done the Kerry Set there, but anyway, I was sure that it would come back to me. I did not realise that numerous sets now exist, many of them recently composed. Brona tried me out and concluded that I had basic steps and rhythm. I was in: that was Thursday evening sorted.

I had put my name down a year before for a senior choir that did not require an audition. Technically I am an alto. I have never had the courage to sing on my own and I find it hard to stick to my own line, particularly if I don't have the tune. I quickly learned that the sopranos usually have the tune. After a few weeks I moved to the sopranos. I couldn't always hit the high notes, but since they usually had the tune I was unlikely to drift.

Choir was on a Thursday morning, which was a bit unbalanced time tabling wise. But it could be worked around.

Doing things that I was good at after retirement was more challenging. I had never managed to acquire basic skills like cooking and cleaning. I had no interest in handicrafts and was useless at DIY. In my 50s having read yet another self-help book which stressed the importance of doing things you were good at, I had asked my sister what she thought I was good at. There was a long pause. I waited expectantly. Finally, she summed up my unique selling point in one word: 'Talking'. If you live on your own in a small village with a population that peaked at less than 2,000 people, the scope for such a skill is limited. Much later, well after my retirement, through Twitter, I was invited on to *Highland Radio in Donegal* every two months or so to join two others discussing specific news items for an hour. I loved that. Talking clearly was my unique selling point.

I was going to be emeritus from the University of Limerick, effectively a retiree. I knew instinctively that I needed another academic identity. I noticed that male colleagues solved this problem by getting affiliations with other institutions through friendship networks. I contacted a former (male) colleague, Professor Chris Whelan and through him got a three-year visiting professorship at the Geary Institute in University College Dublin. The position was of course unpaid, and it was not clear if it would translate into work at a day-to-day level. But it was important psychologically since I did not want to be defined by my retirement. I was very belatedly learning how things worked. I didn't agree with it, but on this occasion, with my battered identity at stake, I went ahead.

Doing things that had meaning brought me back to work. I had always liked the views of the 1960s mystic, Gibran, on the meaning of work:

> 'You work that you may keep pace with the earth and the soul of the earth. For to be idle is to become a stranger unto the seasons ... When you work you are a flute through whose heart the whispering of the hours turns to music. Which of you would be a reed, dumb and silent when all else sings together in unison?'[70]

---

70   Kilbran, G. (1972). *The Prophet*, p. 20. Norfolk: Fakenham Press.

Work in some form or other would be key to meaning. In the emotional turmoil coming up to retirement I had accumulated a number of articles that needed to be revised and resubmitted, so that offered possibilities. The Women in Higher Education Management Network had got a contract for a book on *Gendered Success in Higher Education* which needed to be done by 2017 (and there would be another book on *Gender Power and Higher Education in a Globalised World* in 2021[71]). As a retired academic, I could not apply for research funding from the Irish Research Council. I lobbied about this, and eventually, four years later, they changed the rules. As a gender equality expert, I got invited on to some Advisory Boards for EU-funded projects and was asked to do some external examining of PhDs. I got invited to advise the then Minister for Higher Education on gender equality. I also got asked to do some seminars in Ireland as well as international talks and expert contributions. Most of these were unpaid. I accepted all invitations, regardless.

Trying to stay healthy and calm was clearly meaningful. That potentially necessitated a yoga or T'ai chi class a week. That was another evening sorted. I eventually found a local Walking Group which was a bit too energetic for me – so much so that I could barely shuffle the following day. But I loved the chats and the well-earned glass of Guinness or wine after the walk. Later, I found an hour-long Women-on-the-Move gym session – that was another evening sorted. Slowly I was putting in place building blocks for this new stage – a sort of retirement.

But retirement exposed an emotional hole at the centre of my life. For the first time in my life, I needed friends. Those still in paid employment in academia were largely unavailable except as co-authors. Not all of my existing local friendships withstood my retirement and the related change in my circumstances. That was sad and disappointing. I had not anticipated that problem. I kept in touch with my scattered network of friends from various stages in my life. Those such as Professor Julia Brannen in the UK who shared my pre-occupation with work and my lack of interest in

71   White, K. and O'Connor, P. (eds) (2017). *Gendered Success in Higher Education: Global Perspectives.* London: Palgrave Macmillan; O'Connor, P. and White, K. (eds) (2021). *Gender, Power and Higher Education in a Globalised World.* Cham: Palgrave MacMillan.

retirement became increasingly important. The set dancing, choir, yoga, walking group and book circle etc. provided distraction. I had early rebelled against the traditional dominance of family. Ironically family now became more important. For years my sister and I had spoken on the phone for over an hour every week. Now my five nieces and sixteen grandnieces and grandnephews began to be more important to me than they had previously. I discovered to my surprise that I particularly liked the small people, to whom, confusingly, I have remained 'aunty'.

As many people discovered during the COVID-19 pandemic, and as I had always intuitively recognised, working from home is socially isolating and psychologically difficult if you are an extrovert. I particularly missed the institutional framework of meaning. Every year since my retirement, I have submitted an annual one-page report on my publications and other academic activities to successive heads of department and deans: overwhelmingly these have not even been acknowledged. As a retired, although still very academically active woman, I was invisible. Spending time working for nothing and ostensibly for no one made no sense to most of the people I met on a weekly basis. At times it made no sense to me. But a kind of stubbornness sustained me.

COVID-19 with its lockdowns completely disrupted my fragile framework. Singing, dancing, the gym and travel were immediate casualties; out-of-doors yoga survived intermittently, as did the book circle and the walking group. During the height of the pandemic, I took up year-round sea swimming since I needed a daily challenge. I did various online courses. I took to twitter. I continued to write and publish, and to talk online whenever and wherever possible. But my anxiety levels – always volatile – increased. My worries centred around health and death – not helped by the daily news reports on numbers of deaths each day, hospital overcrowding and respiratory difficulties among those classified as vulnerable on the basis of age.

I had been abroad for work or holidays several times a year prior to COVID-19 – but even as it waned I was still afraid to travel. My courage, which had always sustained me, failed. I turned down opportunities to go to Bordeaux and Thessalonica at the end of 2021. Then I was invited by Professor Teresa Carvalho, a friend and colleague to give a keynote at a conference in Aveiro in April 2022 (with an EU Advisory Board meeting beforehand). I went, and got COVID there. I was not very sick, but it unnerved me and I did not go abroad for the rest of the year. I have now accepted invitations for 2023, and went to Barcelona in January and to Bordeaux in June. Those went well. We shall see.

The fragility of my life and life style has become clearer post pandemic. I have now lived longer than either of my parents. Death at my age is no longer a theoretical possibility. But I still think it is a bad idea. I have continued to write and publish and to be a member of a number of research advisory boards, as well as doing the kind of service activities (including reviewing and PhD evaluation) that are a normal part of academic life. I have continued post-COVID to be a daily sea swimmer, often with a neighbour and friend, Catherine Griffin: enjoying the camaraderie and the challenge of that experience (and the hot bath immediately afterwards). I have gone back to choir and still do a weekly yoga class. I very much enjoy my intermittent panel participation on *Highland Radio* commenting on topical news items. The book circle has gone back to its sociable face-to-face format. I have joined the Waterford film society and the Minaun Community Theatre group where we write and perform short plays (re-activating interests that had lapsed since the 1980s). These activities have opened up new networks. Somewhat to my surprise I have started to make new friends.

I wonder if I will have the time and the energy to reinvent myself again?

CHAPTER 7

Reflections

Context

Ireland has changed in many ways during my lifetime. The influence of the institutional Roman Catholic Church has declined substantially but 69 per cent still identify themselves as roman catholic.[72] In 2018, a thirty-year struggle for reproductive rights for women ended with the passing of the (sixth) referendum in the area, making abortion at least theoretically available, and deleting the 1983 Eighth Amendment to the constitution which granted equal right to life to the mother and to the foetus. However, during the COVID-19 pandemic, male-dominated and masculinist decision-making structures re-emerged in Ireland, with a total failure to deal with the child care needs even of frontline workers at a time when all schools and creches were in lockdown, and those over 70 were 'cocooning' (i.e. required not to leave their homes) and so unable to provide much-needed help with child care. No one in government appeared to recognise that most of those working in the overstretched hospitals were women and particularly for those who had young children, the choices were impossible. In higher education, there was little interest in ameliorating the gendered impact of this situation either in general or specifically on women's research activities, with consequences for their future promotional prospects.

---

72 CSO (2023). Census Results, https://www.cso.ie/en/statistics/population/cen susofpopulation2022/censusofpopulation2022-summaryresults/, accessed 3 June 2023.

Seven years on since my retirement, I continue to publish – in many cases co-authoring with colleagues in Ireland and around the world, giving me external stimulation and validation. The tension between my disciplinary knowledge of the structural and cultural constraints that exist and my sense of individuality and agency persists. Here I reflect on some of the academic questions and personal issues that have underpinned much of my life and that continue to interest me. As one might expect of someone who has lived their life mainly in their head, I explore some academic issues first including whether discrimination exists in academia; whether who is in senior positions there matters and the usefulness of asking questions as a way of challenging the status quo. I then reflect on some more personal ones around place, identity and mental health – themes which have subtly underpinned much of my life.

Does discrimination really exist in academia?

When I graduated with a first-class-honours undergraduate degree in Social Science at 19, I was totally and naively convinced that knowledge not power was what was most important. I wish it was so, but I know now that it is not. Many women academics in male-dominated higher education institutions have similar illusions, assuming that their competence and achievements will be recognised and valued by those in power.

Looking back to the start of my academic career, it is clear that there have been some changes. In 1973/74, five per cent of those at full professorial level nationally were women. This fell in the 1980s, rising to four per cent in 1993/94, shortly before I was appointed a full professor in the University of Limerick. Increases in the proportion of women who are in such academic positions have been steady but limited: rising from 18 per cent in 2012 to 31 per cent in 2022. (well-above the EU average)[73]. Even

73   Higher Educational Authority (HEA). (2023). *Institutional Profiles by sex and gender*. https://hea.ie/policy/gender/statistics/, accessed 11th Nov 2023. See also European Commission (EC). (2021). *She Figures*. Luxembourg: EU Publications Office. https://data.europa.eu/doi/10.2777/06090

yet, 15 per cent of the male academic cohort is at full professorial level in Irish universities compared with just under eight per cent of their female counterparts. Thus, academic men in Ireland (like those in the EU) have a twice better chance than their female counterparts of being in these well-paid, influential positions. Broadly similar patterns have been identified in New Zealand: controlling there for research output, age, discipline and university.[74] Does this reflect a systemic devaluation of women in higher education?

Within Irish universities, the 429-year pattern of male dominance of the position of president/rector ended at the start of the COVID-19 pandemic. Was their appointment a response to this crisis? It is certainly provocative that seven of the eight people who were approved by the relevant governing authorities for appointment to these positions between 2020 and 2023 were women. Currently, seven of the twelve people with ten-year appointments as presidents/rectors are women – considerably higher than the EU average. The fact that this change has occurred over three years (from 2020 to 2023) undermines explanations for women's previous absence rooted in women's lack of confidence, political 'nous', ambition, leadership skills, caring priorities or biology. It remains to be seen what impact this change will have and how sustainable it will be. Professor Kerstin Mey in the University of Limerick is one of those women. She was appointed as vice-president academic affairs and student engagement there in 2018, then acting president and finally president in 2021. Did her appointment reflect the changing culture within higher education in Ireland in general, and within the University of Limerick in particular? Is it realistic to think that I might have contributed to this change?

Five of these seven women presidents/rectors are from a STEM background (as are three of the five men in such positions). Compared with other disciplines which look at the extent and impact of power structures, such areas have often struggled to recognise gendered sources of

74   Brower, A. and James, A. (2020). 'Research Performance and Age Explain Less Than Half of the Gender Pay Gap in New Zealand Universities'. *PLOS One*, 15 (1), 1–13.

organisational discrimination and privilege.[75] Four of these seven women
in presidential/rector positions have had no formative higher educational
experiences in Ireland (doing neither their undergraduate nor their post-
graduate degrees here). This is true of none of the five men in similar positions: implicitly raising questions about the valuation of home grown female
as opposed to male talent.[76] Does the appointment of these women signal
a change in the organisational culture? or simply strategic compliance by
higher educational institutions to state pressure, in the context of the crisis
posed by COVID-19?

The proportion of the female academic staff cohort who are at full
professorial level is higher in universities that have a female president,
possibly reflecting an underlying change in gender stereotypes in these institutions. In any event, looking at the ratio of male and female professors
to those in the positions below them, women's 'chances' vary across time,
and even yet, between universities (from 1:24 to 1:9). On the other hand,
men's 'chances' of a full professorship have not changed since 2013–15, and
they still vary little between these universities (1:4 to 1:7). This implicitly
suggests that these patterns reflect variations in organisational culture. Is
the underlying message that women can be 'allowed' to advance – but not
at men's expense?[77]

Higher educational institutions are still organisations that are created
by and for men.[78] This is reflected in their structure and culture. Thus, the
areas where male academics predominate are valued more highly than those
where women predominate. This is reflected for example, in the differential availability of senior posts; in the workload allocation models and the

75   With notable exceptions such as MIT which published a ground breaking re-
     port: *A Study of the Status of Women Faculty in Science at MIT* (1999) http://web.
     mit.edu/fnl/women/women.pdf, accessed 12 May 2001.
76   O'Connor, P. and Irvine, G. (2024). 'Why Are Seven of the 12 Presidents in Irish
     Universities Now Women? What Does It Mean?' Unpublished ms/book chapter.
77   Hodgins, M. and O'Connor, P. (2021). 'Progress, but at the Expense of Male Power?
     Institutional Resistance to Gender Equality in an Irish University', *Frontiers of
     Sociology*, https://doi.org/10.3389/fsoc.2021.696446.
78   O'Connor, P. (2020). 'Why Is It So Difficult to Reduce Gender Inequality in Male
     Dominated Higher Education Organisations?', *Interdisciplinary Science Review*, 45
     (2), 207–28.

stereotypes underpinning them. Thus, for example, women typically are seen as more suited to undergraduate teaching, pastoral care and administration and this assumption is reflected in the work allocated to them. These activities are essential – but are undervalued in promotional competitions. Recruitment practices frequently lack transparency (not only in Ireland – but in Denmark,[79] the Netherlands[80] etc.). The criteria for such recruitment/promotion in Irish universities officially includes teaching, research and service – but in practice research is prioritised. Men are likely to produce more publications; have higher citations and more research funding – at least partly because of the implications of the fact that they are men in male-dominated institutions.

The culture of higher educational institutions is still gendered. The achievements of men and women are differently evaluated. Thus, for example, both men and women in a research-intensive university in the United States, when assessing identical CVs, one with a man's name and the other with a woman's name, favoured the CV with the man's name, and at a higher starting salary.[81] Day-to-day informal interactions facilitate men's careers (e.g. through sponsorship where senior managers leverage their own power, reputation and influence to advance the career of their protégé). Thus, men get sponsorship to move up: women at best get mentors to help them to change themselves.[82] Half of those in a national survey of

79 Nielsen, M. W. (2016). 'Limits to Meritocracy? Gender in Academic Recruitment and Selection Processes', *Science and Public Policy*, 43 (3), 386–99.

80 Van den Brink, M. and Benschop, Y. (2012a). 'Slaying the Seven-Headed Dragon: The Quest for Gender Change in Academia', *Gender, Work & Organization*, 19 (1), 71–92; Van den Brink, M. and Benschop, Y. (2012b). 'Gender Practices in the Construction of Academic Excellence: Sheep with Five Legs', *Organization*, 19 (4), 507–24.

81 Moss-Racusin, C. A., Dovidio, J. F., Brescoll, V. L., Graham, M. J. and Handelsman, J. (2012). 'Science Faculty's Subtle Gender Biases Favor Male Students', *Proceedings of the National Academy of Sciences*, 109 (41), 16474–79.

82 O'Connor, P., et al. (2020). 'Mentoring and Sponsorship in Higher Educational Institutions: Men's Invisible Advantage in STEM?', *Higher Education Research and Development*, 39 (4), 764–77; see also Parsons, C. and O'Connor, P. (2023). 'You've Heard of Mentorship in Science, but What about Sponsorship?', *Nature*, 19 January, https://www.nature.com/articles/d41586-023-00123-z.

staff in Irish higher educational institutions described being treated differently and/or being put down or condescended to because of gender,
with women being at least twice as likely to have these experiences as their
male counterparts.[83] The kinds of sexist hostility or microaggressions they
referred to included being devalued or marginalised as well as more overt
gender-based violence and harassment. Power is often exercised covertly
and in subtle ways. Early career researchers on temporary contracts, who are
totally dependent on senior (typically male) academics for their positions,
references and future opportunities are particularly vulnerable. Challenging
this 'stealth power'[84] can endanger fragile acceptance by masculinist power
holders and the limited benefits that come with that. Hence, as women,
we can frequently be under considerable internal and external pressure to
collude with our own oppression.

I was well into my 40s before I recognised that discrimination existed
in academia. In a world where gender is a key marker, where constructions
of masculinity involve dominance over women and a privileging of men
relative to women, my experience over forty-six years in academic institutions is that identification with women seems to be difficult for most men,
no matter how well-educated they are. I have met men who have been able
to do this – Professor Damian Hannan, my first boss at the Economic
and Social Research Institute; Denis Doherty CEO of the Midland and
Midwestern Health Boards; Professor Chris Whelan a former colleague at
the Economic and Social Research Institute; Professor Paul Walton from
the University of York; Professor Edmond Magner, dean of the faculty of
Science and Engineering in the University of Limerick, among others (as
well as those outside academia, such as Gerry O'Higgins, the man who
built my little house). I have been struck by how often these men's ability

83   MacNeela, P., Dawson, K., O'Rourke, T., Healy-Cullen, S., Burke, L. and Flac, F.
     F. (2022). *Report on the National Survey of Staff Experiences of Sexual Violence and
     Harassment in Irish HEIs.* Dublin: HEA, p. 16. https://www.gov.ie/en/publicat
     ion/09bb5-report-on-surveys-of-experiences-of-sexual-violence-and-harassment-
     in-higher-education/, accessed 6 June 2023.
84   O'Connor, P., Martin, P. Y. Carvalho, T., et al. (2019). 'Leadership Practices by
     Senior Position Holders in HERIs: Stealth Power in Action?', *Leadership*, 15 (6),
     722–43.

to move beyond identification with other men has been rooted in their understanding of other kinds of discrimination, often based on class or religion, which they have been able to transfer to gender.

An important part in perpetuating the system is played by men who see discrimination but who do not actively challenge it.[85] They fear that to do so would disrupt their relationships with their male colleagues and undermine their own chances of advancement. They may well be right. But they are complicit in perpetuating the system. I saw how the wheels of power are oiled by men's deference towards and support for each other: creating ties of indebtedness in the expectation of future rewards, while at the same time extolling the importance of 'merit'. The language of care, of 'looking after' and of 'seeing people right', is used to obscure what can only be described as nepotism and bias by men in favour of men. Group-think and male bonds (especially male sponsorship of other men) seem particularly strong at the top of Irish society, although some of the same indicators, such as not encouraging women to go for promotion, have been identified in academia in other countries.[86]

I saw how many women's tendency to focus on the job in hand, rather than on the development of a power base contrasted strongly with the actions of some men.[87] As someone who was politically naive but had an unconsciously commanding presence, I have seen how a failure to mark out 'turf' could be taken as weakness and lead to the erosion of one's position. Men quite simply stepped in and took over if there was the slightest hint of ambiguity. It was very difficult to reclaim that power. I noticed many men's reluctance to 'go out to bat' for a woman. Good men would

85 O'Connor, P. (2008). 'The Challenge of Gender in Higher Education: Processes and Practices'. *Proceedings of the 4th International Barcelona Conference on Higher Education, Vol. 3. Higher Education and Gender Equity*. Barcelona: GUNI. l3_pap_OConnor.doc (core.ac.uk).

86 Graves, A., Rowell, A. and Hunsicker, E. (2019). *An Impact Evaluation of the Athena SWAN Charter*. Loughborough University; Ortus: https://s3.eu-west-2.amazon aws.com/assets.creode.advancehe-document-manager/documents/ecu/Athena-SWAN-Impact-Evaluation-2019_1579524189.pdf, accessed 20 August 2020.

87 O'Connor, P. (2019). 'An Autoethnographic Account of a Pragmatic Inclusionary Strategy and Tactics as a Form of Feminist Activism', *Equality, Diversity and Inclusion: An International Journal*, 38 (8), 825–40.

approach me privately and say they would not oppose me, but only the strongest and most exceptional would publicly support me. That reluctance was heightened in senior management, especially if the main power holder had not publicly declared support for my position. I was surprised by most men's lack of moral courage, something which contrasts with the male stereotype. I found that the system is maintained by men's desire to be men in a situation where being a man involves at the very least, a lack of open support for women, individually or collectively.

The sites of oppression, particularly for young women also include the sexual area with masculinity defined in terms of male dominance/female objectification and femininity in terms of subordination/submission. These ideas legitimate the enactment of gender-based violence and harassment, particularly against those women who 'dare' to enter any public space including male-dominated areas in higher education. Students can become targets, with nearly three in ten of them saying in a recent national survey that, it had been implied that they would get 'better treatment' if they were 'sexually co-operative', with female students being three times more likely than their male counterparts to experience various kinds of sexual coercion; and one-third of the female students who responded to follow -up questions about sexual violence having effectively been raped.[88]

Yet, I persist in believing that change is possible. One indicator of this is change in the gender profile of the professoriate. In Trinity College Dublin the percentage of women in the full professoriate was, with the University of Galway, lowest in Ireland at 14 per cent in 2013. By December 2022, 37 per cent of those at full professorial level in Trinity College Dublin were women, compared with 25 per cent of those in the University of Galway, making Trinity College Dublin the fastest to change. However, change is neither inevitable nor irreversible. In the University of Limerick 34 per cent of those at full professorial level were women in 2012, but it fell to 28

---

88   MacNeela, P., Dawson, K., O'Rourke, T., Healy-Cullen, S., Burke, L. and Flac, F. F. (2022). *Report on the National Survey of Students Experiences of Sexual Violence and Harassment in Irish HEIs*. Dublin: HEA, pp. 14, https://hea.ie/assets/uplo ads/2021/04/Summary-report-Students-Jan-2022.pdf accessed 6 June 2023.

per cent subsequently and has only now reverted (at 31 per cent) to near the 2012 level.[89]

Make no mistake about it: discrimination still exists in academia. The barriers and the bias may be less overt but they are still there.

Does it matter who holds senior positions in academia?

For many people the fact that I have spent so much time researching and writing about the absence of women in senior positions in higher education is unintelligible. They argue that higher education is a niche area of little interest to most of society. They argue that a focus on elite positions is too narrow and that changing their gender profile will not do anything to tackle social problems related to poverty or violence. Others are critical of the focus on women and see this as reinforcing binary constructions of gender. For yet others the key issue is that similar or even greater problems are experienced by those who vary in terms of race/ethnicity or other bases of discrimination. All of these criticisms have merit.

We all begin from where we are. For right or wrong I have spent forty-six years in higher educational institutions, whether as a researcher, teacher or manager. In an important sense higher education has been my world. Hence it is perhaps not surprising that I am interested in its structure, culture, limits and possibilities. Up to twenty-five years ago Ireland was a largely homogenous society in racial/ethnic terms, with Travellers being the only identifiable minority ethnic group. That situation has changed dramatically, but gender remains a key marker.

Although I have been concerned with the position of women in higher education for almost twenty-five years,[90] I have had other intellectual preoccupations during my academic career, although typically they have also

89 Higher Educational Authority (HEA) (2023). *Institutional profiles by sex and gender* https://hea.ie/policy/gender/statistics/ accessed 11th Nov 2023.

90 O'Connor, P. (1999). 'Women in the Academy: A Problematic Issue?' In A. B. Connolly and A. Ryan (eds), *Women and Education*, pp. 17–48. Maynooth: MACE.

involved gender. Indeed, I came late to a focus on public power and to questions such as: Who has it? How is it exercised? To whose benefit? These questions still seem important. I am interested in societal change, and if it is to occur without bloodshed, then a key role must be played by those who are highly educated, in leadership positions and/or who have power. There are examples (such as the ending of apartheid in South Africa) where the self-interest of the dominant group was redefined to bring about structural transformation. Such examples are rare, but they do exist. They underline the importance of understanding power and the role played by leaders in bringing about societal and cultural change.

I am constantly amazed at those who dismiss the importance of having women in senior positions and who see no contradiction between such attitudes and the recognised importance of role models in sport, whether GAA, soccer, rugby, horse riding, boxing, running etc. These areas have until very recently been dominated by men. Furthermore, it is often sport that acts as a 'bonding mechanism' for men in positions of power in all areas. Why does the logic that 'If you can't see it, you can't be it' not also apply to women's occupancy of positions of power?

Men's occupancy of these positions is still normalised. Some people have been appalled by the toxic masculinity of Putin, Trump and Johnston but many others, both men and women, have remained in thrall to them. Yes, we have seen more women leading governments internationally and in other senior positions, even young women like Jacinta Ardern in New Zealand or Sanna Marin in Finland. But the tendency for their activities to be judged more harshly than that of their male colleagues remains, with their limitations seen as indicating the unsuitability of women in general for such positions. This is ironical since even Putin or Trump's behaviours are not seen as raising questions about the appropriateness of men in general as leaders.

Increasing the proportion of women in these positions will not necessarily bring about organisational or societal transformation, although their presence does reduce gender-based violence and harassment. It can also bring particular issues into sharp relief. In the society we live in, many men have very different priorities to their female counterparts: for example, in Ireland state funding for horse and greyhound racing appears much more important to our male-dominated political parties than funding for child care or for domestic violence refuges. These priorities reflect the gendering of their lives rather than their biology. They affect their stereotypical gendered assumptions about appropriate targets for public funding. Higher educational institutions play a part in legitimating those patterns and assumptions.

The priorities of male elites have been reflected in the prioritisation of research in the universities; in the normalisation of exploitative knowledge creation models, particularly in STEM (where the careers of permanent academics are enhanced by the work of a large number of precarious early career researchers with no possibility of permanent jobs) and by research funding models and career structures that perpetuate these exploitative power relationships.[91] In Ireland it is now clear that across the higher education system, the majority of those on temporary contracts are researchers or those supporting them.[92]

I was in my 50s when I visited the Pergammon Museum in Berlin. When I saw the huge heads of gods and giants on the frieze around the Pergamon Altar I was astonished to find an up to then unrecognised tension easing from my shoulders. The heads included both men and women. In the second century BC, women were recognised as just as powerful as men. They could be gods. It was a moment of visceral relief. And yet also one of surprise at my own response. The impact of catholic iconography, and its depiction of the appropriateness of the subordinate position of women had taken its toll. The dominance of men in senior positions in Ireland still persists not only in the institutional Roman Catholic Church but also in the civil service, in the Dáil, in the media etc. It is depicted simultaneously

91   O'Connor, P., Le Feuvre, N. and Sumer, S. (2023). 'Cross-national Variation in Postdoc Precarity: An Enquiry into the Role of Career Structures and Research Funding Models', *Policy Futures in Education*, 1–19, https//:doi.org/10.1177/147821 03231177483; O'Connor, P. (2022). 'Probationary Citizenship in STEM in an Irish University: A Disrupted Patriarchal Bargain?', *Irish Journal of Sociology*, 30 (3), 286–307.

92   O'Connor, P. (2023). 'The Precarious Employment of Staff in Irish Higher Educational Institutions and Its Policy Implications', *PublicPolicy.ie*, 6 June.

as 'natural' and irrelevant. I was surprised to find that, even for me, it was a relief to see physical evidence to the contrary.

My pre-occupation over the past twenty-five years with power in higher education is not perhaps as irrelevant as some might like to think.

Asking questions …

The titles of a lot of the articles that I have written include a question mark.[93] This has occurred too often to be pure chance. Asking questions is a way of challenging power. It problematises the taken-for-granted arrangements on which the legitimacy of power rests. Many of these questions have their roots in the question that underpinned much of my early life: whether power or knowledge was most important. My mother believed firmly in the importance of knowledge since it had transformed her experience of life. My father was equally convinced that relationships with power holders were key. Backing the wrong ones had changed his life. Power and knowledge always seemed in tension.

Later I was puzzled by the gap between the ideologies which tell us how things should be and the realities of women's lives. In 1960s and 1970s Ireland we were told that women's lives were in the home, and that women found identity and satisfaction there. This was not the reality I observed in my own home and the other homes I knew. So, I researched it for my Master's thesis. In my PhD I tackled another 'sacred cow'. Husbands it was asserted were their wives' best friends in what was then depicted as

---

93   For example: O'Connor, P. (2000). 'Ireland: A Man's World?', *ESR*, 31 (1), 81–102; O'Connor, P. (2011). 'Irish Universities: Male Dominated? Limits and Possibilities for Change?', *EDI*, 31 (1), 83–96; O'Connor, P. (2015). 'Good Jobs – but Places for Women?', *Gender and Education* 27 (3), 304–19; O'Connor, P. (2012). 'Is Senior Management in Irish Universities Male Dominated?', *IJS*, 18 (1), 1–21; O'Connor, P. (2018). 'Gender Imbalance in Senior Positions: What Is the Problem? What Can Be Done?', *Policy Reviews in Higher Education*, 3 (1), 28–50; O'Connor, P. (2020). 'Creating Gendered Change in Irish Higher Education: Is Managerial Leadership up to the Task?', *Irish Educational Studies*, 39 (2), 139–56.

companionate marriages created by love (contrasting with the marriages of my grandparents' generation with their dowries). All other relationships were dismissed as unimportant. But I noticed the big part played in women's lives by mothers, sisters and close friends. It seemed to me that in the absence of those ties, women's lives were much harder and lacking in joy. As well as the book on *Friendships Between Women*, which was widely seen as innovatory, it led to other publications on the contexts in which friendships were created and maintained[94] and on the similarities and differences between kin and friendship ties.[95] I found that those women who had both a very close confidant whom they saw every two to three weeks, as well as a confiding relationship with their husband, were least likely to have a psychiatric affective disorder.[96] Almost thirty years later, the importance of friendships in contributing to physical and mental health is at last being recognised. I wondered about women's power within marriage[97]; about their experience of motherhood[98] and of marital sexual pleasure.[99]

When I came back to Ireland after ten years in the UK, I wondered how much had actually changed in women's lives, particularly as regards paid work and family. So *Emerging Voices: Women in Contemporary Irish Society* came to be written.[100] Later I wondered if young people's lives were still mapped by gender and this led to a book on *Irish Children and Teenagers*

---

94   O'Connor, P. (1999). 'Women's Friendships in a Post-Modern World'. In R. Adams and G. Allan (eds), *Placing Friendship in Context*, pp. 117–26. Cambridge: Cambridge University Press.

95   O'Connor, P. (1990). 'The Adult Mother/Daughter Relationship: Uniquely and Universally Close?', *The Sociological Review*, 38 (2), 293–322.

96   O'Connor, P. (1991). 'Women's Confidants Outside Marriage: Shared or Competing Sources of Intimacy?', *Sociology*, 25 (2), 241–54.

97   O'Connor, P. (1991). 'Women's Experience of Power within Marriage: An Inexplicable Phenomenon?', *The Sociological Review*, 39 (4), 823–42.

98   O'Connor, P. (1993). 'Women's Experience of the Mother Role', *The Sociological Review*, 41 (2), 347–60.

99   O'Connor, P. (1995). 'Understanding Variations in Marital Sexual Pleasure: An Impossible Task?', *The Sociological Review*, 43 (2), 342–62.

100   O'Connor, P. (1999/98). *Emerging Voices: Women in Contemporary Irish Society*. Dublin: Institute of Public Administration.

in a Changing World.[101] When I was dean, I saw that although universities were supposed to be places where merit and excellence were objectively assessed, this did not seem to be what actually happened. I wondered what was going on and this led to a book on *Management and Gender in Higher Education.*[102]

Possibly because of book publishing conventions, the titles of my books (unlike my articles) do not feature question marks. However, the gap between ideology and day-to-day reality, particularly women's day-to-day reality, has driven a lot of my research. Paradoxically it has taken me a long time to recognise that this gap reflects the interests of those (predominantly men) in positions of public power. Who wanted us to think that all women find identity and satisfaction in housework and child care? Who wanted us to think that women don't need close friendships? Who wanted us to think that paid work and family are totally different than they were in the 'bad old days'? Who wanted us to think that universities are meritocratic institutions? When I put the questions so baldly it is obvious that it is those with power who want us to deny the reality of our day-to-day experiences.

Male-dominated power is still reflected in the devaluation of predominantly 'female' areas. Having spent nearly twenty years in the academic worlds of child care and women's studies, I am acutely aware of the ways in which those involved in them are marginalised and their work dismissed as simultaneously 'natural' and 'not really important'. Quite unselfconsciously, and without a feminist frame, but possibly reflecting a perspective which problematised the 'normal', these areas and activities seemed to me to be important and valuable from an early stage in my career. But they were not seen in that light. The low valuation of these areas (as well as of nursing, midwifery, primary teaching etc.) is reflected in their pay and conditions and ultimately reflects the values and priorities of the predominantly male power holders in the public area. Many women who work in them do not notice for quite some time that they are less well-resourced and have fewer 'perks', poorer career paths, and lower positions in organisational power

---

101   O'Connor, P. (2008). *Irish Children and Teenagers in a Changing World.* Manchester: MUP.
102   O'Connor, P. (2014). *Management and Gender in Higher Education.* Manchester: MUP.

hierarchies. The under-representation of men in these 'female areas' of paid work is frequently seen, even by trade unions (such as the Irish National Teacher's Organisation), as a problem – with men in such contexts being seen as a scarce and valuable resource: thus, further militating against individual women's career progression.

The situation in predominantly male professions and sectors, such as higher education, reveals a different face of power. At first glance it appears to be easier for women to thrive there since the value of these areas is largely uncontested. However, the universities' funding models continue to value male-dominated subjects (such as engineering and information communications technology) more than female-dominated ones (such as nursing and midwifery), with more professorial posts in male-dominated areas 'in the national interest' (defined by men at the top of the government and the civil service). Although women can get into these male-dominated areas, it is difficult for most to move up, and their acceptance is conditional and limited within these structures.

It is, I now think, more important to study power and privilege than discrimination and oppression, since the former creates the latter. It is also more dangerous. Social media, such as Twitter/X and the global #MeToo and #Black Lives Matter facilitate challenges to power, without paying the ultimate price as a whistle-blower. For a long time although I asked troubling questions, I dodged the stark reality of public power. Thus, in looking at women's attitudes to being housewives and mothers in my Master's thesis, I differentiated between traditional and modern attitudes: implicitly suggesting a progressive model of change. By focusing on types of very close relationships and their impact on women's mental health I also unconsciously hoped to avoid the issue of power – although asking if these ties could compensate for poor marital relationships was coming close to dangerous territory, since it implicitly challenged the cultural importance of such relationships. Since friendships are an acceptable and important part of young people's lives, and since young people are marginal in terms of power, looking at their life styles and identities was another safe exercise. In looking at higher educational institutions, I have at last focused on public power: who has it and how is it exercised.

Challenging power is fraught with danger in the face of external and internal pressures. It is not clear if the destabilisation of male-dominated masculinist power will lead to the creation of a feminist world. It is a risk – but what is the alternative?

Would I want to live here?

Life under lockdown during the COVID-19 pandemic reminded me of the narrowness of many people's lives in 1950s Ireland, their drabness, lack of excitement and colour. Seeing new places and having new experiences gives me that sense of colour and opens up the possibility of imaginatively entering into other lives and times. Sitting in the ruins of St Clemens Church in Visby in Gotland in July 2005, I saw a musical production about the struggle between Christianity and the old pagan ways there in the twelfth century, and wondered why things were so different there to the Irish conversion to Christianity in the fifth century. One of the advantages of my life style was that I had no responsibilities and so could and did travel in Europe, Asia, Australia and North America. For much of this time, my peers were busy raising children and minding husbands and aged parents and had neither the time nor the money to join me. I was always worried when going away on my own, but I still went.

I have no problem accepting that, in such contexts, I am a tourist – that many of my experiences as a tourist are 'plastic', commodified, predigested; that they are not like the 'real' day-to-day experiences of those living there. But to me that is part of the whole point of the experience: it is an escape from one's own 'real' existence – a different kind of 'plastic'. Although I always try to get a handle on the social, economic and historical contexts of the places I go, their sheer physical beauty or quirky charm are also important. As is the opportunity to switch off my drive and my usual pre-occupations and to be more receptive to chance experiences.

My first trip to Europe was to Austria with two friends after my graduation. I nearly drove them crazy wanting to see every four-star sight in the then green Michelin guide. It was like being a child in a sweet shop. I wanted so much to stuff my face that I barely had time to eat. Those days are past. Now I know that it really does not matter if I do not get to see X or Y: indeed, that part of the holiday is that I do not have to do so. I early learned that I do best on holidays where physical demands, however limited, are combined with mental stimulation. I have sailed, climbed, cycled, walked and taken public transport on holidays. I love Guide Books – although it is a pity that increasingly they usually do not now provide the kind of sociological data that they used to (e.g. birth rate; women's participation in paid employment etc.). Although I know that most of what I learn will disappear shortly after I return, the struggle to learn keeps my mind busy and the knowledge itself, however superficial, makes the trip much more enjoyable and interesting.

In my 30s my trips were mostly around Europe. In addition to sailing, there were cycling holidays around the Chateaux of the Loire; the Rhone Valley, the Netherlands, Denmark – anywhere that was flat. I loved France and spent some wonderful holidays there. There was no internet then and no mobile phones and booking hotels was a nightmare. I had 1960s Leaving Certificate French and a great capacity to shrug my shoulders and gesticulate but dealing with the endless choices of single or double bed; with or without a shower; with or without breakfast, on a public phone, was a considerable challenge. Eating alone there was also a trial. Inevitably when I arrived in the dining room or restaurant I would be greeted by a sad look and a question in French: 'You are alone? You want to eat alone?' There was no greater tragedy. Eventually I solved the problem by pretending to be a restaurant critic – making discreet notes on the food throughout the meal. This ended the pitying glances and improved the service.

I used to love going away without making plans or booking accommodation. But one Bastille Day (14 July) in the 1980s changed all that. My travelling companion and I on a whim had taken a train from Paris to Sarlat that day. We arrived there around 19.00 hours and proceeded to reject hotels on various grounds (no pool; too posh; not posh enough etc.). By the time we settled on one it was booked up ('We are full. I am so sorry' said in French). As it grew dark, our predicament became very clear. We ended up in a centre for the homeless on rather dirty mattresses. Hanging loose did not seem such a good idea after that.

In my 40s, I typically went to one conference outside Ireland every year to present a research paper. The thought of tying my holidays to these events had never occurred to me until a UK colleague, Professor Suzan Lewis suggested it. It was a great idea. It was what led me to New Orleans in January 2000. It is hard to say why some places creep into your soul. It is perhaps because something in you finds an echo in them. Bourbon Street at first glance was tawdry and run down. But the New Orleans Jazz session in Preservation Hall, with its plain timber benches, no alcohol, where black and white musicians played together: each one rising spontaneously from the group to lead and then to be submerged and succeeded by another, reconciled race and individual and group tensions. Music was everywhere: even the down-and-outs in the main square had a violin or a double base. The worlds of the dead and the living seemed permeable, with the dead surfacing from their graves if the levees did not hold. Fortune telling was a major pre-occupation. The swamps with their snoozing crocodiles and the widows' weeds on the trees added to the eerie surreal atmosphere. I felt easy somehow there. It was unlike anywhere else I had ever been – and yet somehow familiar.

Old Istanbul was another such place. I had heard of the whirling dervishes for years but had no idea that they still existed until I saw them. Walking along a street, I heard strange unearthly music coming from a church-like red brick building. Going inside I saw men swirling in their long white dresses, brown tomb-like hats on their heads, blood-red sheep skins laid out on a green lit revolving circular glass disc. It felt sacred and mesmeric. In the old part of Istanbul, there was the constant background call to prayer; the bare beauty of the mosques and the lushness of Topkapi Palace. Who would not want to see these places? I did not want to live there – nor indeed in Japan, despite its efficient bullet train and impeccable standards of hygiene reflected in its outdoor shoes, toilet shoes and heated toilet seats. The extraordinary beauty of Kyoto captivated me: the multitasking Goddess with all the hands, and 400 smaller but gilded multitasking goddesses in front of her; the gardens with circles of raked stones denoting the life course. I was astonished at the gentleness of the people and yet the ferocity of the cries of 'we are in ecstasy' (shouted in Japanese) as open shirted bare-chested young men in white shorts with black bandanas carried the sacred Shinto relics during the 2014 Gion Masuri festival from one location to another.

Wherever I went, I would think: Would I want to live here? Scandinavia seemed an option, and Stockholm, with its one-third water, one-third green and one-third built environment seemed very attractive. But I was horrified to find that attitudes to women in leadership positions were as bad there as in Ireland. Norway and Iceland's maternity leave policies were extremely impressive, but being a foreigner in those small countries was problematic, and the acceptance of women in academic leadership positions again seemed to be no better than in Ireland. Being a woman in the UK in the 1970s was much easier than being a woman in Ireland at that time but other identities became problematic (e.g. being Irish at the time of the IRA bombing campaign and the Falklands war).

In my 50s I went to China. It rained hard in the afternoon in Beijing in July 2004 and although labour was very cheap, hotels had simple metal boxes into which guests could insert their umbrellas and get them covered with a plastic bag so that there were no drips anywhere. It was fifteen years later before I saw this simple gadget in Wexford Opera house. I was awed by the Terracotta warriors standing in their open pits below ground level in Xian and amused by the playful, green rounded hills like fingers in Guilin. But sociability in the group of twenty people with whom I travelled after the conference was surprisingly limited and conversation almost nil, since each national group spoke their own language to each other. There were no Irish or English people on the trip and the Americans were for the most part in new second relationships and preoccupied with each other.

I returned to China a few years later-this time to Yunnan, on the borders of Tibet, the most ethnically diverse of the provinces where we had three different guides all from non-Han groups, all married to Han spouses. At this time the one-child policy affected all Han families, but those who identified as non-Han could have two or three children, at the cost of their political influence and economic well-being. I went there because I had read Namu's account of her childhood around Lake Lugu in 'The Country of Daughters'.[103] Unfortunately we did not make it to Lake

---

103   Namu and Mathieu, C. (2004). *Leaving Mother Lake*. London: Abacus.

Lugo where a small Mosu tribe still exists. Family life was reputed to revolve around mothers and daughters, inheritance was through the female line, and male lovers were chosen freely by the women but were tangential to family life. This seemed to me to offer a lot more stability to children than in western societies where marriages are typically based on romantic love which may well fade with time, and where single parents are overwhelmingly mothers and are very likely to experience poverty. The Mosu's arrangements avoided male sexual or economic control, while retaining women's agency in choosing sexual partners. Men knew they were not wanted when the woman's door remained closed and the sign that they had been replaced was another man's spear outside her door.

I had always been suspicious of the tendency to define 'the family' as a homogenous structure. Like many Irish people I had seen families created through the dowry system (reflecting an economic model), with inheritance and descent traced through the male line, with women marrying into and isolated in their husband's family and 'home place'. That system retained male power and was not only patriarchal, but patrilineal and patrilocal. In the 1980s I read Fox's study of marriages on Tory Island[104] where couples continued to live apart after marriage if they had aged parents to care for; and Bettelheim's description of the children's houses and the very different organisation of the family in the Kibbutz.[105] In retrospect I can see that this interest in alternative structures reflected my gut feeling that the existing organisation of the family was problematic – a view reinforced by reading Minturn and Lambert's book on child rearing across six cultures[106] which showed that the then 'normal' model of a mother being at home full-time rearing children was more conducive to poor mental health than any other system. This was reinforced by research at the Social Research Unit in Bedford and Royal Holloway College in London where having three children under 14 years, not being in paid employment and lacking a close confidant were all identified as factors which increased women's likelihood of depression. The discourse of 'the family' in Ireland has since

104   Fox, R. (1979). 'The Visiting Husband on Tory Island', *Journal of Comparative Family Studies*, X (2), 163–92.
105   Bettelheim, B. (1971). *The Children of the Dream*. St Albans: Paladin.
106   Minturn, L. and Lambert, W. W. (1964). *Mothers of Six Cultures*. London: Wiley.

been replaced by 'families' with the increased prevalence of those headed by women as single parents, and of blended or single sex families. However, these are still a lot less empowering for women than those in the 'country of daughters'.

In Yunnan, the circle dances in the evening in the squares, frequently led by elderly women, and their graceful T'ai Chi moves in the early morning raised fundamental questions about our western attitudes to the elderly. Pollution however was out of control and in Yunnan, a ten-year campaign on toilets was just beginning. In restaurants, even in world heritage cities, there were signs up for diners telling them 'Pee no Poo'. I can still remember the smells and open stalls in Tiger Leaping Gorge, a famous beauty spot where the Tigers were not alone in leaping. I felt that I had seen the future in China and I did not like it.

For a while in my 60s my travel companion was a friend who loved long-distance trips and whose husband did not travel. Our attitudes to holidays were similar, except that she prioritised food and found good places to eat no matter where we were. This was a very convenient solution to my lazy indifference to food, and so for a number of years we travelled very happily: visiting Cuba, Vietnam, Cambodia etc. I would have liked to have gone to Machu Pichu to mark my retirement but the fear of altitude sickness deterred me. Looking for a similar sort of cultural tradition but without the altitude, I enrolled on a holiday exploring Mayan civilisation. To my surprise I was considerably older than anyone else on the trip; the only other solo traveller was a man in his 30s. We got on really well. I refused to reveal my age to any of the group until near the end of the trip, and when I did do so, he was very disconcerted.

Yes: travelling is a challenge for a solo woman of a certain age ... But the chance to see the world is not one to be missed ... even if nowhere seems to be better as a place to live ...

What is in a name?

Names are obviously important as an expression of our identity. Traditionally in Ireland many of the same names were re-used in families in each generation. That pattern has largely disappeared. The focus now is on unusual names reflecting individuality, although for the most part we still do not choose our own names.

My mother as a young woman in the early part of the twentieth century was so determined to forge her own identity that she changed her name by deed poll from Julia to Sheila (the Irish version of Julia) reflecting her nationalist attitudes. When my sister was being christened, she was refused permission by the priest to call her Stella (there was no saint of that name she was told). My sister was christened Mary Bernadette but was always called Stella. I was christened Patricia and was called Patricia. I have a vague recollection of being told by my mother that I was called after a nun whom she was very fond of- Sister Patrick. Many years later I discovered that my maternal grandfather was called Patrick. He died a couple of years before I was born, and we heard nothing positive about him. It has recently struck me that I could have been called after him. Perhaps if I had been told that, I might have seen it as reflecting a wish for a boy? If that was my parents' wish it was never apparent to me. Having a son to inherit the land was a non-issue. Both my parents had early signed themselves out of their right to inherit any part of their families' farms: partly because they did not like farming and partly because they felt it would not be fair to those siblings who had stayed in the 'home places' and worked the land.

There was another Patricia O'Connor in my class when I was in secondary school. To distinguish us, I became Patricia A and she became Patricia M. I continued to be called Patricia through school and university. But when I got involved with Seán while in college, he decided to call me Pat. I cannot remember when it started nor why. Unusually for me, I did not object. I suppose I must have liked it: it was simple, short, straightforward. For several years I remained Patricia to everyone except him. When I went to work in London in my early 20s, I decided to be Pat in work, while remaining Patricia with my family. For many years my bank and credit cards were a mix of Pat and Patricia, causing panic when booking Ryanair flights since the name on the ticket had to be identical to the name on the bank card and passport. To avoid all that hassle I decided to change all documents to Pat and to remain Patricia with my family. This still causes confusion when family and friends meet and uncertainty as to what in-laws should call me. But over time Patricia became my intimate name and I disliked it if people (and they were usually men) decided to call me Patricia in work. Pat as my work name seemed much less vulnerable. The two names gave me distance and, I felt, some kind of protection in work. Pat was a name that, in written communication, concealed my gender. I thought it was funny when people assumed that I was a man and were abashed when they discovered that I was a woman.

Many years later I discovered that publications with identifiable female names were less likely to be cited than those with male names. I had not even considered this when I shortened my name to Pat. I also belatedly learned that those names which included a second initial were most likely to be cited. Blissfully ignorant of this I instinctively preferred to entirely obscure gender in references so that I was simply P. O'Connor. This reflected what I now see as a naive hope that gender could be irrelevant. Maybe such a world will exist in the future, but it certainly does not exist now.

Over the years, I had become vaguely interested in eastern ideas about health and well-being as well as those related to yoga, the self, the chakra system and even reincarnation. For someone who has always been self-willed, it may seem odd that in my 50s I became interested in numerology. In part I think it reflected a flight from freedom or at least a question about whether or not freedom was an illusion. What if our paths were laid down at birth? It would save a lot of time and energy to know what those paths were rather than trying to forge ones that were bound to end in cul-de-sacs or rejection. Although I have spent my life in rational scientific circles I had long concluded that there were limits to that kind of thought. Over the years I have become more confident making decisions based on my gut feelings than on rational assessments.

In my 50s I needed a new challenge but I did not know where to go career -wise. It seemed to me that numerology was worth exploring. In numerology, my christened name (Patricia Ann O'Connor) identified my personality as an 11, a prime number, 'the number of the Light Bearer who brightens the darkness so that others may see the way safely through ignorance and darkness': with illumination being the key word.[107] Kovan suggests that those with this personality face 'many challenges, particularly emotionally ... [they] are very tense ... They possess a rare combination of detachment and interest which gives them a unique ability to advise and teach others'.[108] My work name, Pat O'Connor, identified my personality as a number five, a free spirit 'linked to freedom and the search for an ideal way' – with the essential key to an optimistic and full life being 'to keep learning, reading and talking'.[109] Many of those who were fives were, like me, teachers in higher education, their favourite subjects including politics and human rights with an interest in cultural pursuits. This was a much simpler and less heroic version than that suggested by my christened name Patricia Ann O'Connor. In retrospect I can see that by changing my name, I tried to simplify myself and potentially my life.

Of course, this did not change what numerology sees as the number that reflects your destiny, which is based on your birthdate. My destiny as a three is someone who 'undergoes a lifelong lesson in learning to trust her own mind' going out 'confidently and hungrily into the world to learn on the hoof travelling and reading, communicating and experiencing all the bounties that life has to offer'.[110] These descriptions of my personality and my destiny seem to me to be very apt.

My flirtation with numerology did not clarify my career objectives. But it did make me wonder about my illusions about my individuality and agency.

---

107   Kovan, D. (2001). *Secrets of Numerology*, p. 61. London: Dorling Kindersley.
108   Ibid., pp. 60–61.
109   Ibid., p. 41.
110   Ibid., p. 108.

Holistic therapies: Have they helped?

All my life I have been challenged by anxiety– not helped by a tendency to ignore my body and live in my head. In my late 40s, perhaps as a reflection of anxiety and/or the menopause, my heart started to race uncontrollably for no apparent reason. I remember sitting on the floor of my little house at 3 a.m. one morning thinking that I was going to die. The only other time I had ever had this kind of experience was altitude sickness in my 20s, but that subsided after a couple of hours. This did not. I was put on beta blockers which I hated. Their purpose was to slow me down and they did that. It was like I had suddenly become 90 years old and everything was an effort. It was clear then that I could no longer ignore my body. I decided to try and become a calm person (an aspiration which friends and colleagues thought hilariously improbable). I started doing a yoga session a week and gave up tea and coffee. For years I drank only tranquillity tea: my colleagues suggested that I sue the manufacturers because of its lack of effectiveness. I said:

'Imagine what I would be like without it?'

'Fair point' they grudgingly admitted.

Sometime later I got off the beta blockers. But my anxieties remained. I continued, as I had done since my teens, to try and live by the maxim of Susan Jeffers, a self-help guru: 'Feel the fear and do it anyway'[111]: such action requiring a continuous huge effort of will and courage.

In my 50s during the Celtic Tiger, people I knew began to use alternative therapies. I tried reflexology. I enjoyed it, although it had the peculiar effect of making me feel as if I was shedding layers like an onion. After each session I could not bear to be in crowded places: I felt fragile and needed space and quiet. Having had weekly sessions for a number of months, when about to go on a two-week holiday, I decided to double up on sessions in

---

[111]   Jeffers, S. (1987). *Feel the Fear and Do It Anyway*. Grear Britain: Cenrury Hutchinson Ltd.

the week before and after that holiday. The effect was catastrophic: I felt that my head was about to explode. The therapist, who had only done a short course in the area herself, was unable to cope with my reaction and suggested that I go to see my doctor. I was unnerved by her abdication of responsibility. Many years later I had a chance to experience reflexology on a trip to China when therapists worked on dozens of tourists seated on a line of couches in hotel foyers. They focused on stimulating circulation rather than pressing key points in the feet. There were no negative consequences from this approach, nor indeed much positive ones. Recently, I have returned to reflexology with a qualified and careful therapist, Kay Boland, and find it gently relaxing. In my experience reflexology can be very powerful but it needs to be done by an expert and with extreme care.

In my 50s having temporarily abandoned reflexology, I started to go for a vigorous Thai yoga massage regularly and did this for a number of years. It combined acupressure and assisted yoga postures, in addition to the masseur walking up and down my spine. The acupressure on my legs was extremely painful but overall, I felt looser and better after a session. Then I came across Anne Jensen at a local yoga centre and a new therapy she had developed called Heart Speak. Anne had done a PhD at Oxford. Re-experiencing trauma, dating it, evaluating its strength and imaginatively dealing with it was the core of the therapy although there was also a focus on muscle testing, but I was less interested in that. It was meant to produce fast results in terms of helping one to break out of fearful old futile patterns. The first session was face to face and I felt light afterwards. Subsequently the sessions were online, and I did them once a month for a few years. I cried a lot after each session, and eventually reached the end of the road.

The feelings of anxiety subsided during my deanship in my 50s but returned when my time as dean ended and I was faced with going away for a sabbatical and coping with the consequent dislocation and lack of structure. I was also acutely aware that I now had no big dream to escape into and that I had to dismantle the paper world I had constructed, foreshadowing my retirement when I was 65 years. I found a registered therapist who did various treatments including Emotional Freedom Technique (EFT: also referred to as tapping) as well as hypnosis and counselling. Mostly she focused on EFT. I continued to see her every month for three years. At one point I got the instructions for tapping slightly wrong and found that I was again experiencing terrible feelings of vulnerability and agitation. After that I insisted that I do the tapping in the face-to-face monthly sessions. This produced an extraordinary effect on her: she got pale and complained of being physically sick and rushed to open the window when we finished a round of tapping. I found this upsetting; it seemed that I could only get well by making someone else sick. I wondered if I had felt that my survival was somehow at my mother's expense, and whether this had bred in me an obligation to succeed, since this was the only way her sacrifice could be even vaguely justified. The therapist briefly tried counselling but my life time's experience of debating and arguing meant that it was unhelpful for me. Hypnosis did not really seem to work either. Free hand drawing was interesting but did not seem to go anywhere. Again, I cried a lot after each session. After three years it was time to move on. I felt that she was relieved to see the end of me and the sickness that I inadvertently transferred to her.

Reiki was my next choice: a lovely gentle woman in the village, Angela Davidson (originally from the UK) did it in my home for several years. Non-intrusive, it made me feel light and calm, but then she moved on to other ventures. I had tried acupuncture briefly when there were Chinese therapists in Waterford, but linguistic difficulties made treatment difficult, although the stress balls in my ears were good. I returned to it with Deirdre O'Carroll, an Irish woman, after I had shingles and found it very helpful not only in relieving that pain but in contributing to my overall emotional well-being. The lockdowns temporarily ended it but I returned to it as the COVID-19 pandemic waned and found it helpful.

These kinds of holistic therapies are for me, routine maintenance, rather like taking the car for a service. None of them have produced a transformation – but over time they have helped. The manifestation of that effect was rather peculiar. When my oldest grand-nephew was born in 2005 I drove a considerable distance to see him, bringing gifts etc. But when my niece offered to let me hold him, I just could not do it. I knew it was very hurtful but I just couldn't hold him. Twelve years later, in a similar situation, I was able to hold a new baby with no difficulty. It is not a very useful change in a life that has remained largely lived in my head. But it is a striking one. There are others. I am less afraid of the dark; easier in my own company; better able to cope with silence and a bit calmer.

I am of course extremely lucky to have been able to afford all these various kinds of holistic therapies. I think that fear is still my underlying problem and from that comes anxiety, agitation and depression. How much of this is due to nature or nurture? How much is due to my parents? to the world I grew up in Ireland of the 1950s? to living a very focused life in opposition to the prevailing male-dominated patriarchal power structures, determined but simultaneously terrified?

I have given up asking those questions. I am as I am, with my strengths and weaknesses.

Epilogue: Don't you hate men?

One of the common misperceptions is that women like me hate men. The truth is rather different. It is because many of us have had the experience of being loved and accepted as equals that we have dared to think we are. It seems extraordinary to me that this still appears to be a radical idea in western society in the twenty-first century.

When I look back to that moment in 1979 when I turned down Seán's third proposal of marriage (or at least deferred it ...) I know that given my background, my assumptions, my hopes and my vulnerabilities, I would do the same again. The #MeToo movement has highlighted many women's dramatic experiences of sexual harassment. My experiences have rarely been of this kind. Like generations of women before me, I experienced a much more subtle and mundane form of discrimination and disempowerment, reflected in relentless devaluation, denigration and marginalisation. Although publicly confident, articulate, warm and outgoing they have taken a toll on me. Despite the gains of the past fifty years, such experiences, even in western societies, are part of the unspoken reality of being a woman. I have had them – despite my whiteness, my education and my many other privileges. Ultimately, they reflect another face of misogyny (i.e. hatred of or contempt for women) manifested in the desire to dominate and subordinate, to keep us women in 'our place'.

For many men this is not a conscious choice, but a learned way of behaving, reflected in the assumption that being a man involves domination of or devaluation of women. Like more overt forms of sexual harassment which are justified by rationales such as 'she asked for it'; the treatment of individual women is excused by legitimating discourses[112] such as that 'she just was not excellent enough'; 'she did not really want the job because of

---

112   O'Connor, P. and White, K. (2021). 'Power, Legitimating Discourses and Institutional Resistance to Gender Equality in Higher Education'. In P. O'Connor and K. White (eds), *Gender, Power and Higher Education in a Globalised World*, pp. 187–207 Cham: Palgrave Macmillan.

family priorities'; 'that it was just slagging' etc. These excuses can appear reasonable in any one case. However, as in the #MeToo situation when a consistent pattern emerges, the underlying misogyny becomes clear. It is maintained by a 'pack' mentality where men support and collude with each other in legitimating attempts to keep us in 'our place'. That 'pack' mentality legitimates men's feelings of entitlement, and their very definition of themselves as men. I have been dismayed to find that so very few men are willing to stand out from the 'pack'. When I turned down the three proposals of marriage, I did not expect misogyny to be quite so endemic in the world of paid employment. Many of my worldly-wise female friends and colleagues knew, even then, that changing one man's evaluation of one woman was a good deal easier than taking on an embedded patriarchal system.

Women like me, who have felt most at home in our heads, occupy a marginal space in a gendered embodied world. We are still women and seen as women; we value that embodiment but it somehow seems less salient than other aspects of our identities. The one advantage of this is that although I have been as afraid as most women of physical attack (and miraculously have been lucky enough to avoid it), on a day-to-day basis I have been able to move around more freely than many women since I seem able to ignore my physical vulnerability.

In all sorts of ways my life has been privileged, in terms of whiteness, education, income and life style. For a woman, I have done very well. For a woman with vulnerabilities and insecurities I have done extremely well. But I cannot resist asking why my gender should be seen as somehow putting a ceiling on my hopes and ambitions? Is it in the best interest of society to discourage and devalue 51 per cent of the population? My story is much less heart-rending than that of many women who are also disadvantaged by race, class, child care or other responsibilities. But if someone like me has these kinds of experiences, how much more likely are they to be felt by these other women? And how much higher a price will they pay for naming and fighting them?

My life has been unusual in being much simpler than that of most women I know since it has minimised the exhausting, time consuming and for some, very satisfying domestic and caring activities that are still largely borne by women. I have spent most of my life doing things I enjoyed in the public area. Some of these were in predominantly female areas (child care, gender/women's studies) and I saw how these areas were devalued and under-resourced, with considerable implications for those who worked in them. The 'important' activities continue to be seen as male-dominated ones, undertaken by men in the public arena. These were the ones I ended up doing, as professor and dean. But of course, I was a woman, and so in these contexts I was often seen as a fish on a bicycle, a marvel but a freak, someone who did not 'fit' and frequently needed to be cut down to size.

For a very long time, the image of those in power has been stereotypically masculine, creating a double bind for women: to be a nice woman meant to be lacking in leadership skills; to be a strong leader was to be a 'ball-breaker' – not a 'proper' woman. Jacinta Ardern, the Prime Minister of New Zealand, a young mother, who determinedly embraced a very different style of leadership, posed a fundamental challenge to the stereotype. The toll exacted on her by relentless gendered pressure culminating in her resigning as prime minister was very disturbing. The existence of other women political leaders and their more effective performance in tackling the COVID-19 pandemic, when contrasted with their macho male counterparts, has been striking and may play an important role in reframing constructions of leadership. However, even where 'being good with people' is valued, as it is in current constructions of leadership, the 'natural' access to senior positions requiring these abilities is through predominantly male career paths.

I recognise that we women are as much products of our society as men. Paradoxically they/we may have even more to lose in risking male protection and support by challenging our categorical devaluation. Because hatred of other women is such an obvious tool to create dependency on men, it has seemed useful to try to avoid this. I remember when I took up that new job in the University of Limerick in the 1990s the then male head of department confided in me that:

'We have great fun here watching the women gut each other'.

Adding to those dramas has never seemed entirely useful. On the other hand, it has seemed useful to highlight a nineteenth-century tradition, going back to John Stewart Mill,[113] of men recognising and valuing women publicly as equals. That is risky for men – but it is absolutely essential in a world where they disproportionately occupy positions of formal power. Such a situation has existed in higher education in Ireland throughout my life. Women have now been appointed to head up seven of the twelve public universities. It is not yet clear whether or not this will help break the equation between masculinity and power there.

When I look back over my life, I am surprised to find that over a period of forty-six years, from 1970 to 2016, in five research or teaching organisations, I never had a woman as a boss. Women reflecting on their careers in thirty or forty-years' time may well have a different story to tell. But this is my story. Paradoxically then it features more men than women. Most of the men who impacted positively on my career were able to see parallels between gender discrimination and sectarian or class prejudice and this affected their attitudes and behaviour. Some were genially patronising, and this was far more preferable than hatred or discrimination. Some saw me as an equal, but only by negating me as a woman. But there were also some who saw me as a woman and as an equal.

It may seem that I have been disloyal to the institutions where I worked, and particularly to the University of Limerick. It took a gamble in promoting me in a bionic leap, from lecturer to full professor, thus giving me a platform to raise the issue of gender equality. I am grateful for the many opportunities it gave me. Should that gratitude buy my silence? Anecdotally I know that many other universities treated women no better, and some considerably worse. But organisations are rarely well-served by silence. If someone like me cannot speak out, who can? It is perhaps important to say that this was an unusual period in the history of the University of Limerick. In a context where the 'normal'[114] duration of a university presidential term is ten years, there were four presidents there over a period of ten years. It is also a fact that poor institutional memory and the practice of appointing academics for three to five years to senior management positions mean that

---

113   Mill, J. S. (1869). *The Subjection of Women*. London: Longmans, Green, Reader and Dyer.

114   Since the 1997 Universities Act, 10 years is the legal duration of a university presidential term.

few people remember who was in what particular position. Similar amnesia exists in other organisations, some of which have been restructured or even disbanded in my lifetime. However, the patterns across time and place are remarkably consistent. Maybe I am naive to persist in thinking that higher educational institutions should be learning organisations, that in particular, they should learn from their own past? I would hate to think that experiences like mine might continue unchallenged for the next fifty years.

So, there it is. We each live with the consequences of our choices in the context of the constraints on us. I still feel that it is entirely unreasonable, illogical and wrong that women are not seen as men's equal. The route I chose was less travelled by women of my generation. It has brought successes and failures, pleasures and pain. But I am no longer the frightened thinker that I was at 23 years in calling that out, despite now knowing the costs and the benefits of doing so. I hope some women will recognise themselves in my story and be comforted and inspired by it and will go on to challenge the power structures embedded in Ireland today. I hope some men will recognise the potential impact of their actions, words and silences on all women, and especially on the women they love.

The metaphor of a procrustean bed continues to be very relevant for Irish women: we are all expected to fit the narrow 'bed' of subordinate femininity. Conformity is the objective, and metaphorical death is the means to achieve this. 'Proper' women fit this procrustean bed.

I never did.

Appendix: Pat O'Connor's Academic Publications[115]

Books

Sinclair, I., Crosbie, D., O'Connor, P., Stanforth, L. and Vicery, A. (1988). *Bridging Two Worlds: Social Work and the Elderly Living Alone*. Hampshire: Avebury.

O'Connor, P. (1992/2002). *Friendships Between Women* New York: Guildford; Hemel Hempstead: Harvester Wheatsheaf. *Nominated by Choice as Outstanding Academic Book*. Reissued by Pearsons on demand.

O'Connor, P. (1999/1998). *Emerging Voices: Women in Contemporary Irish Society*. Dublin: Institute of Public Administration.

O'Connor, P. (2008). *Irish Children and Teenagers in a Changing World*. Manchester: MUP.

O'Connor, P. (2014). *Management and Gender in Higher Education*. Manchester: MUP.

White, K. and O'Connor, P. (eds) (2017). *Gendered Success in Higher Education: Global Perspectives*. London: Palgrave Macmillan.

O'Connor, P. and White, K. (eds) (2021). *Gender, Power and Higher Education in a Globalised World*. Cham: Palgrave MacMillan.

Whitehead, S. with O'Connor, P. (2023). *Creating a Totally Inclusive University*. London: Routledge.

Refereed journal articles

O'Connor, P. and Brown, G. W. (1984). 'Supportive Relationships: Fact or Fancy?' *Journal of Social and Personal Relationships*, 1, 159-76.

Sinclair, I., Stanforth, L. and O'Connor, P. (1988). 'Factors Predicting the Admission of Elderly People to Local Authority Residential Care'. *British Journal of Social Work*, 18 (3), 251-67.

O'Connor, P. (1989). 'Images and Motifs in Children's Fairy Tales'. *Educational Studies*, 15 (2), 129–43.

O'Connor, P. (1990). 'The Adult Mother/Daughter Relationship: Uniquely and Universally Close?' *The Sociological Review*, 38 (2), 293–322.

115 Since the publications reflect the questions tackled at different stages, a decision was made to present them chronologically regardless of first author.

O'Connor, P. (1991a). 'Women's Confidants Outside Marriage: Shared or Competing Sources of Intimacy?' *Sociology*, 25 (2), 241–54.

O'Connor, P. (1991b). 'Women's Experience of Power within Marriage: An Inexplicable Phenomenon?' *The Sociological Review*, 39 (4), 823–42.

O'Connor, P. (1992). 'Child Care Policy in Ireland: A Provocative Analysis and a Research Agenda'. *Administration*, 40 (3), 200–19.

O'Connor, P. (1993a). 'The Professionalisation of Child Care Work in Ireland: An Unlikely Development?' *Children and Society*, 6 (3), 250–66.

O'Connor, P. (1993b). 'Same-Gender and Cross-Gender Friendships amongst the Elderly'. *The Gerontologist*, 33 (1), 24–31.

O'Connor, P. (1993c). 'Women's Experience of the Mother Role'. *The Sociological Review*, 41 (2), 347–60.

Turner, T. and O'Connor, P. (1994). 'Women in the Zambian Civil Service: A Case of Equal Opportunities?' *Public Administration and Development*, 14 (1), 79-92.

O'Connor, P. (1994a). 'Salient Themes in the Life Review of a Sample of Frail Elderly Respondents in London'. *The Gerontologist*, 34 (2), 224–30.

O'Connor, P. (1994b). 'Very Close Parent/Child Relationships: The Perspective of the Elderly Person'. *Journal of Cross-Cultural Gerontology*, 9, 53–76.

O'Connor, P. (1995a). 'Defining Irish Women: Dominant Discourses and Sites of Resistance'. *Eire: Ireland*, 30 (3), 177–87.

O'Connor, P. (1995b). 'Same Gender and Cross-Gender Friendships among the elderly'. *The Table*, Quarterly Japanese publication [Translation of 1993 article into Japanese].

O' Connor, P. (1995c). 'Tourism and Development in Ballyhoura: Women's Business?' *The Economic and Social Review*, 26 (4), 369–401.

O'Connor, P. (1995d). 'Understanding Continuities and Changes in Irish Marriage: Putting Women Centre Stage'. *The Irish Journal of Sociology*, 5 (1), 135–63.

O'Connor, P. (1995e). 'Understanding Variations in Marital Sexual Pleasure: An Impossible Task?' *The Sociological Review*, 43 (2), 342–62.

O'Connor, P. (1996a). 'Gendered Structures in Action: "Male" versus "Female" Agendas in a Family Rights Project'. *Administration*, 44 (3), 107–25.

O'Connor, P. (1996b). 'Organisational Culture as a Barrier to Women's Promotion'. *The Economic and Social Review*, 27 (3), 205–34.

O'Connor, P. (1996c). 'A Support Group for Families Who Have Children in Care: An Evaluative Case Study'. *Children and Society*, 10 (1), 64–76.

O'Connor, P. (1998). 'Criacao social de problemas e solucoes'. *Sociologia: Problemas e Practicas*, 27, 79–96.

O'Connor, P. (1999a). 'Emerging Voices'. *Canadian Journal of Irish Studies*, 25 (1), 147–63.

O'Connor, P. (1999b). 'Ireland: A Country for Women?' Special Issue of *Jouvert:Ireland,,* ed. by M. Pramaggiore.

O'Connor, P. (2000a). 'Changing Places: Privilege and Resistance in Contemporary Ireland'. *Sociological Research Online*, 5, 3. http://www.socresonline.org.uk/5/3/oconnor.html.

O'Connor, P. (2000b). 'Ireland: A Man's World?' *The Economic and Social Review*, 31 (1), 81–102.

O'Connor, P. (2000c). 'Resistance amongst Faculty Women in Academia'. *Higher Education in Europe*, 25 (2), 213–19.

O'Connor, P. (2000d). 'Structure, Culture and Passivity: A Case Study of Women in a Semi-state Organisation'. *Public Administration and Development*, 20 (3), 265–75.

O'Connor, P. (2001a). 'A Bird's Eye View … Resistance in Academia'. *Irish Journal of Sociology*, 10 (2), 86–104.

O'Connor, P. (2001b). 'Dealing with Organisational Nuts and Bolts: The Relevance of Organisational Practices to Women's Promotion'. *Irish Journal of Feminist Studies*, 4, (1), 1–16.

O'Connor, P. (2001c). 'Supporting Mothers: Issues in a Community Mother's Programme'. *Community, Work and Family*, 4 (1), 63–85.

Goldthorpe, J., O'Dowd, L. and O'Connor, P. (2002). 'A Sociology of Ireland: A Review Symposium'. *Irish Journal of Sociology*, 11 (1), 97–111.

O'Connor, P., Kane, C. and Hayes, A. (2002). 'Young People's Ideas about Time and Space'. *Irish Journal of Sociology*, 11 (1), 43–61.

O'Connor, P. and Haynes, A. (2004). 'Relational Discourses: Social Ties with Family and Friends'. *Childhood: A Global Journal of Child Research*, 11 (3), 361–82.

O'Connor, P. (2005). 'Local Embeddedness in a Global World: Young People's Accounts'. *Young: Nordic Journal of Youth Research*, 13(1), 361–82.

O'Connor, P. (2006a). 'Globalization, Individualization and Gender in Adolescents' texts'. *International Journal of Social Research Methodology*, 9 (4), 261–77.

O'Connor, P. (2006b). 'Private Troubles, Public Issues: The Irish Sociological Imagination'. *Irish Journal of Sociology*, 15 (2), 5–22.

O'Connor, P. (2006c). 'Young People's Constructions of the Self: Late Modern Constructs and Gender Differences'. *Sociology*, 40 (1), 107–24.

O'Connor, P. (2007a). '"Doing Boy/Girl" and Global/Local Elements in 10–12 Year Olds' Drawings and Written Texts'. *Qualitative Research*, 7 (2), 229–47.

O'Connor, P. (2007b). 'Still Changing Places: Women's Paid Employment and Gender Roles'. *The Irish Review*, 35, 64–78.

O'Connor, P. (2008). 'The Elephant in the Corner: Gender and Policies related to Higher Education'. *Administration*, 56 (1), 85–110.

Ozlem, O., de Lourdes Machado, M., White, K., O'Connor, P., et al. (2009). 'Gender and Management in HEIs; Changing Organisational and Management Structures'. *Tertiary Education and Management*, 15 (3), 241-57.

O'Connor, P. (2011). 'Irish Universities: Male Dominated? Limits and Possibilities for Change?' *Equality, Diversion and Inclusion: An International Journal*, 31 (1), 83–96.

O'Connor, P. and White, K. (2011). 'Similarities and Differences in Collegiality/ Managerialism in Irish and Australian Universities'. *Gender and Education*, 27 (3), 903-19.

O'Connor, P. (2012a). 'Irish Young People's Narratives: The Existence of Gender Differentiated Cultures'. *Irish Journal of Sociology*, 17 (1), 95–114.

O'Connor, P. (2012b). 'Is Senior Management in Irish Universities Male Dominated? What Are the Implications?' *Irish Journal of Sociology*, 18 (1), 1–21.

O'Connor, P. (2014). 'Understanding Success: A Case Study of Gendered Change in the Professoriate'. *Journal of Higher Education Policy and Management*, 36 (2), 212–24.

O'Connor, P., Carvalho, T. and White, K. (2014). 'The Experiences of Senior Positional Leaders in Australian, Irish and Portuguese Universities: Universal or Contingent?' *HERD*, 33 (1), 5-18.

O'Connor, P. (2015). 'Good Jobs – but Places for Women?' *Gender and Education*, 27 (3), 304–19.

O'Connor, P. and Carvalho, T. (2015). 'Different or Similar: Constructions of Leadership by Senior Managers in Irish and Portuguese Universities'. *Studies in Higher Education*, 40 (9), 1679-93.

O'Connor, P. and Goransson, A. (2015). 'Constructing or Rejecting the Notion of Other in Senior University Management: The Cases of Ireland and Sweden'. *EMAL*, 43 (2), 323–40.

O'Connor, P., O'Hagan, C. and Brannen, J. (2015). 'Exploration of Masculinities in Academic Organisations; A Tentative Typology'. *Current Sociology*, 63 (4), 528–46.

O'Connor, P. and Fauve- Chamoux, A. (2016). 'European Policies and Research Funding: A Case Study of Gender Inequality and Lack of Diversity in a Nordic Research Programme'. *Policy and Politics*, 44 (4), 627–43.

O'Connor, P. and O'Hagan, C. (2016). 'Excellence in University Academic Staff Evaluation: A Problematic Reality?' *Studies in Higher Education*, 41 (11), 1943–57.

O'Connor, P., O'Hagan, C. and Gray, B. (2018). 'Femininities in STEM: Outsiders Within'. *Work, Employment and Society*, 32 (2), 312–29.

Montes Lopez, E. and O'Connor, P. (2019). 'Micropolitics and Meritocracy: Improbable Bedfellows?', *EMAL*, 47 (5), 678–93.

O'Connor, P., Martin, P. Y., Carvalho, T., et al. (2019). 'Leadership Practices by Senior Position Holders in HERIs: Stealth Power in Action?' *Leadership*, 15 (6), 722–43.

O'Hagan, C., O'Connor, P., et al. (2019). 'Perpetuating Academic Capitalism and Maintaining Gender Orders through Career Practices in STEM'. *Critical Studies in Education*, 60 (2), 205–25.

O'Connor, P. (2019a). 'An Autoethnographic Account of a Pragmatic Inclusionary Strategy and Tactics as a Form of Feminist Activism'. *Equality, Diversity and Inclusion: An International Journal*, 38 (8), 825–40.

O'Connor, P. (2019b). 'Gender Imbalance in Senior Positions: What Is the Problem? What Can Be Done?' *Policy Reviews in Higher Education*, 3 (1), 28–50.

O'Connor, P. and Irvine, G. (2020). 'Multi- level State Interventions and Gender Equality in Higher Education Institutions: The Irish Case'. *Administrative Sciences*, 10, 98. https:// doi.org/ 10.3390/ adm sci1 0040 098.

O'Connor, P. (2020a). 'Creating Gendered Change in Irish Higher Education: Is Managerial Leadership up to the Task?' *Irish Educational Studies*, 39 (2), 139–56.

O'Connor, P. (2020b). 'Why Is It so Difficult to Reduce Gender Inequality in Male Dominated Higher Education Organisations? A Feminist Institutional Perspective'. *Interdisciplinary Science Reviews*, 45 (2), 207–28.

O'Connor, P., et al. (2020b). 'Micro- Political Practices in Higher Education: A Challenge to Excellence as a Rationalising Myth?' *Critical Studies in Education*, 61 (2), 195-211.

O'Connor, P. (2021). 'Naming It: The Problem of Male Privileging in Higher Education'. *Academia Letters*, July. https://doi.org/10.20935/AL1653.

O'Connor, P., et al. (2021). 'Organisational Characteristics that Facilitate Gender- Based Violence and Harassment in Higher Education?' *Administrative Sciences*, 11, 138. https://doi.org/10.3390/ admsc 11040138.

Hodgins, M. H., O'Connor, P. and Buckley, L. A. (2022). 'Institutional Change and Organisational Resistance to Gender Equality in Higher Education: An Irish Case Study', *Administrative Sciences*, 12, 59. https://doi.org/10.3390/adminsci1 2020059.

O'Connor, P. (2022). 'Probationary Citizenship in Science, Technology, Engineering and Mathematics in an Irish University: A Disrupted Patriarchal Bargain?' *Irish Journal of Sociology*, 30 (3), 286–307.

O'Connor, P. (2023) 'Is gendered power irrelevant in Higher Educational Institutions? Understanding the persistence of gender inequality'. *Interdisciplinary Science Reviews,* https://doi.org/10.1080/03080188.2023.2253667

O'Connor, P. and Drew, E. (2023). 'The Tenure Track Model: Its Acceptance and Perceived Gendered Character'. *Trends in Higher Education*, 2 (1), 62-76.

O'Connor, P., Le Feuvre, N. and Sumer, S. (2023). 'Cross- national Variation in Postdoc Precarity: An Inquiry into the Role of Career Structures and Research Funding Models'. *Policy Futures in Education*, 1 - 19. https://doi.org/10.1177/14782103231177483.

Parsons, C. and O'Connor, P. (2023). 'You've Heard of Mentorship in Science, but What about Sponsorship?' *Nature*, 19 January. https://www.nature.com/articles/d41586- 023-00123-z.

Edited Journals

O'Connor, P. (ed.) (2018) *Gender and Leadership*, Special Issue of *Educ Sciences 8, 93* doi:10.3390/educsci8030093.

O'Connor, P. (2018) 'Introduction and a Future Research Agenda' *Gender and Leadership*, Special Issue of *Education Sciences* 8, 93. https://doi.org/ 10.3390/ educsci 8030093.

Harford, J. Fitzgerald, T. and O'Connor, P. (eds.) (2020) *Creating Change: Gender, Leadership and Higher Education,* Special Issue of *Irish Educational Studies*, https://www.tandfonline.com/toc/ries20/39/2.

O'Connor, P., Harford, J. and Fitzgerald, T. (2020). 'Mapping an Agenda for Gender Equality in the Academy'. Special Issue of *Irish Educational Studies*, 39 (2), 131 - 38. https:// doi.org/ 10.1080/ 03323 315.2020.1754 880.

Book chapters

O'Connor, P. (1996). 'Havent the Men Won Out? Organisational Culture as a Barrier to Women's Promotion'. In S. Lewis (ed.), *Balancing Employment and Family Life*. Ljubljana: CWS.

O'Connor, P. and Shortall, S. (1999). 'Does the Border Make the Difference?' In R. Breen, A. Heath and C. T. Whelan (eds), *Ireland: North and South: Social Science Perspectives*, pp. 285-318. Oxford: Oxford University Press.

O'Connor, P. (1999a). 'Women in the Academy: A Problematic Issue?' In A. B. Connolly and A. Ryan (eds), *Women and Education*, pp. 17-48. Maynooth: MACE.

O'Connor, P. (1999b). 'Women's Friendships in a Post- Modern World'. In R. Adams and G. Allan (eds), *Placing Friendship in Context*, pp. 117-36. Cambridge: Cambridge University Press.

O'Keefe, B. and O'Connor, P. (2001). 'Out of the Mouths of Babes and Innocents'. In A. Cleary, M. NicGhiolla Phadraigh and S. Quin (eds),

UnderstandingChildren: Changing Experiences and Family Forms, Vol. 2, pp. 207-28. Dublin: Oaktree Press.

O'Connor, P., Smithson, J. and Das Dores Guerreiro, M. (2002). `Young People's Awareness of Gendered Realities'. In J. Brannen, S. Lewis, A. Nilsen and J. Smithson (eds), *Young Europeans, Work and Family*, pp. 89-115. London: Routledge.

O'Connor, P. (2003a). `Discrimination', `discrimination legislation', `disability', `employment legislation', `equality', `equality authority', `labour force, female participation', `occupational segregation', `racism', `women's movement', `rape crisis centres', `suicide', `travellers and prejudice', `the X case'. In B. Lalor (ed.), *Encyclopaedia of Ireland*, pp. 300, 301, 361, 600, 801, 909, 914, 1024-25, 1073, 1150, 1155. Dublin: Gill and Macmillan.

O'Connor, P. (2003b). `Faculty Women: Making our Mark'. In V. Batt, S. Ni Fhaolain and R. Phelan (eds), *Gender Matters in Higher Education*, pp. 11-30. Galway: NUIG/WSC.

O'Connor, P. (2003c). `Feminism and the Politics of Gender'. In M. Adshead and M. Millar (eds), *Public Administration and Public Policy in Ireland*, pp. 54-68. London: Routledge.

O'Connor, P. (2008a). `The Challenge of Gender in Higher Education: Processes and Practices'. *Proceedings of the 4th International Barcelona Conference on Higher Education, Vol. 3. Higher Education and Gender Equity*. Barcelona: GUNI. https://upcommons.upc.edu/handle/2099/5744 (core.ac.uk), accessed 12 June 2023.

O'Connor, P. (2008b). `The Irish Patriarchal State: Continuity and Change'. In M. Adshead, P. Kirby and M. Millar (eds), *Contesting the State*, pp. 143-64. Manchester: MUP.

O'Connor, P. (2010). `Gender and Organisational Culture at Senior Management Level: Limits and Possibilities for Change?' In J. Harford and C. Rush (eds), *Women and Higher Education in Ireland Have Women Made a Difference?* pp. 139-46. Germany: Peter Lang.

Kelleher, P. and O'Connor, P. (2011). `Men on the Margins: Masculinities in Disadvantaged Areas in Limerick City'. In N. Hourigan (ed.), *Understanding Limerick: Social Exclusion and Change*, pp. 169-84. Cork: Cork University Press.

O'Connor, P. (2011). `Where Do Women Fit in University Senior Management? An Analytical Typology of Cross-National Organisational Cultures'. In B. Bagilhole, K. White (eds), *Gender, Power and Management: A Cross Cultural Analysis*, pp. 168-91. London: Palgrave Macmillan.

O'Connor, P. (2012). `Reflections on the Public Intellectual's Role in a Gendered Society'. In M. P. Corcoran (ed.), *Reflections on Crisis: The Role of the Public Intellectual*, pp. 55-73. Dublin: RIA.

O'Connor, P. (2013). `A Standard Academic Career?' In B. Bagilhole and K. White (eds), *Gender and Generation*, pp. 23-45. London: Palgrave Macmillan.

O'Connor, P. (2015). `A Premature Farewell to Gender: Young People "Doing Boy/Girl"'. In L. Connolly (ed.), *The 'Irish' Family*, pp. 86-105. London: Routledge.

O'Connor, P., Carvalho, T., Vabo, A. and Cardoso, S. (2015). `Gender in Higher Education: A Critical Review'. In J. Huisman et al. (eds), *The Palgrave International Handbook of Higher Education, Policy and Governance*, pp. 569-85. London: Palgrave MacMillan.

O'Connor, P. (2017a). `Changing the Gender Profile of the Professoriate: An Irish Case Study'. In K. White and P. O'Connor (eds), *Gendered Success in Higher Education*, pp. 91-110. London: Palgrave Macmillan.

O'Connor, P. (2017b). `Towards a New Gender Agenda and a Model for Change'. In K. White and P. O'Connor (eds), *Gendered Success in Higher Education: Global Perspectives*, pp. 255-82. London: Palgrave Macmillan.

O'Connor, P. (2020). `Accessing Academic Citizenship: Excellence or Micropolitical Practices?' In S. Sumer (ed.), *Gendered Academic Citizenship: Issues and Experiences*, pp. 37-64. Cham: Palgrave.

O'Connor, P. and O'Hagan, C. (2020). `The Academic Career Game and Gender Related Practices in STEM'. In P. Cullen and M. Corcoran (eds), *Producing Knowledge, Reproducing Gender*, pp. 25-46. Dublin: UCD Press.

Sumer, S., O'Connor, P. and Le Feuvre, N. (2020a). `Conclusions: Gendered Academic Citizenship as a Promising Research Agenda'. In S. Sumer (ed.), *Gendered Academic Citizenship: Issues and Experiences*, pp. 229-46. Cham: Palgrave Macmillan.

Sumer, S., O'Connor, P. and Le Feuvre, N. (2020b). `The Contours of Academic Citizenship'. In S. Sumer (ed.), *Gendered Academic Citizenship: Issues and Experiences*, pp. 1-36. Cham: Palgrave Macmillan.

O'Connor, P. (2021). `Gender Equality: A Neglected or Rhetorical Dimension of Rankings in Higher Education'. In E. Hazelkorn and G. Mihut (eds), *Research Handbook on University Rankings: Theory, Methodology, Influence and Impact*, pp. 150-62. Cheltenham: Edward Elgar.

O'Connor, P. and Barnard, S. (2021). `Problematising Excellence as a Legitimating Discourse'. In P. O'Connor and K. White (eds), *Gender, Power and Higher Education in a Globalised World*, pp. 47-69. Cham: Palgrave Macmillan.

O'Connor, P. and White, K. (2021). `Gender Equality in Higher Education: The Slow Pace of Change'. In P. O'Connor and K. White (eds), *Gender, Power and Higher Education in a Globalised World*, pp. 1-23.Cham: Palgrave Macmillan.

O'Connor, P. and White, K. (2021). `Power, Legitimating Discourses and Institutional Resistance to Gender Equality in Higher Education'. In P.

O'Connor and K. White (eds), *Gender, Power and Higher Education in a Globalised World*, pp. 187-207. Cham: Palgrave Macmillan.

O'Connor, P. (2022). `A Typology of STEM Academics and Researchers' Responses to Managerialist Performativity in Higher Education'. In C. S. Sarrico, M. J. Rosa and T. Carvalho (eds), *Research Handbook on Academic Careers and Managing Academics*, pp. 189-201. Cheltenham: Edward Elgar.

O'Connor, P. and Montes- Lopez, E. (2022). `Excellence?'. In F. Jenkins, B. Hoenig, S. M. Weber and A. Wolffram (eds), *Inequalities and the Paradigm of Excellence in Academia*, pp. 150-65. London: Routledge.

Bosek, J. and O'Connor, P. (2023). `Gender and Academic Careers in Ireland: Towards Greater Gender Equality'. In J. Briscoe, M. Dickman, D. Hall, W. Mayhofer and E. Parry (eds), *Understanding Careers around the Globe*, pp. 172-81. Cheltenham: Elgar Publishing.

Selected Reports

O'Connor, P. (1995). *Barriers to Women's Promotion in the Health Boards.* Limerick: MWHB.

O'Connor, P. (1996). *Invisible Players? Women, Tourism and Development in Ballyhoura.* Limerick: Women's Studies.

Lewis, S., O'Connor, P., et al. (1999). *Futures on Hold: Young Europeans.* Brussels: EC.

O'Connor, P. (1999a). *The Glass Ceiling: Report on the Position of Women in Udaras Na Gaeltachta.* EU: ADAPT.

O'Connor, P. (1999b). *Parents Supporting Parents: An Evaluative Report on the NPSP.* Limerick: Van Leer Foundation and MWHB.

Kelleher, P., Kelleher, C., O'Connor, P. (2008). *Uncertain Futures: An Exploratory Study of Men at the Margins.* Limerick: University of Limerick Press.

O'Connor, P., et al. (2010). *Evaluation of 2008 Linnaeus Grant.* Stockholm: Swedish Research Council & Formas.

O'Connor, P., et al. (2014). *Evaluating the Research Programme Nordic Spaces.* Stockholm: RJ.

HEA. (2016). *National Review of Gender Equality in Irish Higher Education Institutions.* Dublin: HEA.

O'Connor, P. (2018). *Gender- Related Challenges in European Education Systems: The Irish Country Report EIGE/ 2016/ OPER/ 08.* Italy: Mediterranean Institute for Gender Studies.

O'Connor, P. (2021). *Briefing doc for Royal Irish Academy on HE in Ireland and Northern Ireland,* 4 June.

Selected recent short policy pieces

O'Connor, P. (2020) 'Are Universities male dominated? What can be done?' *PublicPolicy.ie* March 8th.

Mc Coy, S. Byrne, D. O'Connor, P. (2021) 'Do teachers and mothers over-estimate boys and under-estimate girl's maths performance' *PublicPolicy.ie* 1st Nov.

O'Connor, P. (2022) 'Science Foundation Ireland's Gender Strategy 2016-2020: A critique' *PublicPolicy.ie* 27th Sept.

O'Connor, P. (2022) 'Postdocs: Who cares about their careers?' *PublicPolicy.ie* 5th Dec.

O'Connor, P. (2023) 'Irish university leadership's gender balance may not persist' *Times Higher Education*, May 23rd. https://www.timeshighereducation.com/opinion/irish-university-leaderships-gender-rebalance-may-not-persist.

O'Connor, P. (2023) 'The precarious employment of staff in Irish Higher Educational institutions and its policy implications.' *Publicpolicy.ie* 6th June.

Index

Reimagining Ireland

Series Editor: Dr Eamon Maher, Technological
University Dublin

The concepts of Ireland and 'Irishness' are in constant flux in the wake of an ever-increasing reappraisal of the notion of cultural and national specificity in a world assailed from all angles by the forces of globalisation and uniformity. Reimagining Ireland interrogates Ireland's past and present and suggests possibilities for the future by looking at Ireland's literature, culture and history and subjecting them to the most up-to-date critical appraisals associated with sociology, literary theory, historiography, political science and theology.

Some of the pertinent issues include, but are not confined to, Irish writing in English and Irish, Nationalism, Unionism, the Northern 'Troubles', the Peace Process, economic development in Ireland, the impact and decline of the Celtic Tiger, Irish spirituality, the rise and fall of organised religion, the visual arts, popular cultures, sport, Irish music and dance, emigration and the Irish diaspora, immigration and multiculturalism, marginalisation, globalisation, modernity/postmodernity and postcolonialism. The series publishes monographs, comparative studies, interdisciplinary projects, conference proceedings and edited books. Proposals should be sent either to Dr Eamon Maher at eamon.maher@ittdublin.ie or to ireland@peterlang.com.

Vol. 16   Zélie Asava: The Black Irish Onscreen: Representing Black and
            Mixed-Race Identities on Irish Film and Television
            ISBN 978-3-0343-0839-7. 213 pages. 2013.

Vol. 17   Susan Cahill and Eóin Flannery (eds): This Side of Brightness: Essays
            on the Fiction of Colum McCann
            ISBN 978-3-03911-935-6. 189 pages. 2012.

Vol. 18   Brian Arkins: The Thought of W. B. Yeats
            ISBN 978-3-03911-939-4. 204 pages. 2010.

Vol. 19   Maureen O'Connor: The Female and the Species: The Animal in Irish
            Women's Writing
            ISBN 978-3-03911-959-2. 203 pages. 2010.

Vol. 20   Rhona Trench: Bloody Living: The Loss of Selfhood in the Plays of
            Marina Carr
            ISBN 978-3-03911-964-6. 327 pages. 2010.

Vol. 21   Jeannine Woods: Visions of Empire and Other Imaginings: Cinema,
            Ireland and India, 1910–1962
            ISBN 978-3-03911-974-5. 230 pages. 2011.

Vol. 22   Neil O'Boyle: New Vocabularies, Old Ideas: Culture, Irishness and the
            Advertising Industry
            ISBN 978-3-03911-978-3. 233 pages. 2011.

Vol. 23   Dermot McCarthy: John McGahern and the Art of Memory
            ISBN 978-3-0343-0100-8. 344 pages. 2010.

Vol. 24   Francesca Benatti, Sean Ryder and Justin Tonra (eds): Thomas
            Moore: Texts, Contexts, Hypertexts
            ISBN 978-3-0343-0900-4. 220 pages. 2013.

Vol. 25   Sarah O'Connor: No Man's Land: Irish Women and the Cultural
            Present
            ISBN 978-3-0343-0111-4. 230 pages. 2011.

Vol. 26   Caroline Magennis: Sons of Ulster: Masculinities in the Contem-
            porary Northern Irish Novel
            ISBN 978-3-0343-0110-7. 192 pages. 2010.

Milton Keynes UK
Ingram Content Group UK Ltd.
UKHW011804120324
439385UK00016B/115